D1808068

THE EUROPEAN
INTERNET COMPANION

A Beginner's Guide to
Global Networking

THE EUROPEAN INTERNET COMPANION

A Beginner's Guide to Global Networking

TRACY LAQUEY

Adapted for the European Market by
Stephan Deutsch of EUnet and
Richard Harris of Hyperion Systems

Foreword by U.S. Vice President Al Gore

AN EDITORIAL INC./ONLINE BOOKSTORE (OBS) BOOK

Addison-Wesley Publishing Company
Wokingham, England • Reading, Massachusetts
Menlo Park, California • New York • Don Mills, Ontario • Amsterdam
Bonn • Sydney • Singapore • Tokyo • Madrid • San Juan
Paris • Seoul • Milan • Mexico City • Taipei

© 1995 Tracy LaQuey and Editorial Inc.
Artwork © 1993 Editorial Inc.

All rights reserved. No part of this publication may be reproduced, stored in a retrieval system, or transmitted in any form or by any means, electronic, mechanical, photocopying, recording or otherwise, without prior written permission of the publisher. Enquiries about electronic rights should be directed to Editorial Inc., Whistlestop Mall, Rockport, MA 01966.

The programs in this book have been included for their instructional value. They have been tested with care but are not guaranteed for any particular purpose. The publisher does not offer any warranties or representations, nor does it accept any liabilities with respect to the programs.

Many of the designations used by manufacturers and sellers to distinguish their products are claimed as trademarks. Addison-Wesley has made every attempt to supply trademark information about manufacturers and their products mentioned in this book. A list of trademark designations and their owners appears on page viii.

Cover designed by Designers & Partners of Oxford
and printed by The Riverside Printing Co. (Reading) Ltd.
Text designed by Arisman Design
Typeset by Cathleen Collins in Meridien, Futura and Courier
Illustrations by Steven Ackerman
Printed and bound in Great Britain at the University Press, Cambridge

First printed 1995

ISBN 0-201-42778-8

British Library Cataloguing-in-Publication Data
A catalogue record for this book is available from the British Library.

Library of Congress Cataloging-in-Publication Data is available

Contents

Trademark Notice

Amiga: Commodore Business Machines

Apple II, AppleLink, AppleTalk: Apple Computer, Inc.

Atari: Atari Corporation

BSD: Berkeley Software Design, Inc.

Cisco: Cisco Systems, Inc.

CityScape: CityScape Internet Services Ltd

CIX: Compulink Information eXchange

ClariNet: ClariNet Communications Organization

CommerceNet: CommerceNet, Inc.

CompuServe: CompuServe, Inc.

CP/M: Digital Research

CSNET: Corporation for Research and Educational Networking

DEC: Digital Equipment Corporation

DECwindows: Digital Equipment Corporation

DELPHI: General Videotex Corporation

Demon: Demon Internet Limited

EINet: Microelectronics and Computer Technology Corporation

Ethernet: Xerox Corporation

EUnet: EUnet Limited

FidoNet: Tom Jennings

GreenNet: GreenNet

IBM: International Business Machines Corporation

IPX: Novell, Inc.

Mac: Apple Computer, Inc.

MCC: Microelectronics and Computer Technology Corporation

MCImail: MCI Communications Corporation

MS-DOS: Microsoft Corporation

NetPages: Aldea Communications, Inc.

NORDUnet: NORDUnet Limited

OBS: Online BookStore, Ltd.

On-Line: On-Line Entertainment Ltd

PICO: University of Washington

PINE: University of Washington

PIPEX: Unipalm Group Plc.

PROCOMM: Datastorm Technologies, Inc.

Prodigy: Prodigy Services Co.

PSI: Performance Systems International, Inc.

SNA: International Business Machines Corporation

Sound & Vision: Sound & Vision BBS

Specialix: Specialix International

Sprint: Sprint

Sun: Sun Microsystems, Inc.

TelePost: TelePost Communication AS

TEX: American Mathematical Society

TGV: Two Guys with a Vax, Inc.

UNIX: American Telephone and Telegraph Company

UUNET: UUNET Canada Inc.

VAX: Digital Equipment Corporation

VMS: Digital Equipment Corporation

VT100: Digital Equipment Corporation

X Window System: Massachusetts Institute of Technology

(It was not possible to identify some of the trademarks by press time, but if the information is forthcoming, it will be added in the next reprint of the book.)

Foreword

Computer networks have been around for over twenty-five years, and in that time they have gone from being a laboratory curiosity to a tool used by millions of people every day. The first network, ARPANET, was used primarily by a few thousand computer scientists to access computers, share computer files, and send electronic mail. Today, scientists, engineers, teachers, students, librarians, doctors, businesspeople, and politicians rely on the Internet and other networks to communicate with their colleagues, receive electronic journals, access bulletin boards, log on to databases, and use remote computers and other equipment.

In the last few years, we have witnessed the democratization and commercialization of the Internet. Today, the network connects not only the top research laboratories and universities but also small colleges, businesses, libraries, and schools throughout the world. The growth of commercial networks has enabled much broader access to the Internet. And that growth is accelerating because the telecommunications and computer industries have recognized the commercial potential of high-speed, interactive networking and have invested hundreds of millions of dollars in developing new switching technology and new applications for networks.

Since I first became interested in high-speed networking almost seventeen years ago, there have been many major advances both in the technology and in public awareness. Articles on high-speed networks are commonplace in major newspapers and in news magazines. In contrast, when as a House member in the early 1980s I called for creation of a national network of 'information superhighways,' the only people interested were the manufacturers of optical fiber. Back then, of course, high-speed meant

56,000 bits per second. Today we are building a global information infrastructure that will carry billions of bits of data per second, serve thousands of users simultaneously, and transmit not only electronic mail and data files but voice and video as well.

Unfortunately, it is not easy to keep track of all the new developments in networking. According to some recent estimates, the amount of traffic on the Internet has been increasing 10 percent per month, and the number of new applications and services has been growing almost as quickly. You can now access thousands of different databases and bulletin boards on everything from medieval French literature to global warming. Just a few months ago, the White House Web server went on-line, and already over a million people worldwide have used it to access U.S. Government information. Since the Internet is a network of networks, there is no one place to go for information on what's available and how to access it. Most users still have to rely on friends and colleagues for information about the Internet.

That is why I welcome the revised edition of *The Internet Companion.* It provides a valuable primer on the Internet, explains the 'rules of the road,' and provides step-by-step instructions on accessing many of the information resources available through the Internet. It should help both new and experienced Internet users learn how to make the best use of the network.

For too many people the Internet has been uncharted territory, and as a result they have hesitated to explore the vast potential of networking. I trust this book will change that.

February 1995   *U.S. Vice President Al Gore*

Preface

The Internet Companion was the first computer trade book to introduce the world to the wonders of the Internet. When it made its debut in 1992, it immediately became a best-seller. Even though today there are other sources of information about the Internet, including training classes and videotapes, new users still look to the *Companion* for guidance and help in getting to know and use this 'network of networks'.

How times have changed! Back in 1992, few predicted the great Internet wave, which ever since has been building momentum, gathering speed. Not long ago, you could recite the 'anonymous FTP' sites from memory, whereas today, there are hundreds of thousands of places to download files, retrieve software, and access online books and services. Only five years ago, people cited IP addresses instead of host names, and there were few graphical user interfaces. Now, in many cases, you don't even need to know computer names, let alone addresses; you just point and click on colorful icons. Although previously you could only complain about the government in online political forums, now you can send email to many politicians, as well as retrieve the latest government press releases and initiatives. It used to be that you could only talk about movies in online forums; today the Internet transmits live video broadcasts and radio shows, as well as movies.

In short, the Internet is continuously changing, growing, and improving, and it is having a tremendous impact on our lives. It's not just a physical computer network anymore, but a publishing medium, a communication channel, and a library. Yet it's both advanced and primitive. As Bruce Sterling, a science fiction writer and Internet philosopher once said, 'Everyone has a different Internet'. What it is to you depends on your expectations, the networking resources available to you, and your motivation to use it. Whatever your fancy, this book will get you started. It introduces you to Internet concepts, applications, and idiosyncrasies and offers you glimpses of how people are using it for the mundane and the marvelous.

This book contains numerous examples and sample commands to try. In general, computer names and email addresses by themselves appear in italic, while new terms are introduced in boldface. Some of the commands are a mixture of bold and italic; in those cases, you should type anything in bold exactly as it appears. The italic represents variable input that only you can supply, such as your email address or your login name.

Keep in mind that although many instructions and examples are given in these pages, this book does not offer step-by-step directions for every case. Remember also that new services are being made available daily, and that even though the resource information was up-to-date when the book went to press, it is very likely that some of it will have changed by the time you read it. Always read any instructions that are given when connecting to an online database, and if you have problems, consult your Internet provider's helpdesk or consulting services.

You may feel as though you're about to be thrown into the ocean with your shoes tied together. But come on in—the water's fine! Millions of people are 'surfing on the Internet', and you can too. And while you're out there, don't forget to drop me a line: *Tracy@editorial.com*. Numerous Internauts have written to tell me how *The Internet Companion* helped them and how they use it, and I look forward to hearing about your Internet adventures.

Many people helped make this book a reality. In particular, I wish to thank Patrick D. Parker, Laura Fillmore, Tim Evans, Eugene Bailey, Mic Kaczmarczik, Guy Steele, Ed Kozel, Virginia Bechtold, David O'Leary, Susan Estrada, Susan and Peter Rauch, Al and Sheri LaQuey, Gerald and Valerie Parker, and all the people who sent me stories about how they use the Internet.

February 1995   *Tracy LaQuey*

Online Publisher's Preface

When I first discovered it in the 1980s, the Internet seemed like an electronic version of the U.S. National Park System, a fabulous undiscovered wilderness, of which all citizens shared ownership but which few knew how to access or use.

In an effort to better understand where the Internet came from, how it works, and what an instantaneous, unmediated, and global electronic communications system might mean for all people, I proposed a general trade book that would answer all my questions. Luckily I found the perfect author in Tracy LaQuey, who proceeded to travel where no author had gone before, and with insight, expertise, and wit wrote this first, standard-setting 'Internet for neophytes' book, which became an immediate bestseller. Now, the book has been adapted for the European audience. In its new incarnation as *The European Internet Companion*, it assumes both paperback and online forms—to better address the needs of today's international Internet audiences.

Although its origins lie in the United States, the Internet has become a global phenomenon with stunning rapidity, for it is no typical export commodity. Not a product (although it contains products), not a service (although it needs services in order to run efficiently), not a company (although, as a global network of networks, it represents the work of countless companies), the Internet is perhaps best thought of as a functional idea whose time has come. Like any good idea, it will not be impeded by physical boundaries of time or space and is easily tailored to the languages, needs, and intelligence of the people who adopt it.

The Internet and the common digital language it uses represent a form of 'Electronic Esperanto', opening up a new global thinking and communications medium to anyone on the planet who has access to a computer, a phone line, and a modem. The publication of *The European Internet Companion* represents an important step toward making this new and empowering technology accessible to the European audience.

Because of the challenges inherent in the new Internet medium, however, this book must also continue to evolve if it is to prove of maximum usefulness. To that end, we invite all its readers, both online and on paper, to participate in this protean work. Come and visit the online Internet Companion site at the Online BookStore (OBS). Find out what's new, and email us your suggestions about how to make this site better suit your Internet needs. We value and acknowledge our readers' ideas: If we implement hypertext links you suggest in our WorldWideWeb Internet Companion site, we will publish your name as a "link contributor" on the copyright page of both the online and, in the future, printed versions of the book.

When accessed online, *The European Internet Companion* offers a different experience than that of a book, which one simply reads from cover to cover; it becomes a responsive cyber-resource that grows and improves with use and reader participation. Online, the reader rules, and with this in mind, perhaps together we can reshape this groundbreaking book into an even more useful Internet resource—at once a starting point and a home base in the new, multilingual digital landscape of the Internet.

February 1995   *Laura Fillmore*
President, Online BookStore
http://marketplace.com/obs/top.htm

Chapter 1

WHAT IS THE INTERNET AND WHY SHOULD YOU KNOW ABOUT IT?

*T*he *Internet is a loose amalgam* of thousands of computer networks reaching millions of people all over the world. In recent years it has grown so large and powerful that it is now an information and communication tool you cannot afford to ignore.

Today the Internet is used by all sorts of people and organizations—newspapers, publishers, TV stations, celebrities, teachers, librarians, hobbyists and businesspeople—for a variety of purposes, from communicating with one another to accessing valuable services and resources. You can hardly pick up a newspaper or magazine without reading about how the Internet is playing a part in someone's life or project or discovery.

To appreciate what the Internet has to offer you, imagine discovering a whole system of highways and high-speed connections that cut hours off your commuting time. Or a library you can use any time of the night or day, with vast stores of books and resources, giving unlimited browsing possibilities. Or an all-night, nonstop party with a corner table of kindred souls who welcome your presence at any time. That's the Internet, and this chapter will tell you why you should know about it.

One thing to bear in mind when reading this or any other book about online services: The Internet is not the Information Superhighway—it's simply the closest thing to it we've got at the moment! The term 'Information Superhighway' grew out of the U.S. National Information Infrastructure initiative launched by

U.S. Vice President Al Gore. This 'Infobahn' (a term becoming more commonly used in Europe) includes the integrated provision of online information and retail services, video-on-demand cable TV, video and audio telephony and conferencing. It also encompasses the high-speed managed networks required to transmit and deliver these services on a national and global basis. Other countries, worried about the prospect of the United States gaining an uncatchable lead in developing the infrastructure and services required for the 'Information Age', have responded with their own initiatives, with a greater or lesser degree of vision and commitment.

As you can see, the services on the current Internet form only a part of the overall vision for the Information Superhighway. The Internet does, however, offer a model and a test bed for the ways in which people, services and information interact. It seems likely that the Infobahn's archaeologists twenty years hence will still be able to identify pieces of the current Internet culture and attitudes reused in the foundation stones of the gleaming towers and roads of the Information Age.

WHENCE IT CAME

The Internet universe was created with an unassuming bang in 1969 with the birth of ARPANET, an experimental project of the U.S. Department of Defense Advanced Research Projects Agency (DARPA). It had a humble mission, to explore experimental networking technologies that would link researchers to remote resources such as large computer systems and databases. The success of ARPANET helped cultivate numerous other worldwide networking initiatives, which intertwined as they grew; 25 years later, these have evolved into an ever expanding, complex organism comprising tens of millions of people and tens of thousands of networks. At the same time that the ARPANET developed in the United States, European networks began linking with each other and to their U.S. counterparts. For a thorough discussion of these networks, see Chapter 2.

Most users describe the Internet as a 'network of networks', but beyond this infrastructure of electronic impulses and digital links is a tool capable of beaming you into another dimension, an invisible world where there are no stop signs or speed limits,

In fiscal 1969 a DARPA program entitled 'Resource Sharing Computer Networks' was initiated. The research carried out under this program has since become internationally famous as the ARPANET. This DARPA program has created no less than a revolution in computer technology and has been one of the most successful programs ever undertaken by DARPA. The program has initiated extensive changes in the U.S. Department of Defense's (DoD) use of computers as well as in the use of computers by the entire public and private sectors, around the world. Just as the telephone, the telegraph and the printing press had far-reaching effects on human interconnection, the widespread utilization of computer networks which has been catalyzed by the ARPANET project represents a similarly far-reaching change in the use of computers by mankind. The full impact of the technical changes set in motion by this project may not be understood for years.

Source: BBN for DARPA (1981). *History of the ARPANET: The First Decade.* Report 4799, available from NTIS, 1-703-487-4650, $27, ADA 115440.

there is no gravity, and time and space have almost no meaning. The Internet, or 'the Net', as it's often referred to in casual conversation, appears to stretch forever. It doesn't just connect you to another computer; it connects you to all other Internet-connected computers. However, it is wrong to think of the Internet as just a bunch of computers. It is a cybersphere, a perpetually expanding universe with its own geography, 'weather', and dynamic cultures. In this cybersphere, people in geographically distant lands communicate across time zones without ever seeing one another, and information is available 24 hours a day from thousands of places. This dimension is also commonly known as cyberspace.

Cyberspace—the Internet—is inhabited by millions of normal people, 'non-techies' who use it daily to communicate and search for information. When this book was first written, in the spring of 1992, the Internet population was mostly researchers and academics, and there weren't many applications and interest groups of relevance to the 'general public'. Two years later, mainstream services dot the Internet landscape and dominate its use; as a result, the Internet is exploding, almost bursting its seams with useful resources and new people climbing aboard.

IT KEEPS GOING AND GOING . . .

It's important to understand the significance of the Internet's growth and popularity. In one sense it could be compared to the proliferation of fax machines in the late 1980s. Our worldwide 'fax system' wasn't built overnight; it started with the appearance of a few fax machines here and there. As businesses realized their usefulness and power, fax machines became more commonplace, increasing the value of each fax machine as more and more became available.

Similarly, stand-alone computers are useful, but their potential is limited by isolated applications—word processors and spreadsheets, for example—and the amount of money you have to spend on disk drives and CD-ROMs. A mere direct (full-time) or dialup connection to the worldwide Internet gives you access to more info-goods, services and people than you'll ever find on your own isolated computer or local-area network. The Internet is already the largest computer network in the world and, in terms of connected networks, people and resources, it's getting larger, and therefore more 'valuable', literally by the minute.

How large is the Internet? The Internet Society (ISOC), a professional organization of Internet developers, people of influence and users, publishes some statistics in its quarterly journal, *Internet Society News*. As of the Winter 1994 issue, the Internet reached 69 countries directly and 146 via email gateways, and consisted of 23,659 networks and 2.217 million computers. (An email gateway is a special connection that allows only electronic mail—'email'—to transfer between two or more networks.)

The bulk of Internet computers and networks still belongs to the research and education communities. This is not surprising, given that the Internet arose from the primordial research ooze. However, many universities are teaming up with businesses to develop online catalogues and archives. And, according to the ISOC journal, 31% of the networks belong to businesses. Of the number of registered—but not necessarily connected—networks, 51% were commercial. There's definitely a rising trend in commercial activity and 'connectivity'; many businesses have realized that they can link their enterprise networks to the Internet and gain instant access to their customers. Some market research indicates that online services—in general—make up almost a billion-dollar industry, with an estimated 25% per year growth, so it stands to reason that providers of these services . . . are migrating to the Internet. (The source of these quoted figures is *The Tampa Tribune*, 13 December 1993, 'Cyberspace Market.')

One example of the impact of the Internet on business possibilities is in the former Soviet Union. Imagine the vast land stretching from the European continent to China and Japan, following the breakup of the U.S.S.R., transformed into many newly independent countries with the need to communicate. But who would be able to provide a telecommunication infrastructure connecting all those people, organizations and companies? Most of the telephone lines were of low quality, and sending a fax to Estonia from London was more difficult than winning poker against a hand holding four aces. In such circumstances the Internet stepped in and was able to open up the former Soviet Union to the world. Using the Internet, one can send email to many major organizations in Russia, even if some of them cannot be reached via the phone. Most of the area is linked with a 2Mbit infrastructure, satellite links and fibre networks. Estimated by the number of customers as well as by the area covered, the Internet providers in the former Soviet Union have achieved a larger size than those in Western Europe by now.

For most of the commercial enterprises in Western Europe it is only possible to communicate with their joint-venture partners in Eastern Europe via Internet services.

The types of resources accessible via the Internet are growing at an astounding rate. The term 'resource' describes anything you can access on the Internet, no matter where it's physically located. Examples of some Internet resources are a database of regularly updated weather information in Michigan, an online bookstore in Berlin, a florist in Lisbon or an archive of daily newspaper articles in Prag [Prague]. A resource can also be a mailing list or a newsgroup that brings together people from all over the world to discuss shared interests such as soccer, books, cooking and poetry. Suffice it to say that there are literally tens of

> In 1991 Bernard Steiner, an employee of EUnet in Germany, considered himself an unimportant person in the world of finance and the stock market, but he found out that other people thought differently of him. He was asked by someone from the Soviet Union if he would be able—and willing—to send stock market information on a regular basis to a person in Moscow. There this information would be used to set stock market exchange rates for the whole of Russia. After considering the possibilities of buying large sums of roubles and changing some rates as they went along the wire, Bernard Steiner forwarded the hot potato to the German stock market organization Deutsche Terminboerse, which was also connected to the network in Germany.
>
> Source: Stephan Deutsch, personal recollections (I read this mail :-) .

thousands of servers, archive sites, mailing lists, newsgroups and databases available on the Internet.

The Success of the Internet

It's hard to imagine how the Internet has grown so fast and been so successful without some ambitious organization or individual managing the project. Yet no one has a monopoly on access to or use of the Internet; there's no monolithic empire called Internet, Inc controlling accounts and application development or roping off the backstage parts of cyberspace. One of the reasons the Internet is so successful is the commitment of its developers to producing 'open' standards. The specifications or rules that computers need to communicate are publicly and freely available—published so that everyone can obtain them. The standards that the Internet uses are known as the TCP/IP protocol suite.

Although you may not think about it often, standards play a big part in your everyday life. Camera film always fits in your camera, and loose-leaf paper bought at the stationer's fits in your file. Libraries catalogue books according to a standard system, so that once you learn it, you can walk into any library and find the books you need. On the contrary, things that don't conform to standards can make your life miserable. Standards are just as important in the computer and networking world. Without open standards, only computers from the same supplier could talk to each other, creating an electronic Tower of Babel. Computers and networks that conform to the same communications standards are able to 'interoperate', regardless of their make.

Cooperation is a major ingredient of interoperability. The Internet nervous system does not have a central brain, such as a powerful supercomputer that controls its operation by feeding it commands and directing its limbs to perform key functions. Instead, all the networks and computers act as peers in the exchange of information and communication. The technology that makes it happen is known as 'internetworking'; it creates a universality among disparate systems, enabling the networks and computers to communicate.

The Packet

Fundamentally, the Internet revolves around the concept of a **packet**, a basic building block or a digital brick. All information and communication transmitted on the Internet are broken into packets, each of which is considered an independent entity. The packets are then individually routed from network to network until they reach their destination, where they are reassembled and presented to the user or computer process.

This method of networking is very flexible and robust. It allows diverse computers and systems to communicate by means of networking software, not proprietary hardware. If a network goes 'down'—meaning it isn't available to transfer information—the packets can be rerouted to other networks in many cases. This dynamic alternate routing of information creates a very 'persistent' means of communication. Indeed, that was the intent of the network engineers developing this technology during the height of the Cold War. They wanted a network that would continue to function even if parts of it were destroyed during a war. No longer enemies, all sides now use this technique to communicate with each other.

While most newcomers probably don't care about these standards and technical details, an understanding of the underlying infrastructure will help in learning to use the Internet properly and in taking full advantage of its powerful capabilities. It goes deeper than that though; understanding from the bottom up how separate computers and networks fit together will give you an appreciation for the Net culture, the sharing, cooperative spirit that is inherent in the Internet. Chapter 2 will further define these concepts of inter-operability and open standards, as well as explain how the protocols and networks come together to make the Internet work.

THE EQUALIZER

You can see how open standards enable businesses and individuals to compete on an equal footing in developing networking software and products. But 'open networking' extends beyond the development of networking protocols and products. Once you, an Internet user, are 'jacked in', you have access to the same resources as the rest of the millions of Internet users, whether you're located in Sydney or Stockholm.

The phrase 'democratization of communication' often comes up in discussions about the Internet, which is, indeed, a truly democratic forum. The network doesn't care if you're president of a Times Top 100 company or a warehouse clerk, a potato farmer or a molecular biologist. Your tidings and opinions are handled the same way, and it's the worth and wit of what you have to say that determines who's willing to listen—not your title.

It's also never been so easy to be both a consumer and a producer of services. If you're ambitious enough and aspire to be an electronic entrepreneur providing commercial services or Internet access, in most countries there's nothing to prevent you—no long lines, no paperwork and no regulations. (Okay, it's not *that* easy; you do need to read this and a few other books first.) Once your network is *directly* hooked into the Internet, all the computers on that network are accessible from every other Internet-connected computer. (See Chapter 7 for an explanation of the different types of Internet connections.)

The significance of this environment is that it empowers the individual; it encourages and stimulates participation, imagination and innovation. There are numerous stories of how just one or two people have utilized the Net to do great things, whether it's to publish a newsletter, make a name, or develop contacts.

And there are thousands of people who are already offering free and for-pay information services. If you don't have access to a whiz-bang, high-speed Internet connection or to a large multi-user computer, that's not a problem. Already there are businesses offering space for hire on their Internet-connected computers and disks. You can lease 'office space' from 'office parks' in cyberspace and set up shop. Your virtual shop may be thousands of miles and two countries away, but it's probably a mere fraction of a second hyperdrive from every location.

In the U.K., the government is currently investigating the potential of developing a 'National Network Infrastructure', to provide a framework for the development of public information services. At the time of writing, the initiative has got as far as delivering a consultative report—which dismissed the Internet in about two paragraphs as not having a central control or billing system and being an open system that just anyone can use!—and sponsoring some business seminars. Meanwhile the main U.K. PTO, British Telecom, has indicated a willingness to fund the estimated £15 billion required to build the infrastructure. However, the terms of BT's operating licence effectively prevent it from delivering any profitable services over that infrastructure. Not surprisingly, BT does not appear willing to make the investment unless it can see a return. At the local level, cable franchises in the U.K. are installing high-capacity fibre-optic cable that will allow a large proportion of homes and businesses to access these services directly, at high speed and low cost. Many of these local services are going online now, although few yet offer Internet connection.

At the end of 1994, British Telecom announced its new Internet service. BT is initially offering high-speed (up to 25Mbps) permanent connections to two PoPs in the U.K., with another ten PoPs and other services to follow in 1995. The company may at some point provide modem-based dial-in services and could possibly offer local rate connections using the 0345 local access numbers.

Communication

What distinguishes the Internet (and other global networks) from traditional communication technologies is the level of interaction and the speed at which you can broadcast your messages. No other

SatelLife

Physicians in Africa are practising medicine and dealing with some of this century's most serious medical challenges in the midst of staggering 'information poverty'. In the mid-80s, the problem caught the attention of Dr. Bernard Lown, founder of International Physicians for the Prevention of Nuclear War and winner of the Nobel Peace Prize in 1985, who felt the high frontier of space should be used for humanitarian rather than military purposes. He started Satel-Life, a non-profit organization committed to promoting health in the developing world by providing improved communication and exchange of information. SatelLife's Health-Net is a computer network linking medical centres in the Southern Hemisphere in much of the developing world, with an initial focus on Africa. Using a microsatellite, email and in-country networks, HealthNet enables physicians and health-care workers in remote areas to upload or download information to each other and to medical research centres in the industrialized countries.

(Continued)

medium gives every participant the ability to communicate instantly with thousands and thousands of people. Consider this: it is possible for you, on your very first net-surfing expedition, to send a message containing your thoughts to several thousand people. What other communication medium gives you that power? Instantaneously? Without prior editing?

The Internet certainly has people talking; everyone has an opinion, and all opinions seem to end up on the Internet. If you're looking to unearth all sides of an issue, there's no better place. The Internet functions as an ongoing consumer report, with people continuously offering up views, experiences, recommendations and warnings. You can use the Internet's communication applications (explained in Chapter 3) to ask for help from thousands of people, broadcast an announcement of an event or a new service, offer your analysis of a situation, or just muse in an interest group. The Internet is a perfect tool for alerting and

For example, a physician treating an AIDS patient in Zambia, Africa, where the HIV-positive rate approaches 25 %, could better treat his patient by communicating with physicians and researchers in other African countries as well as with colleagues in other parts of the world. Through HealthNet, he can get a free electronic copy of *The New England Journal of Medicine*, with the latest research results, rather than waiting six months to receive a copy that might cost half his monthly salary. Using the HealthNet system, this physician can query researchers about new developments, such as the possible connection between polio vaccines and AIDS in Africa, or about new drugs developed for AIDS treatment.

Staffed by people in Cambridge, Massachusetts, SatelLife received a major contribution for its first satellite from NEC Corp. SatelLife's second satellite was launched in 1993. With ground stations in Africa, Cuba and Brazil, SatelLife connects to the Internet through a gateway in Newfoundland.

Source: Based on an interview with Charles Clements, M.D., Executive Director of SatelLife.

assembling large numbers of people electronically. Information relating to a certain event can be transmitted immediately, making it a very effective rousing device. There are plenty of forums that exist for this very purpose—announcing late-breaking bulletins about an event or sparking a debate about the most recent controversies.

Now, this online free-for-all doesn't come without a few 'netiquette' rules. As in any social situation, there is an accepted mode of behaviour, and you will do well to make note of it before diving in and instantly distinguishing yourself as a barbarian. Chapter 3 contains a must-read guide to some well-known network conduct codes.

Another aspect of cooperation between people discussing, talking, and exchanging information on the Net is the aspect of language. Unfortunately there is no central translator and not all persons have a 'Babel fish' (see *The Hitchhikers Guide to the Galaxy*,

Douglas Adams, 1978) in their ear. English is mostly used on the
Net and you should use it if you don't know if the people you
want to talk to know your language. But even if English is a standard on the Net, you are not bound to use it. There are a lot of
user groups using other languages as well.

The writing of non-English languages (if its letters are included
in the American Standard Code for Information Interchange—
ASCII) is handled via 'letter set extensions'. Most applications and
services solve the problem for you and you do not have to bother all
the time about German 'ue's or French 'e's. And if you want to read
your Internet news in Kanji (Japanese) letters, you are free to do so!

Information

United States President Bill Clinton said in May of 1993: 'We are
moving very rapidly in all forms of production and services to a
knowledge-based economy in which what you earn depends on
what you can learn. Not only what you know today, but what
you are capable of learning tomorrow.' (As mentioned before,
the European political heads don't have the Infobahn written on
their flag, but that does not mean that they are not aware of the
impact. Several programs and projects of the European Union—
former EC—deal with this topic as well.) The deeper we plunge
into the online age, the more apparent the shift of power is—
from the hands of the most wealthy, learned, and influential to
anyone who has access to timely facts and the latest news, and
can effectively assimilate and analyze this information. What you
can learn depends on the information resources to which you
have immediate access. No one can know everything all the time
in this fast-paced world (although some people definitely try).
The people who will succeed in today's and tomorrow's world
will be those who can effectively use the resources and tools
available to them. The Internet is there to help you.

There is an ever-growing number of valuable information resources being made available via the Internet. These include free
and public archives, library catalogues, government services and
commercial databases. The Internet is liquid, changing every second; as news rains down, differing views, reports and opinions
irrigate archives and forums. Powerful search tools, with names

like Gopher, WorldWideWeb (WWW) and Wide Area Information Server (WAIS), explained in Chapter 4, can help you harvest information at its source.

These digital devices give you the power to bypass the middleman on your way to the source. It's not good enough anymore to turn on the 24-hour news service on your radio or TV and *wait* for a forecast of the local weather. On the Internet, you can check the latest weather and order goods and services online when you need them, rather than wait until they're shown on the TV channels. You can browse online guides looking for properties available for sale instead of first going to an estate agent. Continuously updated databases across the country and archives around the world give you access to the very latest news, opinions and articles when *you* want them, not when they're fed to you in eight-second bites or mentioned once a day in the morning paper. You can make your own opinions based on the sources, not the summaries. The Internet *can* help you make intelligent choices. However, be aware that no network will show you the best path; it's up to you to compile and analyze what's available, and then make the intelligent decision. But *you* are in charge. *You* make the call.

Virtual Communities

The Internet excels in bringing people closer together. Since geography is no longer a delimiter, people from different countries and varied backgrounds are able to join together according to common interests and projects. The Internet is responsible for an untold number of associations between people and groups; this kind of interaction on such a wide scale without a computer network is impossible.

For example, the WorldWideWeb server of the University of Dortmund provides students with information about the menus for lunch and dinner, pricing and opening times. They can browse through online CD-ROM catalogues of the university's library and get telephone numbers of university employees, as well as study plans, schedules for seminars and so on. Under the point 'several' they also find information about the correct value of stamps to put on a letter and, if nothing else, they find information about constitutional law for emergency cases dealing with their university professors. So the Internet can help them to have an easier life at university and therefore has become a necessary social tool.

Internet 'netizens' have circled their computers around virtual campsites, communing and cultivating friendships. Because it's so simple to join or leave a group, your own virtual village may change on a daily or hourly basis. You are a native to your own web, your own cyber-sphere of influence, but it is easy to be a tourist, visiting and interacting in other communities. Beaming yourself around incognito is also possible; you can become a digital cyborg, assuming other personalities. As a well-known cartoon proclaimed in 1993, 'On the Internet, no one knows you're a dog.'

PEELING BACK THE LAYERS: DIFFERENCES BETWEEN NETWORKS

There are many conceptual leaps people have to make in order to understand computer networking. Trying to understand the differences between the Internet and other online services and networks is just one of them. It's especially difficult if you've had experience with one but not the others.

There are literally thousands of different 'networks' that you can access. Some of them have been around for almost 20 years. Why then, has the Internet risen above all of these bulletin board systems and commercial services to become the top dog amongst networks?

One of the biggest misconceptions about the Internet is that it's 'free'—both access and resources. In the early days of the ARPANET and the Internet, most of the links and networks were paid for by U.S. Government agencies as part of large research projects or experimental networks. Many of the individuals working or studying at these research universities, labs and agencies had unlimited free access to the Internet through these regional or nationwide networks. The National Science Foundation was one of the agencies that built a backbone network, the NSFNET, to which mid-level networks connected. NSF developed an acceptable use policy that prohibited activity of a commercial nature, such as advertising and invoicing. That was fine with the original users; they gave their research and papers away for free anyway. And so began the tradition of making information—papers, standards documents, software, images, sounds—available in public archives on the Internet.

Due to the lack of government sponsorship of the Internet in Europe, only employees of connected organizations paying for the access (and therefore often restricting the use to business) and some students of universities originally got the opportunity to access the Internet. But most of the universities restricted—and are restricting—the use of the Internet for students as well. Because of that, use of all Internet services is mostly considered under the aspect of efficiency and cost—the free and open environment that exists in the United States does not exist in Europe. This might be a reason that private persons on the Internet are not as common in Europe as in the States, but this situation is changing rapidly. Now most of the Internet providers offer you a low-price full-service Internet connection that you can use like a telephone account to communicate with people all over the world.

During the growth of the network of networks, other commercial services and bulletin board systems (BBSs) were built outside the Internet. Commercial services, like CompuServe and Applelink, not only charged for access through hourly charges and monthly fees, but also charged for entrance to many of their databases. For many people with a desire to communicate but without a lot of cash, bulletin board and conferencing systems filled a void—thousands of these sprang up around the world, many of them offering free or low-cost access to their services.

It's no surprise, then, that the Internet is often compared to a large BBS. But the Internet is much more than that; it provides a high-speed highway between separate services such as BBSs and commercial databases. Unlike moving from one BBS to another, you don't have to hang up and redial to access separate services on the Internet.

Companies like Prodigy and CompuServe are not really networks in the sense that the Internet is; they're commercial information service providers, each owned and controlled by a company. To get access to one of these, you call up the company, provide your credit card number, and set up an account. You can then use your computer and modem to dial what is often a local number to get access to the service. The services are documented, support is available, and the pricing structure for usage and access is well defined. Each of these services is run by a business.

Not so with the Internet. Remember, it's a network of networks, a transport service, an information highway, *not*, as a whole, a commercial information service. It's a distributed, anarchic system, and much larger than all the commercial information systems put together in terms of people and diversity of services. Support, quality and pricing for Internet connectivity and services are not regulated or defined throughout. There are many ways to get access from local, national and international Internet transport providers or from dialup commercial access systems.

This flexibility has advantages and disadvantages. In most cases you're not limited to one solution. If you don't like one Internet provider's service, you can easily get access to the Internet another way. This can be frustrating, though, because there are, in certain countries, so many choices in providers that sometimes it's difficult to make a decision. In other countries, it's still very much a Hobson's choice.

Another difference to keep in mind is the diversity of services you get on the Internet. For example, to provide an information service through a commercial information provider, a person or organization most likely has to get permission and make special arrangements with the company that owns the service. The Internet, on the other hand, doesn't have a controlling organization that denies or approves involvement. As a result, individuals and companies are making new resources available every day. In fact, many of the commercial databases you might access through a commercial information service have already made (or are planning to make) direct connections to the Internet. Several providers on the Internet even go so far as to offer a 'commercial BBSs are also in your bag' solution, such as CompuServe and German PTT Datex-J (formerly Bildschirmtext, which is a national information access service much like a BBS and is famous in Germany). So you do not have to deal with all of them directly but may handle things easily with your Internet account. (Be aware, though, that you still need to set up an account with some of them to use their services.)

The Internet connects both free and commercial resources. Because of this, many commercial information services will be pressured to provide direct access to the Internet, including a nice graphical interface to the Net in addition to their own offerings.

CONVERGENCE: A TRAFFIC CIRCLE ON THE INFORMATION HIGHWAY

The Internet is providing the common ground for information service providers to do business. It's also blurring the lines between what used to be separate and distinct applications.

To understand what this convergence craze is all about, let's back up a bit and explain the different types of communication. TVs and telephones transmit information (your voice, the evening news and so on) using an analogue signal—that is, the information is represented by a continuous signal of varying strength.

Computers, on the other hand, work with binary digits, or bits. A bit is simply a 1 or a 0. That's it. Digital information is simply represented by patterns of these ones and zeros. By digitizing communication—representing everything in ones and zeros—computers can deal with multimedia and data in the same way. Furthermore, if computers are connected to a network of some kind, they can enable interactive digital audio and video communication between people. Your computer can become an all-purpose communications appliance that combines the functions of a telephone and TV, and also lets you use applications like a word processor or email program.

Digitizing (the translation of audio and video information from analogue to digital format) of multimedia technologies has the communications, broadcasting and publishing industries all aflutter, ushering in the chaotic days of convergence mania. The traditional roles of the telephone, television and cable companies with which we're so familiar are rapidly ceasing to exist, and ultimately all of these companies will be in the same business: that is, either providing the content—entertainment, *interactive* communication and information services—or access to these. The

On 23 May 1993, a historic moment occurred when a cult movie entitled *Wax: Or the Discovery of Television Among the Bees* was broadcast over the Internet to a small worldwide audience who watched and listened to it live on their computers. The video was fuzzy and in black and white, and the audio sputtered in and out, but this digital moon walk marked another small, yet significant, step toward the much-heralded convergence of audio, video and data. The movie was about a beekeeper who ends up being kept by the bees, and perhaps this is poetic justice, as today many Internauts are held captive by the digital bits buzzing through wires and telephone lines.

Since then, the number of groups and artists using the Internet as a marketing medium has mushroomed. Parts of a recent Rolling Stones concert were transmitted over the Internet, and the record company responsible for the latest release from the choral ensemble Megadeath report that providing clips from the CD on the Internet has led to a significant increase in sales of the album itself.

Source: Richard Harris, personal recollections from Newsgroup postings.

broadcast and entertainment industries have only just begun warming up by advertising possible new interactive services, while communication companies consider new alliances and mergers. The publishing industry is also repositioning itself.

And through it all, the Internet has been a testing ground, in a sense amalgamating everything in its path by bringing technologies together and letting them loose in a digital playground. The Internet may not be providing 500 TV channels, but it is possible today to participate in interactive video and audio 'conferencing' from your computer, and to share the same 'whiteboard' for illustrations and notes. You can listen to Internet radio shows while simultaneously downloading software. You can read online articles or books with hyperhooks that 'mind-bind' you on-demand to text, video clips, still images and audio. All of these applications have only recently been made available, but they're rapidly becoming more popular, and are making up a

The Big Crunch

'I'm reminded of an idea of Stephen Hawking, the British physicist. . . . Hawking has speculated about a distant future when the universe stops expanding and begins to contract. Eventually all matter comes colliding together in a "Big Crunch", which scientists say could then be followed by another "Big Bang"—a universe expanding outward once again.

'Our current information industries—cable, local telephone, long-distance telephone, television, film, computers and others—seem headed for a Big Crunch/Big Bang of their own. The space between these diverse functions is rapidly shrinking—between computers and television, for example, or interactive communications and video.'

Source: From a speech given by U.S. Vice President Al Gore on 11 January 1994, at Royce Hall, UCLA, Los Angeles, California.

significant percentage of the traffic and use on the Internet. Unfortunately, many of these applications demand powerful workstations and a high-speed connection to the Internet—requirements beyond what most people by themselves can meet. So if you want to see the future, go to a university. But it's important to know that these things *are* possible, because it probably won't be long before you can participate.

BUSINESS USE

There are myriad reasons why the business community should be connected to the Internet; indeed, one of the fastest-growing segments of the Internet today is commercial. The Internet is providing a wonderful environment in which to do business; there are many stories of small and big businesses that have leveraged their relatively small investment in connection costs to search the Internet for information, keep in contact with customers, or provide online services and operate virtual shops. Those businesses that claim they listen to their customers' needs can now do so on the Internet. Companies exploring telecommuting

... military forces in the former Soviet Union are trying to destroy the reform course of the Gorbachev administration and start a revolt against the Russian government. The rebels have cut off all information channels and control the TV, radio stations and press. Normal reporting of events is no longer possible and only rebel propaganda reaches outside the country. The political opposition has to try to smuggle information over the border. Over a computer network that an organization in Moscow shares with a Western European Internet provider, a speech by Boris Yeltsin covering the situation in Russia is exchanged. Via email this speech is forwarded to ClariNet, a Canadian network provider specializing in supplying reports to TV, radio and news agencies throughout the world. The impact of the information flow along those lines (the message was not to be the first or the last) on the situation and development of the revolt in the former Soviet Union is open to speculation. However, what counts is that the revolt was unsuccessful and the liberalization of the Eastern continent continued.

Source: Stephan Deutsch. personal recollection. Chris Schmidt, of the EUnet Germany staff, got the electronic mail first in August 1991.

options for their employees should definitely evaluate the Internet's capabilities.

Often communication via Internet services is the only solution for the information exchange necessities of commercial enterprises. Transmitting data at an acceptable performance level has to be supported by an incredibly expensive infrastructure that relies not only on financial but also on the organizational resources of a company. Many small commercial companies cannot afford to maintain their own telecommunications network. Internet providers offer these structures under acceptable conditions, and a company can do business through the Internet fast and without further knowledge. And because the Internet includes all new technologies and communication tendencies, your investment in the future is safe.

Just as there is a Net code of conduct, there is also an accepted way of doing business over the Internet. The basic tenet of participation is that 'you should give as well as receive', but emailing direct-mail advertisements in hopes of receiving more sales is not considered 'giving' by the Internet community. Businesses that do well provide information in a 'passive' manner— that is, by making available an archive of their information and catalogues so people can search when they want to. People definitely don't appreciate being bombarded with glowing descriptions of products. However, an outsider giving an objective review or recommendation is considered acceptable.

Interest in and demand for online interactive services is definitely heating up. The types of virtual corporations that are emerging include online bookstores that let you peruse or download online books or order a hard copy book. There are similar services for record stores and online magazines. And virtual shopping malls are rapidly appearing.

What makes the commercial aspect of the Internet really interesting is the cooperation of business areas that are not related in any way to computers and networks. In the Ruhr area of Germany, for instance, the public transport service (VRR—Verkehrsverband Rhein/Ruhr) offers pricing information and ticket purchase via the Net. Lawyers can apply new decisions of the German supreme court to special cases. And the more companies step in, the more services you can use.

Given the history of the Internet in Europe, it seems to be easier for the European Net community to accept the commercial direction in the development of the network of networks. By building up projects that are supported by both industry and commerce, the European Internet tends to accept new commercial aspects on the Net more readily than people on the American Internet. There are a few heroes from the early days of the Internet engaging in a hot debate about the impact of commerce on the development of the Net, stating that the Internet is the network of freedom and should not be intruded on by commercialism. All these discussions influence the growth of the Net and make more people aware of it.

Europe, despite its being hampered by a heavy (and slow) regulatory environment from national public telephone operators

'It does not require a crystal ball to predict that business use of the Internet will expand significantly over the next few years. . . . The electronic highway is not merely open for business; it is relocating, restructuring and literally redefining business in America.'

Source: Mary J. Cronin, *Doing Business on the Internet* (New York: Van Nostrand Reinhold, 1994).

(PTOs), is not far behind the United States. In the U.K. and Germany, the most deregulated of the European countries, there are a large number of organizations providing local and nationally focussed Internet access and a variety of value-added services.

France is in some ways the odd one out—having had its own equivalent of the Internet, the Minitel service, for some years. This service is based on France Telecom's provision in the 1980s of small terminals to homes, businesses and public places throughout France. These provide services ranging from an electronic phone book to email, online databases and chat lines. As a result of this, France has been relatively slow in developing Internet services, although there are now links between the Internet and Minitel.

BACKING OUT OF THE DRIVEWAY

The Internet is 'The Great Equalizer', but unfortunately, the first hurdle is the highest—that is, actually getting off on an even footing.

A transport provider will give you access to the Internet and, as mentioned above, there are many ways to get 'connected'. Whether you have a PC or a Cray supercomputer, a gigabits-per-second speed network or a plain old telephone line, you can get connected to the Internet. There are two basic methods of access available for individuals: through an organization's network, or through a computer, modem and telephone line. The basic costs are explained below. Chapter 7 discusses some of the available options in more detail, and also tells you the general steps to take if you wish to connect your organization's network.

Costs

For some people around the world, the Internet is like an 'all-you-can-eat' buffet—there are no worries as to how much they use because they use a university access or are employed by a large company. For the majority of the European Internet, people and organizations have to pay for their usage, usually by volume charge. In the United States, telecommunications is a free market, with telephone companies fighting each other—advertising for customers, raising special programs and offering discounts for every conceivable reason—all of which often looks like paradise to the European telecommunications customer. The situation in Europe is more complicated, as often there is one monopolistic telecommunication provider (for example, a state-owned company); consequently, the prices for telecommunication infrastructures of leased lines are very expensive. Prices vary considerably from country to country. You can order a leased line in Great Britain and pay about UK£1,500. The line (same speed, same length) in Germany would cost about UK£2,000. That is one reason why Internet costs are different from country to country, but a general decrease in costs over time can be observed in Europe as well as in the United States.

Commercial Providers

Individual users who don't have the benefit of organization apron-string links, in contrast, must get their access from commercial Internet providers, public-access Internet sites, or a digital rich uncle giving away access through public accounts. Access for those with a computer and a modem is usually through a local telephone call to a modem-pool/terminal server or to another computer. The costs can vary, but many commercial providers charge a flat-rate monthly fee that isn't bad considering the potential gain of instant worldwide communication.

Demon Internet in the U.K. is one such provider, with a modem dial-in Internet service that costs £10 per month for unlimited connect time to the Internet. Callers are still liable for phone calls to the nearest Point of Presence (PoP) of their service provider. Demon's dial-in customer base rose from 2,000 to more than 10,000 during 1994, and the growth in demand consistently

'The Internet in particular and the global telecommunications infrastructure in general are expanding at a historically unprecedented rate. Prices are plummeting as national
markets are deregulated, bandwidth is rising, connectivity is
spreading, providers are proliferating, access is becoming
more and more available to people with an increasing diversity of technical capabilities and funding appetites, and
interoperability is being recognized as a crucial element in
nearly every major provider's business strategy. All of these
things are good, and are happening naturally as a conse-
quence of the natural forces of technological evolution and
the marketplace'.

Source: Chip Morningstar, Electric Communities, 3339 Kipling, Palo Alto, CA
94306, (415) 856-1130, *chip@amix.com*.

outstrips its ability to supply new connections. Demon has just
entered into an agreement with the U.K. PTO Energis for the
supply of fast fibre-optic backbone capacity to meet future
demand.

There are a number of other national and regional providers
in Western Europe, ranging from national and multinational organizations such as EUnet and PIPEX to local-area providers,
who are themselves often resellers of capacity from a primary
service provider.

In the same way that different railway networks linked together for mutual benefit in the last century, Internet service
providers are starting to share capacity on a more formalised and
managed basis rather than just allowing other suppliers to route
across their network on a tit-for-tat basis. In late 1994 the London Internet Exchange (LINX) opened in the U.K. capital's
Docklands, providing a shared and managed service to its members, the primary service providers.

As the Internet market matures, the major PTOs and cable
companies are starting to provide Internet access, the most significant being the entry to the U.K. market of British Telecom in
late 1994. Although on a relatively small scale initially, with its
massive and modern telecoms network it may ultimately be able
to provide local dial-in or fixed-link access to the Internet from

any location in the U.K. Elsewhere in Europe, where there is less competition, major telecom companies have been rather slower to take up the challenge.

But, just as the telephone system still doesn't quite reach everyone worldwide, Internet access is not always easily available or reasonable. Many people in remote areas must make expensive long-distance calls to send and receive email or to access resources. Often isolated, and desiring human contact and access to information, they find the extra cost worth it—*if* they can afford it.

THE FUTURE

The Internet's crystal ball doesn't yield many clues to what will happen in the future. The developers of the early ARPANET envisioned it as a way to bring expensive hardware resources closer to researchers. What they didn't expect was that email would become so heavily used by researchers at geographically distant sites who want to talk and collaborate with each other. Other high-speed networks that were built to connect supercomputers are now used more for collaboration and access to information.

Today communication and access to information are still the most popular applications, but the Internet is getting a face-lift. We will start to see more user-friendly interfaces—front ends that make this worldwide web 'transparent'. That is to say, the network and computer are becoming integrated in the home and office, performing important, vital functions without making users aware of the nitty-gritty details.

One such interface is known as Mosaic, and it's been referred to as the new 'killer application' of the Internet. Mosaic and similar applications have worked wonders for the Internet's user-unfriendly reputation, but it is considered a 'wide load' on the Infobahn—meaning, it's hogging the road. It requires a lot of transfers of sometimes large amounts of data across the networks, and this can cause congestion, not unlike the traffic jams we experience on today's streets and highways.

Our experience with Mosaic is providing us with insight into the future. Tomorrow's applications will require faster networking technology, and network researchers are working on building higher-speed networks. High speed in the near future will be gigabit-per-second speeds. For example, an entire encyclopaedia could be transferred in a few seconds on a gigabit-per-second network.

The encyclopaedia metric is often used to describe how fast the network will be, but it's important to realize that although some advanced applications, such as video conferencing, will require high speeds, this increased capacity will also be used to handle the growing number of people who will be using the network. You can compare this additional capacity to a ten-lane highway. The number of lanes does not enable you to drive ten times faster. It just allows more cars to travel at the same time.

We will need to widen the road, especially if the Internet continues to grow at its present rate (and it doesn't show any signs of slowing down). It's estimated that in a few short years, there will be 100 million people interconnected via the Internet. Most likely, they will be communicating with one another by using interactive video and audio applications or email that incorporates multimedia; already there are such applications being used in schools, universities, research labs and some businesses.

With that, you're probably revving your engines and ready to race toward your computer. However, before you start typing, there's some background material and a few fundamental concepts you have to learn before graduating from Internet 'newbie' to 'Top Gun'. So on to Chapter 2, for the lowdown on the Internet.

Chapter 2

INTERNET: THE LOWDOWN

sk an Internet wizard what this network is all about and you'll probably get a long and dusty discourse studded with acronyms and techspeak. The Internet is friendly if you approach it right, but potentially huge and terrifying, especially to people who don't know its ways. This chapter will explain some of the basic principles that underlie the Internet. Fortunately for you, the most important principle of all is that you don't have to *fully* understand how the Internet works to use it. Plenty of blissfully unaware Internet users are pounding away at keyboards and communicating merrily, with absolutely no knowledge of how the Internet fits together. However, although ignorance may be bliss, the more you know, the more doors will open up to you. So here goes.

A NETWORK OF NETWORKS

The Internet is a global web of interconnected university, business, military and science networks. Why the term 'web'? Isn't the Internet just one network? Not at all! It is a *network* of networks. The Internet is made up of little local area networks (LANs), citywide metropolitan area networks (MANs) and huge wide area networks (WANs) that connect computers from organizations all over the world.

These networks are hooked together with everything from standard dialup phone lines to high-speed dedicated leased lines, satellites, microwave links and fibre-optic links. And the fact that they're "on" the Internet means that all these networks are interconnected. This network web extends all over the world, but

---

What the Experts Are Saying . . .

'It's a biological phenomenon. The Internet is not a vertebrate. It acts a lot like slime mold, growing in all directions without anyone in charge. Every time I try to describe the Internet to anyone, everyone assumes I'm having a hippie mystic vision!'

—John Perry Barlow, National Net '93

'I'm starting to think of the Internet as a kaleidoscope. It is just so much broken glass and trinkets. Users turn the mirrors and lenses and, suddenly, meaning snaps into place for them where before there was only chaos. My job at NYSERNet is tuning the mirrors and polishing the lenses.'

—Jean Armour Polly, Manager of Network Development and User Training, NYSERNet, Inc.

---

trying to describe all of it and how it fits together is a bit like trying to count the stars. In fact, so many networks are interconnected within the Internet that it's impossible to show an accurate, up-to-date picture. Some network maps show the Internet as a cloud, because it's just too complex to show all of the links. To complicate matters, new computers and links are being added every day. It's estimated that a new network is added every 10 minutes.

So think of the Internet as a 'cloud of links'. The cloud hides all the ugly details—the hardware, the physical links, the acronyms and the network engineers. Remember that you don't actually need to know all the details to communicate and use resources on the Internet.

Speed of a network is often referred to as **throughput**—how fast information can be propelled through the network. The Internet isn't just *one* speed because, as explained above, it can accommodate both slow networks and the latest technology. There are now networks on the Internet that are capable of transmitting 155 megabits per second (about 17,000 typescript pages).

In Europe the most typical network connection ranges from 64Kbps, for small organizations, up to 2Mbps for larger organizations. A 64Kbps connection can be realised through leased lines as well as through dialup to the popular Integrated Services Digital Network (ISDN). Grades in bandwidth are 128Kbps, 256Kbps, 512Kbps and so on. New services offering 34Mbps connections have just been announced. Gigabit-per-second network speeds currently being tested will allow for even more advanced applications and services, such as transmission of complex weather prediction models produced by supercomputers to weather centres. Or for the transmission of extremely large databases (tens or hundreds of megabytes)—for example, earthquake data transferred from a collection site to the Institute of Geophysics and Planetary Physics for analysis. Or for enabling a video conference including people from all over the world.

IN THE BEGINNING

The Internet was not born full-blown in its present worldwide form of thousands of networks and connections. It had a humble—but exciting—beginning in the United States as *one* network called the ARPANET, the 'Mother of the Internet'. The ARPANET, described in Chapter 1, initially linked researchers with remote computer centres, allowing them to share hardware and software resources, such as computer disk space, databases and computers. Other experimental networks using packet radio and satellites were connected with the ARPANET by using an internetwork technology sponsored by DARPA. The original ARPANET itself split into two networks in the early 1980s, the ARPANET and Milnet (an unclassified military network), but connections made between the networks allowed communication to continue. At first this interconnection of experimental and production networks was called the DARPA Internet, but later the name was shortened to just 'the Internet'.

Access to the ARPANET in the early years was limited to the military, defence contractors and universities engaged in defence research. Cooperative, decentralized networks such as UUCP, a worldwide Unix communications network, and USENET (User's Network) came into being in the late 1970s, initially serving the

Living on the Fault Line

One California energy company, Unocal Corp., uses the Internet extensively to give it a competitive edge in the energy exploration business. Earthquakes shake things up in the oil business, so Unocal's seismic engineers transfer the latest earthquake data from Caltech to help find potential payoff in their existing geothermal fields. Data from a recent California earthquake was in the hands of engineers within minutes of its release by Caltech.

The company also uses the Internet to get state-of-the-art software for modelling seismic data and technical consulting on the uses of fractals in seismic work. Access to the research community through the Internet keeps the company up to the minute in a very competitive business.

Source: Peter Ho, Unocal Corp. (Note: All opinions are Ho's and in no way reflect Unocal's position.)

university community but, later, serving commercial organizations in the United States and Europe as well. In the early 1980s, more-coordinated networks, such as the Computer Science Network (CSNET) and Because It's Time Network (BITNET), began providing networking to the U.S. academic and research communities. These networks were not part of the Internet, but later special connections were made to allow the exchange of information between the various communities.

The next steppingstone in the history of the Internet was the birth in 1986 of the National Science Foundation Network (NSFNET), which linked researchers across the United States with five supercomputer centres. The NSFNET soon expanded to include mid-level and statewide academic networks connecting universities and research consortiums; in thus doing, the NSFNET began to replace the ARPANET for research networking. In March 1990, the ARPANET was honourably discharged (and dismantled). CSNET soon discovered that many of its earlier members (computer science departments) were connected via the NSFNET, so it, too, ceased to exist in 1991.

The development of European internetworking grew on the back of several initiatives: the construction of national X.25-based network infrastructures such as PSS (Packet SwitchStream) in the U.K. and Transpac in France. National and transnational academic networks such as JANET (Joint Academic NETwork) in the U.K., inspired by the DARPA model, were built upon these infrastructures during the late 1970s and 1980s. Interestingly enough, JANET adopted an addressing schema similar to the Internet DNS, except that the domain hierarchy was reversed! For example, a JANET username of richardh@rlpa.uk.ac places the country domain (.uk) before the functional domain (.ac, for academic community). It appears likely that JANET will go over to Internet standard addressing format and adopt TCP/IP as its native protocol.

In parallel with these projects was the less formal but effective and widespread linking of computers that used the Unix operating system, with the support of the various European Unix User Groups (UUGs). These used UUCP (Unix-to-Unix Copy Protocol) built into the Unix operating system to provide the standard for the transmission of email and files between machines, using a variety of networks, from phone lines to the academic networks. For this system to work, it was not necessary for a computer to make a connection to every other computer to which it needed to pass information. The whole thing worked on a cooperative routing principle similar to the Internet itself, where if the recipient for a mail item or a file was outside your local group of computers, the information was passed on to the machine that provided the 'gateway' to the next group of systems. In the early nineties, most of the UUG and academic networks migrated to the Internet protocols and joined the rest of Europe in the Internet.

The majority of the institutions that built the backbones of the physical infrastructure of the UUG nets were based at research institutes and universities sponsored by de facto customer organizations. This may be the reason that the Internet in Europe is far more connected to industry than to government. The past few years have seen the development of an even more commercial nature to the Internet, as many of the initiators of the UUGs became commercial companies that created EUnet, a multina-

tional pan-European Internet provider. Other national and regional Internet services providers followed, and now new players
are appearing on the European stage as U.S. providers turn their
attention to this market.

European governments were not involved in the formation
of the Internet itself, although the German, French and Italian
governments sponsored academic networks that, in fact, provided much of the physical infrastructure for the UUGs. They instead took a great interest in the development of international
standards for communication protocols, under the umbrella of
the CCITT (Consultative Committee for International Telegraph
and Telephone) and ISO (International Standards Organization).
The communications standards resulting from this work are
based upon the ISO/OSI (International Standards Organization/
Open Systems Interconnect) model, rather than on the Internet's
TCP/IP standard. Most of the European national academic and
commercial networks are based on this model, using the X.25
protocol. With the demand for interconnection with the Internet, most of these networks have sufficient gateways to be re-
garded as integral parts of the Internet and have, in most cases,
adopted the Internet addressing conventions. When one looks at
the combination of private and public networks based upon different standards and the regulatory environment in Europe, the
situation appears very confusing. There are, however, lots of new
options (see Chapter 7) and, in most cases, you can get there
from here by one means or another.

HOW COMPUTERS TALK

The computers on a network have to be able to talk to one
another. To do that they use **protocols**, which are just rules or
agreements on how to communicate. Standards were mentioned
in Chapter 1 as an important aspect in computer networking.
There are lots of protocol standards out there, such as DECnet,
SNA, IPX and Appletalk, but to actually communicate, two computers have to be using the *same* protocol at the *same* time. TCP/
IP, which stands for Transmission Control Protocol/Internet Protocol, is the language of the Internet. You may speak Japanese
and I may speak English, but if we both speak French, we can

communicate. So any computer that wants to communicate on the Internet must 'speak' TCP/IP.

Developed by DARPA in the 1970s, TCP/IP was part of an experiment in **internetworking**—that is, connecting different types of networks and computer systems. First used universally on the ARPANET in 1983, it was also implemented and made available free of charge for computers running the Berkeley Software Distribution (BSD) of the Unix operating system. TCP/IP, developed with public funds, is considered an open, non-proprietary protocol, and there are now implementations of it for almost every type of computer on the planet. 'Non-proprietary' means that no one company—not IBM, not DEC, not Novell—has exclusive rights to the products needed to connect to the Internet. Any number of companies, including those just mentioned, make the hardware and software necessary for the network connection.

TCP/IP isn't the only protocol suite that is considered 'open'. Since the early 1980s, the International Standards Organization has been developing the Open Systems Interconnection protocols. While many of the OSI protocols and applications are still evolving, a few are actually being used in some networks on the Internet, and more are planned. So even though most of the computers speak TCP/IP, the Internet is officially considered a 'multi-protocol' network.

The whole idea of protocols and standards can get complicated, but as an Internet neophyte, all you need to be concerned with are the applications that TCP/IP offers. The difference between applications and protocols is that you don't actually *see* the protocols (they're invisible to the end user); however, you will access the Internet using the applications that conform to these standards.

The Internet Toolbox

Three TCP/IP applications—electronic mail, remote login, and file transfer—are the Internet equivalent of the hammer, screwdriver and spanner in your toolbox. There are plenty of fancier applications using variations on or combinations of these basic tools, but wherever you roam on the Internet, you should have

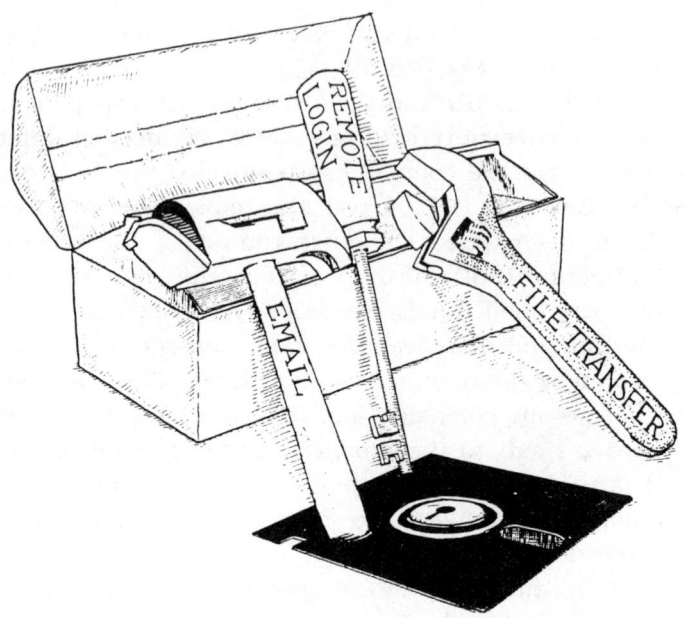

Electronic Mail, File Transfer, and Remote Login are the three basic applications you'll use on the Internet.

the Big Three available to you. The three basic Internet services, as well as the more powerful and colourful applications, are covered in later chapters, but here's a quick introduction to get you on your way.

Electronic mail, also known as **email** or **messaging**, is the most commonly available and frequently used service on the Internet. Email lets you send a text message to another person or to a whole group of people. For example, a student in the Netherlands can send an email message to a student in Bulgaria to ask how kids spend their free time there. Or a group of teachers can have an email conference on using the Internet in the classroom.

Remote login is an interactive tool that allows you to access the programs and applications available on another computer. For example, say that Sven, a student at the University of Oslo, is going on a skiing holiday in the Rocky Mountains and wants to check the weather conditions and snowfall there. An Internet computer at the University of Michigan houses a weather database called the Weather Underground, with temperatures, precipitation and even earthquake alerts for the entire U.S.A. Sven uses the remote login tool to connect to this computer and interactively query the Weather Underground for the information he needs.

File transfer, the third of the Big Three tools, allows files to be transferred from one computer to another. A file can be documents, graphics, software, spreadsheets—even sounds! For example, you may be interested in information on Chernobyl from the Library of Congress's 'Glasnost' online exhibition of documents from the former Soviet Union. Using file transfer, you can download articles from the computer where they're stored onto your own personal computer, where you can read them, print them out or clip and incorporate parts of them into a paper you're writing.

There are quite a few applications available today that use a combination or variation of these three tools to hide details even further. These operate on a client/server model—that is you use the client on your computer, and it contacts servers for directions and information. Clients and servers don't have to be located in the same geographical area, and in many cases on the Internet, they aren't. This technology is very flexible; during one session, your client may access servers all over the world to help you find information. The client/server concept is explained further in Chapter 4.

As the Internet grows larger, locating the information you need will become difficult unless you're using information discovery and retrieval tools. The major resource discovery tools, which operate on the client/server concept, include archie, Gopher, WWW and WAIS. Chapter 4 provides explanations for all of these and gets you started in using them.

How Does TCP/IP Work?

When you're actually using the above-mentioned tools, information of various types is being transferred from one computer to another. TCP/IP breaks this information into chunks called **packets**. Each packet contains a piece of the information or document (several hundred characters, or **bytes**), plus some ID tags, such as the addresses of the sending and receiving computers.

Suppose that you wanted to take apart an old bridge in England and move it lock, stock and barrel to California (people *do* do these things). You would dismantle the sections, label them *very* carefully and ship them out on three, four, maybe even five different trucks. Some take British Airways and some American Airlines, others go by ship, all to be loaded to trucks in New York. The trucks get to California at various times, with one arriving a little later than the others, but your careful labels indicate which sections go up first, second and third.

Each packet, as IP handles it with its addressing information, can travel just as independently. Because of all the network interconnections, there are often multiple paths to a destination. Just as you might drive a different route to work to save a few minutes here or there, the packets may travel different networks to get to the destination computer. The packets may arrive out of order, but that's okay, because each packet also contains sequence information about where the data it's carrying goes in the document, and the receiving computer can reconstruct the whole shebang. That's why the Internet is known as a **packet-switched network**. The switches are computers called **routers**, which are programmed to figure out the best packet routes, just as a travel agent might help you find the best flights with the fewest stops. Routers are the airport hubs of the Internet; they connect the networks and shuttle packets back and forth. The packet is just a chunk of information; it doesn't care (or know) how fast it travels. So it can travel over a 'fighter-jet' network— running at Mach-whatever speeds and connecting supercomputers—that interconnects with a 'biplane' network operating a lot slower.

The Networks That Make Up the Internet

The Internet network connections don't follow any specific model, but there is a hierarchy of sorts. The high-speed central networks are known as **backbones**. The electronic equivalent of the autobahn system, they accept traffic from and deliver it to the mid-level networks. An example of such a backbone system is Canada's CA❀net, a nationwide network that connects all its province networks. The Australia Academic and Research Network (AARNet) is a nationwide network connecting its member organizations. EUnet in Europe connects 34 countries from Iceland to Vladivostok and from the Arctic Circle to Africa. Mid-level networks, in turn, take traffic from the backbones and distribute it to their own member networks, the neighbourhood roads of the networking world. The Verein zur Foerderung eines deutschen Forschungsnetzes (DFN) is a mid-level network, connecting over 100 universities and research facilities in Germany. The organizational networks that connect to these nationwide and mid-level backbones may be very big networks themselves. For example, Vienna University in Austria has a large campus network that connects its university departments.

Each of the network links has speed limitations, but speeds are determined by the technology used (not by some 'packet policeman'). Wide-area connections are usually slower than local-area networks. A WAN link is typically 2Mbps down to 64Kbps. (There are more and more wide-area networks, however, that are starting to operate at 45Mbps or in Europe at 34Mbps.) Local-area networks are usually much faster. Ethernet, a popular LAN technology, runs at 10 or 100 Mbps, while another local-area networking technology, Fibre Distributed Data Interface (FDDI), runs at 100Mbps. An easy way to understand these speeds is to imagine each of these technologies as a system of water pipes. More water can be pumped through bigger pipes during a given period of time, so they have more bandwidth. Local-area network pipes are usually pretty large, and therefore more water (or data) can be blasted through them than can be pumped (transmitted) during the same amount of time through a wide-area network pipe.

Seamless Worldwide Networking

Once all the pipes—networks—are in place, the Internet, which is actually tens of thousands of networks, looks seamless to the user. By means of internetworking—that is, connecting networks together to enable communication and information exchange— all the details are hidden from you: the packets, the routers and all those interconnections. Despite legions of different computers and disparate networks, somehow the whole web works, and any computer directly connected to the Internet can talk to all the other computers on the Internet. So you, working on a computer in your office in Israel, or in your spare bedroom in Los Angeles, can communicate with a colleague in South Africa or a friend in Calgary. It's as if you are directly connected by one wire.

WHO RUNS THE INTERNET?

Who controls this web, this cloud, this network of networks? Well, no one, really. The Internet seems to be both institutional and anti-institutional at the same time, massive and intimate, organized and chaotic. In a sense the Internet is an international cooperative endeavour, with its member networks kicking in money, hardware, maintenance and technical expertise.

The NSFNET (initiated by the National Science Foundation) was often referred to as the overall organization and backbone of the Internet. This is both true and false. The NSFNET, funded by the U.S. Government, increased interconnection in the United States, thus pushing the Internet forward. With the connection of different international network providers to U.S. mid-level networks, users throughout the world are able to access academic resources in the United States.

The Internet Society

The standards process of the Internet is more centralized, but no less exciting. Development and improvement of TCP/IP protocols is sanctioned by the Internet Society (ISOC), a nonprofit professional organization run by its members (both individuals and organizations in various communities, including academic, scientific and engineering). ISOC is dedicated to encouraging cooperation among computer networks to enable the creation of a global research communications infrastructure. The society sponsors several groups that determine the needs of the Internet and propose solutions to meet them. One of these groups is the Internet Architecture Board (IAB), which provides direction to two principal task forces: the Internet Engineering Task Force (IETF) and the Internet Research Task Force (IRTF). The IETF is concerned

Context Is All

'Explaining the magic of networks, Mike Bookey of Digital Network asks you to imagine a car plunked down in the jungle. Checking it out, you might find it a very useful piece of equipment indeed. A multipurpose wonder, it would supply lights, bedding, radio communications, tape player, heat, air conditioning, a shield against arrows and bullets and a loud horn to frighten away fierce animals. In awe of the features of this machine, you might never realize that the real magic of a car comes in conjunction with asphalt.

'For the first 10 years of the personal computer era, according to Bookey, we have used our computers like cars in the jungle. We have plumbed their powers for processing words and numbers. All too often, home computers have ended up in the cupboard unused. We have often failed to recognize that most of the magic of computing stems from the exponential benefits of interconnection.'

Source: Extracted from "The Issaquah Miracle" by George Gilder (George Gilder's Telecosm), *Forbes ASAP*, pp. 114–123.

with operational and technical issues of the Internet, and the IRTF is involved in research and development matters. Standards documentation, as well as useful information that the working groups of the IETF develop, are called Request For Comments (RFCs). These are available in public archives on the Internet. (See Appendix for more information.)

Anyone interested in promoting the Internet can become involved in ISOC. Similarly, anyone with great ideas for protocol development and improvement can join the IETF. All you need is desire, the ability to travel to meetings three times a year, and the willingness to volunteer your time in working groups.

In Europe the Research Internet Protocol Europeene (RIPE) is the administrative organization handling operational and technical issues of the Internet. RIPE is located at the CWI in Amsterdam. In cooperation with RARE (the European organization for ISO/OSI-based networking activities) and with European inter-

national and national Internet provider organizations, RIPE over-
sees internetworking interests in Europe.

The Commercial Internet

Of particular interest to business users are the commercial
Internet providers that have sprung up around the world: in the
United States, companies such as UUNET Communications Services, Performance Systems International (PSI), Advanced Network & Services, Inc., and in Europe, companies like EUnet and
PIPEX as international providers, SwipNet, XLINK, Switch and
others as national providers. Many of the commercial networks,
such as UUNET, PSI, Sprint, CERFnet, PIPEX and EUnet have interconnected their backbone networks to form the Commercial
Internet eXchange, or the CIX (pronounced 'kicks') not to be
confused with Compulink Information Exchange, one of the
most widely used U.K. Internet-linked conferencing systems,
which has goals similar to those of the NSFNET but is independent from government funding and therefore capable of providing commercial data highways. For European users, the parallel
availability of the CIX and NSFNET leads to a more transparent
use of both commercial and academic resources.

In addition to connecting organizations' networks, all of these
commercial providers offer users with modem-equipped PCs and
Macintosh computers individual access to the Internet. Other
projects have the interests of businesses in mind. These include
the Enterprise Integration Network (EINet), spearheaded by
Microelectronics and Computer Technology Corporation (MCC).
EINet uses UUNET's nationwide backbone, Alternet, to offer
value-added services, creating an infrastructure purely in support
of business and commercial applications. EINet addresses sensitive and complex issues that face organizations who do business
online, including security and enhanced email services.

Another group interested in electronic commerce on the
Internet is CommerceNet, a coalition of Silicon Valley organizations in Northern California. CommerceNet's focus is on commercial use of the Internet, with an emphasis on reliability, security
and ease of use. The coalition hopes to accomplish these goals by

developing protocols that address business requirements. Third-party providers can then develop business applications based on these protocols.

ACCEPTABLE USE

As you can imagine, with all the people, networks and government agencies participating in the Internet, there are bound to be rules, restrictions and policies for parts of it. Probably the best-known document outlining some rules is NSFNET's Acceptable Use Policy (AUP), which basically states that transmission of 'commercial' information or traffic (any for-profit activities) is not allowed across the NSFNET backbone, whereas all information in support of academic and research activities is acceptable.

The NSF's AUP is rapidly becoming a non-issue as the networking landscape changes in the United States. The NSFNET is being phased out, and all mid-level networks will obtain their interconnection from commercial providers. At this point it will not matter what type of traffic is sent across—commercial, research, or academic. However, you will probably hear references to the NSF AUP from time to time.

The situation is changing in places, and the country or network from which you gain your Internet access may have specific restrictions (such as no commercial use) and acceptable-use guidelines (such as for research and education use only). The Internet as a whole continues to move to support—or at least to allow access to—more and more commercial activity. Users may have to deal with some conflicting policies while that process evolves, but at some point in the near Internet future, free enterprise will most likely prevail, and commercial activity will have a defined place, rendering the issue moot. In the meantime, if you're planning to use the Internet for commercial reasons, make sure that the networks you're using support your kind of activity.

Even though the Internet is becoming more commercial, there are still 'unwritten' laws that frown upon certain activities, such as direct email advertising. Chapters 3 and 5 discuss some common mistakes to avoid if you're planning to use the Internet for business.

INTERNET CONCEPTS

You'll soon learn how to plunge into the Internet, but before then—as with almost any new adventure in a foreign land—you'll need to acquire some new vocabulary. The basic concepts are simple, and because the network protocols do much of the work, you don't have to become an Internet wizard to travel its highways and byways.

Names and Addresses

If you've ever travelled in a country where you couldn't read the street signs or figure out how the houses are numbered, you'll understand the wisdom of learning the Internet's name-and-address system. Most computers on the Internet can be identified in two ways. Each computer, or **host**, has a name and a numerical address (both unique), just as most of us can be located by our names or numerically by our phone numbers. It's easier to remember a name than a phone number, and it's the same on the Internet. An Internet computer name is usually several words separated by full stops, such as *planet10.yoyodyne.com*. An Internet address—technically an **IP address**—is four numbers also separated by full stops, for example, 161.44.128.70.

When you're saying these names and addresses out loud, you should substitute 'dot' for the 'full stops' to sound as though you belong. This is known as **dotspeak**, and there's a whole lot of it in the Internet. In the examples shown above, you would say 'planet10 dot yoyodyne dot com' and '161 dot 44 dot 128 dot 70'.

The idea is for people to use the computers' names when accessing resources, and to let the computers and routers work with the IP addresses. Each Internet-connected organization keeps a database of the names and addresses of all the computers connected to its own networks. As there are so many computers on the Internet and there is no real central authority, name assignment is best left to the local networks. Imagine if everyone in Europe had to get their new phone numbers from Brussels!

The InterNIC Registration Services, run by Network Solutions, Inc. of Herndon, Virginia, provides a central registering authority in the United States for organizations' second-level domain names and network numbers. The InterNIC also registers countries' top-level contact information. Each organization or country then assumes responsibility for assigning names and numbers to its computers.

There are registries for Canada, Europe, Asia-Pacific and Australia (see the Appendix for contact information). If you're outside the United States, you can contact the U.S. InterNIC, which will forward your request to the registration services in your country. You can also query the InterNIC's WHOIS database to find out the contact yourself. Chapter 5 provides direction for European organizations and users needing registration services.

If you're an individual user with a PC or Macintosh and a modem, you probably don't have to worry about registering anything; your Internet provider will take care of that for you. The InterNIC does more than register networks and domains, though; Chapter 5 explains about other InterNIC services, including user services, resource guides and training. See the Appendix for InterNIC contact information.

So how does this hostname/IP address stuff work? Suppose you want to find out about the metro systems of other major cities. To do so, there's a Subway Navigator on the *metro.jussieu.fr* computer to which you can connect using the remote login tool (you'll learn about Telnet in Chapter 4, but the exact command is **telnet metro.jussieu.fr 10000**). Before you can access this service, a database in France is consulted to find out the IP address of that computer. The address (not the name) is passed on to the routers so that they can make the connection. This is done quickly, automatically and transparently to you.

Why, then, do you need to know about IP addresses when the system was designed so that you shouldn't ever need to concern yourself with them? The answer, as you may suspect, is that things don't always work perfectly, and there may come a time when you will need to know an IP address to access a resource. For this reason, many resources are listed with the computer's name and its IP address. The recommended practice is always to use the computer name, since IP numbers—like telephone numbers—can change, while names tend to stay the same.

Directory Assistance for Computers. There will probably be occasions when you need to get a computer's IP address. (Perhaps the hostname you've been using just doesn't work anymore.) The necessary tools may or may not be available on your system; if they're not, check to see if an alternative tool is offered. Two well-known tools are *nslookup* and *dig*; to use either, just invoke them with the name of the computer. For example, **nslookup glas.apc.org** will return the IP address: 193.124.5.33, or the command **dig metaverse.com** will return 140.174.161.1 (unless those numbers have changed, which is entirely possible).

Domain Name System. There's actually a method to these names and addresses—a naming system known as the Domain Name System (DNS). The DNS is also the worldwide system of distributed databases of names and addresses. These databases provide the 'translation' from names to numbers and vice versa, a sort of international *Who's Who* of computers.

DNS names are constructed in a hierarchical fashion, which you can think of as a worldwide organization chart. At the top of this chart are top-level specifications, such as EDU (educational), COM (commercial), GOV (government), MIL (military), ORG (organizations), and NET (networks), and also two-letter country codes, such as US for the United States and CH for Switzerland. EDU, COM and so on are common in the United States. In Europe country codes (such as .be for Belgium) are used at the top level, with the organization type at the next level down. In most places outside the United States the .edu domain is replaced by .ac. Also, .co tends to be used rather than .com . It's also possible for non-U.S. companies to get a .com registration (usually for marketing purposes).

	U.S.	**Europe**
educational	.edu	.ac.country
commercial	.com	.co.country (or .com)
non profit-making	.org	.org.country (or.org)
organization network	.net	.net
government	.gov	.gov.country

Computer names on the Internet are organized according to the
Domain Name System.

An organization can register for a **domain name**, selecting
one of the top-level specifications mentioned above that describes it best, and then preceding it with a recognizable version
of its name. For example, a hypothetical Subway Spa, located in
Italy, would have a domain name like *subway.co.it*. From there, it
can divide itself into subdomains, extending the organization
chart to department levels, or it can just give all of its computers
names in the *subway.co.it* domain.

Once you understand how this naming system works, you
can remember names more easily, and you can also tell things
about a computer, such as to what organization it belongs. The
names do not, however, always indicate geographical location.
For example, *main.subway.co.it* may be the main computer at the
home office in Rome, while *venus.subway.co.it* might be located at
a division in Milan.

Now you probably have a few questions. After learning about the DNS, every new Internet user first wants to get a list of all the computers on the Internet. After all, you have a telephone directory of all the people in your home area. But there is no exact, up-to-date Internet name and address list available in hard copy or online anywhere.

In the early days of the ARPANET, a list was maintained, but the Internet grew too rapidly to keep up with all the additions and changes. The distributed domain name system has replaced this centrally managed list and has allowed the Internet to grow gracefully.

Internet Resources

While a list of computer names would not be very helpful, a list of online resources is. **Resources** on the Internet are all of the useful things that you can access: hardware such as super-computers, graphics labs, computer centres or printers and on-line information, such as the wealth of databases, documents, software, archives, pictures and sounds available. Resources can also be people. If you can talk to a group of people to figure out the answer to a question or problem, they are a resource; so are mailing lists and conferencing systems. An online forum on school networking or a work group on molecular biology are both Internet resources. Your understanding of the astonishing array of Internet resources, and how to get at them, will grow as you learn your way around the Internet.

Internet or Outernet?

To better understand what the Internet is, you also need to un-derstand what the Internet is *not* and which networks are *not on* the Internet. There are a number of worldwide networks that use protocols other than TCP/IP and provide their own sets of ser-vices. Some don't allow remote login, while some employ differ-ent file transfer methods, but many have a special connection to the Internet. These connections are not, however, the seamless web that was mentioned earlier, where the participating net-works interoperate to allow the same services. Instead, these are

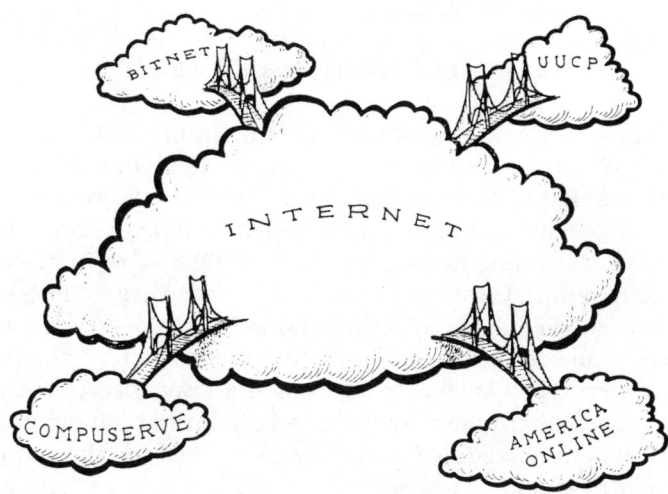

Email gateways allow Internet users to send electronic mail to people
on other networks.

connections of convenience, that—like marriages of the same
sort—have their purposes but not a lot of other interaction.

Networks on the outside are called **outernets**, but understanding the distinction between outernets and the Internet can be
difficult. Owing to the differing governments and languages involved in the Internet and the outernets, there's only one basic
service—email—that currently can be guaranteed to move between them. Email moves from the Internet to the outernets
through **email gateways**, the connecting points that translate the
different email protocols of each network. This worldwide system
of networks and gateways is sometimes called the **Matrix**. Some
network cartographers apply this term to the electronic regions
discovered during their virtual journeys all over the world via
electronic undergrounds and mazes; it's meant to encompass all
the possible email passageways.

The Matrix is also sometimes called the **Net** by citizens of all
networks. This term is ambiguous because it doesn't refer to any
one network, but it works well in referring to the overall worldwide situation. If you hear someone say that he's 'on the Net', it
probably means that he can at least be contacted by email.

'Enough of White Man's ASCII'

Dave Hughes, who is somewhat of an Internet evange-list, took to the foothills of the Rocky Mountains to work with a group of Native American teenagers at the American Indian Science and Engineering Society's summer school in physics. According to Hughes, the kids, who were from the Navajo, Zuni, Crow, Tohono, Sioux and Picurus Pueblo tribes, 'showed polite, quiet interest as I explained the tech-nology and made a local call to the Internet (Colorado Supernet). They laughed a bit, read and responded to email sent especially to them by Dr. George Johnston, physicist at MIT, whom I asked to directly "welcome" them to the world of mathematics and physics by telecom.

'Then I said, "enough of white man's ASCII", and started calling up the Indian art, the Crow Dance poetry, the new pieces by Lorri Ann Two Bulls, via modem, at 2400 baud. They *really* got excited! Putting questions to me, walking

(Continued)

It's interesting to note that many computers on outernets these days have DNS names, so it may only *look* as though they're connected to the Internet. There's a nifty feature in the DNS that allows for **Mail Exchange** (MX) computers. An MX computer is a gateway that's connected to the Internet and that is willing—meaning that an arrangement has been made—to transfer email to an outernet computer. Instead of finding an IP address for the outernet computer in the database, the DNS ob-tains an **MX record**, or the name of the Internet computer that will deliver the email to the outernet computer. All of this should be invisible to you, making it easier to send and receive email between the Internet and outernet networks. Which outernets have email gateways to the Internet? More every day, but some of the well-known international networks are FidoNet, a coop-erative network made up mostly of microcomputers linked via telephone lines; BITNET, an academic and research network; and UUCP, a network of computers that talk to one another over up to look closer at the full-colour VGA monitor, their dark eyes laughing, all smiles, and half of them standing up for the rest of the hour-long session. When it was over, a crowd gathered around the machine, picking up copies of the *Online Access Magazine* and *Boardwatch Magazine* I brought, and there were more questions. And from their obvious tribal knowledge, they were saying 'That's Crow, that's Sioux!' from the colours and symbols in the various pieces of art.

'A heart-warming session with 40 Indian kids who seemed to get a glimpse of a future even they could participate in. And if I am right, by reaching these youths, starting with their own "images of their inner selves" as Indians produced by such technologies, they may be better able to move on into the world of science, mathematics, and the cold regions of technological and white man's society, while still not losing their identity or associations with each other. Perhaps even doing their life's work as professionals, from the reservation, thanks to these little devices.'

Source: Adapted from a posting by Dave Hughes to the Consortium for School Networking Discussion Forum List (*COSNDISC@BITNIC*) on 10 July 1992.

dialup connections using UUCP (Unix-to-Unix Copy Protocol). Commercial networks, including CompuServe, MCImail and Genie, have made connections too. As time goes on, more and more commercial networks are connecting directly to the Internet and are offering full Internet services to their customers. America Online and DELPHI are two such services.

Network News

Another service available on many of these networks is called **network news**. 'News' in this context doesn't refer to current events from the news wires but to discussions; it usually means interest groups and conferences. There are over 12,000 different discussion groups on topics ranging from artificial intelligence to recipes, from politics to sex, from ornithology to skydiving— some collectively generating the equivalent of a book about the size of this one each day. News is transmitted on the USENET network, which has special relationships and connections with some of the networks previously mentioned. For example, USENET news can be transmitted across and between the Internet and UUCP networks, allowing citizens of both cultures to participate. The protocol that is used to transport news over the Internet is called Network News Transfer Protocol (NNTP). USENET is 'on its own', however, and no one person or organization controls it. It's a huge cooperative anarchy, with several million people participating worldwide.

Even though USENET is closely related to the Internet, and a lot of its traffic travels over the Internet, USENET is *not* the Internet. Many people who have access to USENET news don't have Internet connections; similarly, Internet connectivity doesn't always provide access to USENET news. Also, note that USENET is a conferencing system, and is not considered an email network.

Now that you know what the Internet is and what it's not, it's time to get on with learning to use it. Conferencing, email and interactive online conversations are the most exciting new developments in communications since the advent of the telephone. If you think the fax machine is great, wait until you try the Internet! With just your fingers on the keyboard, you can reach around the world.

Chapter 3

COMMUNICATING WITH PEOPLE

A *network neophyte*, faced with a cryptic computer prompt, may find it hard to picture the Internet as a friendly, peopled place. But every day, hundreds of thousands of people are communicating through the Internet—conversing, collaborating, working, playing and letting off steam. Friendships—even marriages—are made and broken on the Internet. Clubs are formed. Problems are solved. Books such as this are written. Jobs are found. Handicaps and disabilities make no difference. Through email and the other methods of online communication, people have become best friends without ever seeing or talking to each other. It is not uncommon for people to turn to the Net for answers; a question posted to online communities—mailing lists and conferences—can yield dozens of tales of invaluable experiences and testimonials within hours.

Online communication, perhaps the ultimate in democratic exchange of information, eliminates barriers. You can't make judgements about a person you're 'talking' to based on appearance, or even on voice. People can be whoever they want to be. Shy people become bold. Children give their views to adults, and the adults listen. Accounts clerks communicate on the same level as company directors.

On the Internet, people can communicate asynchronously and in real time. Translation? **Asynchronous** (Greek for 'not at the same time') communication means that someone can type in a message and send it off, but the recipient doesn't have to be around to receive it. This type of communication has some real benefits. You can send messages whenever you want to, they

---

Springtime in the Ukraine

More and more schools are getting access to the Internet
and are seeing its usefulness in teaching geography and social
studies, mathematics and science. But the benefits run
deeper. A school teacher wrote to us about a project in which
her students communicated with students in the former Soviet Union. 'Besides such an obvious social studies application, I was deeply moved by a romantic exchange of notes on
springtime in our city and springtime in the Ukraine between
a young adolescent girl with cerebral palsy and a young man
whose name was Albert.' There are no handicapped travellers on the Internet.

---

reach their destination quickly and the recipients can read and
respond when *they* want to. Answering machines and voice mail
are everyday examples of asynchronous communication. In contrast, **real-time**, interactive communication (such as the Internet Relay Chat facility mentioned later in this chapter), means
that as someone is 'talking'—that is, typing—you see it on your
screen as it is typed. Real-time audio and video conferencing is
starting to become more prevalent on the Internet too. Both
types of communication, asynchronous and real-time, are covered in this chapter.

ALL (OR ALMOST ALL) ABOUT ELECTRONIC MAIL

Electronic mail is the most popular application on the Internet
today. It's a very powerful tool that's simple to use and easy to
understand. Using email can give you a real feeling for the energy and reach of the Net. It's hard to imagine any other form of
communication that can be so intimate and yet so wide-reaching,
so focussed or so expansive. You can communicate as easily with
someone across twelve time zones as with someone in the same
building. Your message can be limited to just one person, or it
can reach hundreds of kindred souls.

Email is sometimes compared to fax, but there are some fundamental differences. A fax is a graphic image that is digitized

and sent over regular telephone lines using modems. Email on the Internet is, for the most part, text that can be sent over a variety of network links—everything from dialup to fibre-optic lines. It usually costs the same to send email to one person as it does to send it to a group of people, while it would cost more (in time and maybe paper) to send a fax to those same people, especially if they're a long-distance call away. Both are asynchronous forms of communication, eliminating 'telephone tag'—that is, it's not necessary for the recipient to be present to receive either email or a fax. Interestingly enough, there are some projects on the Internet that combine the capabilities of both fax and email, and while interest is growing, the ubiquitous ability to fax over the Internet is not available just yet. Even so, these technologies will continue to collide, and someday soon you won't be able to tell the difference between them. One such project is a worldwide experiment in remote printing involving several countries. For example, a librarian using this experimental system in Canberra, Australia, could send a fax from his Internet-connected workstation to a remote printer (fax machine) in Riverside, California. (To obtain an article that explains this experiment, send email to *tpc-faq@town.hall.org*.)

Historically, Internet email has been text-based without some of the frills that many local-area, network-based email systems have. Text-based means that the message is only words—just like what you're reading right now—and can't include graphics, forms and so on. However, Internet email is starting to branch out with some implementations, including the ability to query distributed directory databases (an online directory service for people's email addresses), to encode/decode messages for privacy purposes (see the 'Security Issues' section in Chapter 5) and to send formats other than just text, such as graphic images, sounds and different character sets (Asian language text, for example) using Multi-purpose Internet Mail Extensions, commonly referred to as MIME.

An extension such as MIME is required, as the current email system does not permit transfer of a nontext file (such as a picture) without making some special changes to it; there are strange characters in these files that can interfere with the email system. If you need to transfer a nontext file via email, inquire whether or not your provider's email application offers MIME

Normal Heroes Always Make a Detour

In 1990, after 15 years as editor, journalist, translator and head of the Moscow News Computer Department, Anatoly Voronov started exchanging mail with Dave Caulkins, an American setting up GlasNet in Russia. Their offices were three blocks apart, but their messages went through the Moscow Teleport host in San Francisco. Voronov ascribed the roundabout routing to the famous principle expounded in the Russian movie classic *Atbolit-66*, 'Normal'niye geroi vsegda idut v obkhod' (normal heroes always make a detour).

GlasNet became fully operational in 1991, with Anatoly on staff. This time the San Francisco connection went through PeaceNet, a 'detour' which proved very helpful during the

(Continued)

---

support. If it does, you can 'attach' sounds, word-processed files or software, and send them off. The only catch is that the recipient of your message must have MIME capability to receive your attachments; unfortunately, it is not yet available everywhere.

There are other ways of sending software and graphics within a message if you don't have MIME support. Many email applications (mentioned below) support automatic conversion of nontext files into ASCII format; that way, those strange codes in the binary file are converted to something the mail system can handle (plain text) without burping. One such program that's sensitive to the Internet's email digestive system and can convert binary files to text is called BinHex, and it's available for both Macs and PCs. To you, BinHex files will look like a bunch of nonsense—random characters—on the screen (they begin with the line, 'This file must be converted with BinHex . . .'). If you receive one of these in your email or through other means (and it's not automatically converted for you), you'll need the BinHex utility to transform the file to its original format, a binary file. See the Appendix for information on obtaining BinHex.

Another one of these programs is UUENCODE/UUDECODE, which comes from Unix operating systems but can also be imple-

August coup d'etat. 'Our traffic grew tenfold,' Anatoly re-
members. 'We got hundreds of "get-well messages" from all
over the world. I remember a posting from a Chinese student
in America, a participant in the Tiananmen Square events in
Beijing, offering to share his personal experiences of how to
beat tanks in the heart of the city.

'People wondered why the KGB didn't cut off our connection. I wonder too. I think they simply didn't know that
we existed. And we had a trick: the UUCP connection was
originated in San Francisco, because at that time a non-
authorized person or organization could not call abroad from
Moscow. And it was impossible even for the KGB to cut the
phone link of the whole of Moscow.

Source: Anecdote from archives of EUnet Germany.

mented in PC and Mac. If you have both BinHex and UUDECODE,
you should be able to handle most of the messages you get with
some nontext in strange characters.

Sending Email

Email is really fast: it is sent and received in seconds, minutes at
the most. The only time this doesn't happen is if you or the recipient of your mail don't have a direct full-time mail connection
to the Internet. In such cases, mail is held on a host machine
(usually that of the Internet service provider) until such time as
the mail gateway computer of the other party calls up to swap
incoming and outgoing mail. (See the discussion of MX records
and outernets in Chapter 2.) Postal mail is often called **snail
mail** by comparison. Sending email is easy, too. All you need is
access to the Internet, an email program and the email address of
the person with whom you wish to communicate.

Access to the Internet. Chapter 2 discussed the differences
between being directly connected to the Internet and being on
an outernet network such as UUCP or BITNET or a commercial

service like America Online or CompuServe. If you have access on any of these networks, then you can exchange email on the Internet.

Email Programs. You'll need an email program that will run on your own microcomputer or on whatever computer you're using. Most large systems and public-access computers offer several email programs (sometimes called email readers or user agents). Some commercial Internet service providers will supply programs to load on your PC or Mac or provide you with information about where to obtain public domain or commercial software for the job. A common characteristic of email programs is that they let you compose and send email, and then read and organize the email you receive. There are many different email programs; some of the more popular ones are listed below. Your choice of a program will depend on how you're accessing the Internet. If you aren't sure what's available, ask your system gurus for assistance.

Post Office Email Programs

If you're accessing the Internet using a PC or Mac, there are several different ways you can read and send email. One of the more popular applications uses the Post Office Protocol (POP). In a nutshell, the POP system allows your personal workstation to get its email from a big computer that serves as a post office, delivering the mail when you (or your computer) ask for it. This eliminates the need for your computer to be on all the time, constantly available to receive email. In order to use a POP-based email application, you need Internet access (via dialup or full-time connectivity) and a POP mail account on a post office computer (ask your Internet provider). All of these applications provide intuitive editors. Listed here are the most popular email programs. Most are free; some are commercial. See the Appendix for information on obtaining these.

Email Addresses. The next big step on your agenda is to learn about email addresses. In order to send someone email, you need to know their address. An email address, like a postal mail ad-

POPULAR UNIX AND VMS EMAIL PROGRAMS

Listed here are some of the most common and popular Internet email applications used on Unix and VMS operating systems. If you have access from a commercial Internet provider, be sure to read their documentation for specifics on the type of email applications and protocols they make available. The only drawback to using email applications on these systems is the editors or message composers (programs that let you type in a message) that come with them; they are not always very user-friendly.

Unix Systems

ELM	The command is `elm`
MH	A set of commands comes with this macro package
XMH	The command is `xmh` (a graphical X11 front end for MH)
PINE	The command is `pine`
Unix Mail Program	The command is `mail`

VMS Operating Systems

DECWindows Mail	Select the mail applications
VMS Mail Program	The command is `mail`

dress, contains all the necessary information needed to deliver a message to someone.

Internet email addresses are, in fact, very simple. They consist of a *local part* and a *host part*. The username refers to the mailbox, login name or userid of the recipient on that computer. For example, if your friend Jacques logs on to his computer as *cousteau,* then that's his username. The host part of the address should be recognizable to you—a series of words separated by dots, as discussed in the domain name section of Chapter 2. The local part and host part of an email address are separated by the '@' sign:

username@hostname

Suppose that you know that Jacques's computer name is *dive.into.ocean.fr.* You could send email to him using this address:

Trading Places: New Dimensions
to Interlibrary Loans

Paula Garrett of Batavia, Illinois, and Katie Wilson of Sydney, Australia, in an effort to see how the other half lives, traded homes and jobs for six months. Both are librarians, so no career changes were involved. However, taking over some-one else's work habits is indeed a learning experience. About the only things the women didn't trade were salaries and mortgage payments!

The venture was a complete success because of the Internet and the Australia Academic and Research Network (AARNet), according to Katie. 'Such exchanges can take place without the Internet, but not as successfully as ours! We found it made a huge difference to be able to keep up with our jobs and keep things flowing smoothly. Six months was not a very long time in which to learn the jobs, which are senior with a lot of responsibility, so the constant email communication helped us hold it all together! Plus we used the Internet to plan the whole thing.' There's no question that the Internet has helped end the cloistered image of librarians.

---

cousteau@dive.into.ocean.fr. (This and the following examples are fictitious.)

Sending It Off. Once you have an email program and know the recipient's email address, you're ready to send a message. Each email program is different, so if you're not familiar with yours, you may have to fumble around a bit or actually read the manual or online documentation. You will need to specify that you want to send a message, either by typing **send**, clicking a *send* button or performing some other wonderful computer incantation. The email program will prompt you for information, asking for the recipient's email address, the key piece of information the program needs to send the message to the recipient. It will also ask for the subject of your message—usually a summary, title or brief descrip-tion. The subject is optional, but you should get into the practice of

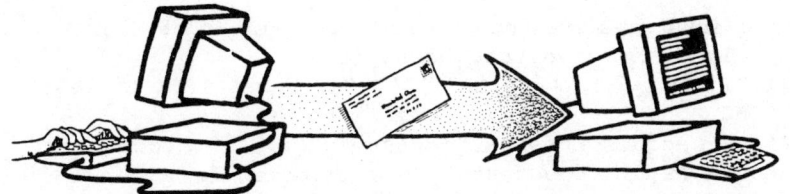

Internet email is usually sent to its destination in seconds.

including it. A good subject description makes the recipient aware of the nature of your message, whether it's important or whimsical. The program may give you the option of sending a 'carbon copy' (cc) message. If there's someone else you think would be interested in the message, here's a chance to include his or her address. (You can send copies to more than one recipient.) If you have the disk space, it's a good idea to send a copy to yourself so you'll have a record of your outgoing messages. (Your email program may also automatically save outgoing messages for you.) There may come a day when you'll need to know exactly what you said to someone!

After you've answered all the email program prompts, you can compose your message, using your email program's editor, which may or may not be similar to the word processor with which you're familiar. It's important to make your message easy to read and understand; some hints for effective communication are discussed in detail in the 'Netiquette' section of this chapter.

Anatomy of an Email Message

An email message has two basic parts, the 'header' information and the body of the message. These pieces are separated by a blank line. In most cases, you'll be interested only in the body, or the actual text, of the message. The headers contain items such as 'Date:', 'cc:', 'From:', and 'Subject:'. Sometimes there are seemingly arcane lines such as 'Received:' and 'Message-Id:'. Normally these are of little concern to you, but they are necessary for the email programs and for debugging purposes. The following is a sample message:

```
From cousteau@dive.into.ocean.fr Sat Feb 4 1:51 EST 1995
Received: by dive.into.ocean.fr
(1.37.109.8/15.2) id AA29108; Sat Feb 4 1:51 EST 1995
-0800
From: Jacques Cousteau (cousteau@dive.into.ocean.fr)
Return-Path: <cousteau@dive.into.ocean.fr>
Subject: Today's diving turn
To: team@dive.into.ocean.fr (Scuba Diving Team of
Jacques Cousteau)
cc: second.team@dive.into.ocean.fr (second Diving Team)
Date: Sat, 4 Feb 95 1:51:07 EST
X-Mailer: ELM [version 2.3 PL11]

Hi team members,

For today's diving turn we still need to fill up the
oxygen bottles, and please don't forget your knives
this time in case a shark comes by to say hello!

Thanks,
Jacques
```

In this example, Jacques Cousteau has sent mail to his diving team, asking them for a favour. Jacques sent this message on Saturday, 4 February, at 1:51 in the afternoon, with the subject **Today's diving turn**. He cc'd the second team (so they have a record of his correspondence with the first team). Later on in this chapter we'll see how the diving team reacts to Jacques' message.

Receiving and Keeping Up with the Mail

Receiving email requires less effort than sending it. Incoming messages are stored in your **inbox**. When you fire up your email program, it fetches your mail from an online mailbox (if there's anything in it), and then usually displays a one-line summary for each message. This summary will include information such as the message number, the date the message was sent, the sender and the subject. You can select which message you want to read by typing the corresponding number, or by selecting it with your mouse.

Here's an example of a message summary line:

```
1   Feb 4   Jacques Cousteau   (21)   Today's diving turn
```

This is message number 1 in the team's email box. It was sent 4 February by Jacques Cousteau. In this example, the number in parentheses indicates the number of lines in the message (21), but it could refer to the number of characters too. And the last column is the subject of Jacques's message, 'Today's diving turn'.

If you think you can't keep up with the junk mail that flows into your snail-mailbox each day, then just wait until you collect dozens of 'keypals' and you're busily exchanging messages every day. Almost everyone *loves* to get email—it will probably give you a tiny thrill to see the message 'You have new mail', when you check your electronic mailbox. However, as it's so easy to send and receive email, you may find that you can't keep up with all the messages you receive! You should set up a good routine for sorting your mail, deleting trivial messages and filing the rest by saving them in separate electronic **folders** sorted by people or topics. If you don't keep up with your email efficiently, your messages will stack up in the inbox as they proliferate, and your email program may slow to a crawl. Your email program may allow you to sort incoming messages by date, sender, subject, size or in other ways; such functions can help you dispense with messages quickly.

Replying to Email

Email programs usually have some kind of 'reply' feature to make responding quick and easy. For your part, this involves typing **reply**, or clicking a *reply* button with your mouse. The reply feature takes care of filling in the address and subject fields (using information in the original message's header), and puts you in the email message composer. A very common convention when replying to messages is to include the original message within your reply message, with each line prefaced by a '>' character (or just three spaces). Your email program may automatically do this for you or provide a command that does it. That way, people can distinguish between their original comments and your response. It may not seem important to reference parts of the original message explicitly, but some people receive so many messages a day that they may not remember your conversation without some background material.

The Whole (Email) Shooting Match

Members of the USENET newsgroup on shooting sports organized the first email rifle competition in early 1992, linking three continents—Australia, North America and Europe—to schedule, stage and score a match between small-bore rifle clubs from Liverpool University and the Australian Capital Territory. The competitors did the shooting on their home ranges and forwarded the scoring via Internet email to the newsgroup moderator in the United States, who judged the contest and announced the results.

According to Geoff Miller of the Australian team, making email history was 'the easy part' of the project; 'then we actually had to get the shooters to the range to shoot their cards'! The Liverpool team, following their leader's red car in a blue minibus, made a faulty fielder's choice at a roundabout and took off after the wrong car. The captain, in the meantime, mistook another blue minibus for his team's and kept it in his rear view mirror all the way to the range. When the team finally got themselves assembled, he discovered he'd left his rifle at home.

In Canberra, lighting problems on the range led to the cancellation of practice shoots and delays in scheduling the competition. The Australians took the field on the first weekend of the new year. Hampered by high winds and the aftereffects of the holidays, the ACT team lost to Liverpool by a margin of 50 points.

Geoff Miller, undeterred by his team's showing, anticipates email matches developing into 'a regular fixture' on the intercontinental small-bore scene, 'providing yet another example of the inexorable march of computers into all areas of life'.

The header lines will alert you to reply messages. For example, a 'Re:' will precede the original subject line, and there may also be an 'In-Reply-to' line. Let's look at the team's response to Jacques:

```
From shark@cave.ocean.fr Sat 4 Feb 1:58 EST 1995
Received: by cave.ocean.fr
(1.37.109.8/16.2) id AA29396; Sat, Feb 4 1995 1:58:11
-0800
From: The dangerous white shark (shark@cave.ocean.fr)
Return-Path: <shark@cave.ocean.fr>
Subject: Re: Today's diving turn
To: Jacques Cousteau (cousteau@dive.into.ocean.fr)
CC: team@dive.into.ocean.fr
second.team@dive.into.ocean.fr
Date: Sat, 4 Feb 95 17:58:11 EST
In-Reply-To: <no.id>; from "Jacques Cousteau" at 4
Feb 95 1:51 pm
X-Mailer: ELM [version 2.3 PL11]

Jacques,

> For today's diving turn we still need to fill up
> the oxygen bottles, and please don't forget your
> knives this time in case a shark comes by to say
> hello!

Fine to hear from you again (a member of your second
team has me on the e-mail list as well). If you will
bring the team and knife, I will bring a fork and
some friends and we can have lunch together . . . .

—see you, Whitey Shark
```

Here Whitey Shark has included part of Jacques's message prefaced by the greater-than-signs (">") because he knows that Jacques receives a lot of email and might not remember exactly what he told his team. He then typed his response to that message. Note that the subject line has a 'Re:' prefacing the original subject.

At this point, if Jacques responds, his email program will again include those greater-than signs. Sometimes you can carry on an entire conversation, keeping track of who said what by how many ">" signs are in front of their comments. You may want to edit out irrelevant parts of the conversation to eliminate any confusion that may be caused.

Bounced Email and Other Errors

Sometimes an email message may not actually reach its destination because of an incorrect address or some other error. Just as postal mail may come back to you stamped 'Returned to Sender', you may get a **bounced message** back wrapped in an **error message** that gives you some clues as to what went wrong. Usually the problem is an error in typing the address. One common error message is *User unknown,* which appears when the message is received by the computer specified in the address but the local part, or username, doesn't match any username or mailbox on the computer. Most often, the cause is a typo or a misspelling, but if you think you typed correctly, then you should contact the person you're trying to reach by another means to find out the correct username.

Another common error is *Host unknown,* in which the hostname is wrong. Again, check for typos first; sometimes parts of the name are missing—for example, perhaps you forgot to include part of the domain name.

Other bounced messages—such as *network unreachable,* (the computer) *can't send for several days, connection timed out* or *connection refused* and *bad file number* generally have something to do with problems on the network or at the destination computer. These problems are usually beyond your control, so you should contact your system consultants or, in the worst case, your Internet provider's email experts who might be able to help you. Mail systems are supposed to support an alias for postmaster, so if I have a problem, I often email to postmaster at a site. This often results in a fix—but sometimes in silence.

Generally, if you type something wrong or have an incorrect address, you will get a bounced message. Sometimes, however, your email will simply disappear into the elusive **black hole**, the place where lost messages go and where they'll never be heard from again—or at least that's what it feels like. There are several possible causes of this phenomenon. The message may arrive at the intended destination, where an error is detected, but your own return address is incorrect, so the bounced message can't be sent to you. Or, the message may arrive safe and sound, but your friend never reads it or decides not to respond to it. Usually, trying again, using another addressing method, or contacting your friend by another means to find out if the message was received will help you figure out what went wrong.

Finding Email Addresses

Possibly the most frequent burning question from new users is how to find out someone's email address. Unfortunately, there's no comprehensive Internet-wide directory assistance available at this time, as there is for finding out telephone numbers in many countries. There are ways, though, to find email addresses, and the more proficient you become in using the Internet, the more tricks you'll be able to use. There's no law, of course, that prevents you from just calling someone and asking. In fact, if you haven't a clue, this is probably the first thing you should do to save yourself some time!

A new trend these days is to include email addresses on business cards, so when trying to reach a business associate, check there first. Or just guess—a frequently used and often successful method, believe it or not! For example, if you know where someone works, you can guess at the domain name (like *kodak.com*). Many organizations now allow email to be delivered to *person-name@domain-name*, where *person-name* is either the person's last name or the first and last name separated by a dot (as in *paul.shafer*). Like the company postroom, an email 'hub' at the domain-name may distribute all the email to the correct computers internally. Again like the company postroom, organizations often have a person who looks after the email hub. This person can usually be reached by using the address convention *postmaster@domain-name* and can help you with queries about addressing. This is not standard procedure, though, so don't count on it working every time.

Online directory service databases are springing up around the Internet. Many organizations have their own online 'white pages', named after the white pages in phone books, but they are by no means universal. Some of these are mentioned in Chapter 5.

Sending Email to Other Networks

As was mentioned in Chapter 2, email is the one application that can be sent between the Internet and outernets. Most networks offer an email service, and many are connecting to the Internet by email gateways. (Remember, email gateways are computers that have connections to both networks and that know how to translate the different email languages between those networks.) For example, if you have a friend or client who has an account on CompuServe, and you're on the Internet, you can send email to him or her, and vice versa.

Sometimes, sending email between networks is a bit tricky because you might have to specify a little bit more information in the email address, such as the actual name of the email gateway. If you have to do that, your email address might look like this:

```
username%hostname@gateway-hostname
```

Here, the email will be sent to *gateway-hostname*, which will then deliver it to the *username* at the *hostname*. For example:

```
shark-friends%deep.hole@cave.ocean.fr
```

This would send the message to *shark-friends* at the *deep* node—which is part of the *hole* (deep in the ocean)—through the *cave.ocean.fr* gateway.

The MX records that were mentioned in Chapter 2 may come into play and bail you out. If the outernet computer to which you're sending email has a DNS name, then you can just use that. You don't need to specify a gateway explicitly; the DNS database will figure it out for you. In fact, it is most likely that you probably won't have to address email this way because nearly everyone has changed over to DNS. But it doesn't hurt to know about it in case someday you have to specify an email gateway.

CONFERENCING: GROUP SPEAK

You can limit your email use to swapping 'letters'—just like your regular snail mail, only faster—but its electronic nature allows another dimension entirely. Imagine a newsletter focussed on your interests, where every subscriber is also a writer, and the articles and information all flow around in hours or days instead of weeks or months. Imagine being able to send a question to a group and receive responses from twelve different people from all over the world in a matter of hours. Online conferencing can do just that. Some discussions and conferences are more opinion-

FROM THE INTERNET TO THE OUTERNETS

Internet to:	*Syntax*
Applelink	*user*@**applelink.apple.com**
ATTMail	*user*@**attmail.com**
BITNET	*user*@*host*.**bitnet** *user*%*host*.**bitnet**@*gateway* May need to specify an email gateway, such as **cunyvm.cuny.edu**
CompuServe	*userid*@**compuserve.com** Convert the "," in the CompuServe userid to a "." Example CompuServ Address: **12345,678** becomes **12345.678**@**compuserve.com**
MCIMail	*userid*@**mcimail.com** Eliminate the hyphen in the userid. Example MCI address: **123-4567** becomes **1234567**@**mcimail.com**
UUCP	*user*@*host*.**uucp** *user*%*host*.**uucp**@*gateway* *user*@*domain-name* (if UUCP node has a DNS name)

In the preceding table, words in bold should be copied literally when constructing an email address. Words in italics should be replaced with the appropriate host, username or gateway name. This table shows common syntaxes for sending email from the Internet to another network. If these don't work for you, contact your system consultants. Note that some commercial services charge a small fee for incoming and outgoing Internet messages. Many, many more networks have connections to the Internet. For more information and references, see the Appendix.

centred than work-centred, like a newspaper's editorial page, except that the opinions, commentary and letters are all online and are sent to every member of the list or newsgroup, not just to the editor. There are interest groups for everyone, centred on business, academia, research, games, humour or hobbies—you name it. The possibilities for information sharing, problem solving and—let's admit it—recreation are staggering.

Email Lists

Once you start using the Internet, you'll notice people talking about joining **lists** and participating in discussions on various subjects. They're referring to **electronic mailing lists**, which are group discussions or interest groups. Email lists can involve as few as two people or as many as tens of thousands. There are literally thousands of different mailing lists on subjects ranging from cooking to etymology, from music to genealogy. And if there's not a list on a subject you are interested in, then you might be able to create one yourself. (To create an Internet email list you must have the necessary resources—a multi-user, directly connected computer and knowledge of email system administration—or know someone who does. Directions for doing this are beyond the scope of this book. Just ask around; perhaps someone will volunteer to help you.)

What Is It? A mailing list is simply a list of email addresses of people interested in a certain subject. Each list has its own distribution address, which looks just like the email addresses described above. All you have to do to get involved in an interest group is to request to be added or 'subscribed' to it by sending email to the list administrator, which is either a normal human being or an automated list-maintenance program. Your email address will be added to the list, and you'll start receiving discussion contributions from other list members. You may reply to these messages or send new thought-provoking topics at any time. Any message you send to the email list address will be distributed to every member of that list. You don't *have* to actively participate by sending messages all the time; you can just 'listen' to the discussion. Such listeners are often called **lurkers** (with no derogatory connotation).

```
The Eggplant Lovers Electronic Mail List
List name:      Eggplant Lovers
Description:    An interest group for people who
                love eggplants.
```

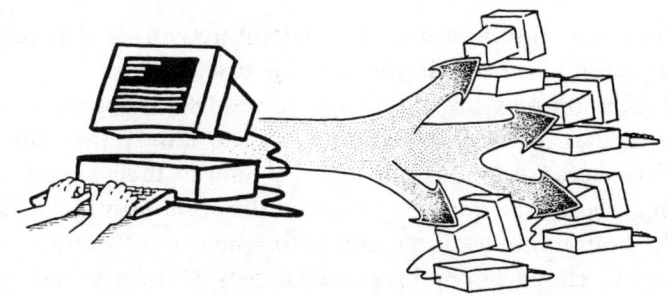

Send one message to many people on an Internet email list.

```
List address:    eggplant@vegetable.org
List members:    melman@sullivan-theatre.cbs.com
                 Stephen_Cavrak@uvm.edu
                 sestrada@aldea.com
                 pparker@oak.zilker.net
                 annie@hiney.com
                 Stephan.Deutsch@Germany.EU.net
                 fn@trinity.radio.open.de
                 jens@garion.uucp
```

Note: Eggplants are also known as Aubergines.

How to Subscribe. To subscribe to an email list on the Internet, generally speaking, you send a subscription request to the list's administrative address, which is different and separate from the actual list address. In most cases, the administrative address name is the list address name, but it will have *-request* added to the end of it. Let's use our Eggplant Lovers list example above. If this list really existed and you wanted to subscribe to it, you would send email to the administrative address:

eggplant-request@vegetable.org

and then state your request in the body of the message. (For example: 'I'd like to subscribe to the eggplant list, please. My email address is . . . .') The list administrator will add you to the list and you'll start receiving any messages sent from fellow eggplant lovers. (You can also *un*subscribe with a similar request sent to that address.) As you might have already observed, it is also possible

for users from the outernets (like UUCP networks) that participate in mailing lists to join the ongoing discussions.

A common new-user mistake is to send subscription requests
to the regular list address—a quick way to annoy the other list
members, because it adds unnecessary mail to their already bur-
geoning inboxes. So don't forget about the administrative address.

The bottom line is to remember to read carefully any instructions or associated descriptions of email lists. Some may tell you to
subscribe (and 'unsubscribe') by sending a sequence of commands
to an automated list program (with names such as LISTSERV,
Majordomo and Listproc, which are discussed below); other lists
are handled by humans. Some lists have very heavy traffic and
therefore strict policies, which are posted regularly on the list itself. All answers have to be sent directly to the questioner who is
responsible for collecting answers and sending a summary to the
list. This prevents unnecessary discussions and traffic jams on
the list. Like most lists, the summaries and interesting issues of
the list are stored in archives that are accessible via other applications on the Internet.

LISTSERV

A cousin to the Internet email list is the BITNET LISTSERV. You
will hear LISTSERV mentioned a lot because there are hundreds
and hundreds of interesting LISTSERV groups. You may want to
join one, so it's important to know what they are. Remember
that BITNET is an outernet-type network, and the only application that can be sent between it and the Internet is email.

LISTSERV, which derives its name from 'list server', is an
automatic discussion list service. It's a program that runs on a
BITNET computer (or BITNET node) and that handles all the list
administrative functions, such as subscribing and unsubscribing
people to and from interest groups. There isn't such a powerful
automatic list maintainer in widespread use on the Internet yet,
where most subscription requests are still processed by an actual
person, a maintainer of each list. However, programs like *listproc*
and *majordomo* are appearing on the Internet and providing Listserv-
like services. These programs operate similarly to Listserv.

A LISTSERV accepts commands requesting different actions, such as subscribing to a list or listing members of a group. On BITNET these commands can be sent to the LISTSERV using an interactive message facility. If you're coming from the Internet, however, you have to send commands within an email message to the LISTSERV address. After the LISTSERV performs the requested functions, it will send you a status report via email so that you will know the outcome.

Now, here's the tricky part. The actual BITNET interest group will also have a different email address from that of the LISTSERV. What this means is that discussion messages are sent to the list address, while commands are sent to the LISTSERV address. Many people get these two confused and end up sending LISTSERV commands to the actual list, where everyone gets a copy of your command message. Here's an example so you'll understand the difference. Say you want to join the Late Night Infomercial Reviews discussion group (fabricated for the purposes of this book, but it does have possibilities!). The list address for this hypothetical example from the United States is *INFO-MERCIAL@CABLETV*. The LISTSERV address is *LISTSERV@CABLETV*.

Note that BITNET addresses are different from Internet addresses. A BITNET computer name is easy to recognize because it's usually one word (no dots) and sometimes is cryptic-looking. When you're sending email from the Internet *to* BITNET, you will need to alert your computer to that fact. Usually you can just append *.bitnet* to the end of the BITNET node name and your system will know how to deal with it. In some cases, however, you may need to specify the actual email gateway, as mentioned above.

Since you want to subscribe to this list, you should send an email message to the LISTSERV address:

`LISTSERV@CABLETV.bitnet`

Remember, you always send list *commands* to the LISTSERV address, *not* to the actual mailing list address. It's the LISTSERV program that takes care of these administrative functions. Within the body of the message (you don't have to put anything in the subject field), you have to type the following command:

SUBSCRIBE INFOMERCIAL Susan Powter

(This is assuming your name is Susan Powter. If it isn't, then substitute your own name.) As you can see in this example, the *LISTSERV SUBSCRIBE* command is easy:

SUBSCRIBE List-Name Your-Name

Your-Name should be your name as you usually write it, *not* your userid or email address. (The LISTSERV gets your email address from the message header, not the body.)

Once you've put this command in the body of the message, you can send it. You should receive a welcome message saying that you are subscribed and giving you some important information about the list. You'll then get messages reviewing the latest in get-rich schemes and weight loss programs. Now, if you want to participate in the discussion—that is, send messages to this list—you should send email to the list address, *not* the LISTSERV address. So you would send your contribution to *INFOMERCIAL@ CABLETV.bitnet.* If you want to unsubscribe, repeat the steps above, sending email to the LISTSERV address, but instead of the *SUBSCRIBE* command, you type *SIGNOFF INFOMERCIAL.* That's it.

There are many other LISTSERV commands besides *SUB-SCRIBE* and *SIGNOFF.* If you're interested in learning more about these commands, send email to *LISTSERV@BITNIC.bitnet,* with the command **INFO REFCARD** in the body of the message. You'll receive an email message containing a list of general user commands from the LISTSERV at the BITNET Network Information Centre (BITNIC).

List Caveats

If you join an Internet email or LISTSERV list, how much traffic will you receive? That depends. Some lists aren't very active at all, so you might see only a few messages a week. Other lists can become very animated, however, and you may receive dozens of messages a day. Many people get really excited about joining lists and so they subscribe to a whole lot of them. Then they get more email than they can handle. It's a good idea to keep track of the lists to which you've subscribed. That way, if you go on vacation for an extended period and don't want to deal with hundreds (or thousands) of email messages when you return, you can unsubscribe to all of the groups on your list (LISTSERV gives you the ability to temporarily turn off or postpone receipt of messages while you're away).

The amount of traffic an interest group generates can be reduced considerably if members avoid sending unnecessary messages to the whole list—for example, subscription requests and 'I agree' or 'Me too' responses. Don't get 'reply happy' and feel that you need to respond publicly to every question that someone sends.

Often people use the reply feature in their mail program to offer a contribution to or continue a discussion, or to send a private message to the originator of the message. A word of warning here. You should *always* check to see to *whom* you're replying: is it the message sender or the entire list? Each email program is different, so you should familiarize yourself with your particular reply feature.

Picture this anguished moment: You see a message from your best friend on an email list; she has made a contribution to a discussion. You want to reply to her personally and tell her about your bad day and how you can't stand your boss, so you hit the *reply* button. You use words you shouldn't. You get descriptive in places. You finish the message and away it goes—to every single person on the list, including your boss! As unbelievable as it sounds, it happens all the time. The moral of the story is that you should always double-check to be sure your reply message is going to the right recipients. Either that, or stock up on the antacid pills.

Finding Lists

There are a lot of lists out there, and they can change quickly. You can download some online 'Lists of Lists' and peruse them to find out which groups are for you. Just browsing the A's in one such List-of-Lists, you can find interest groups on addictions, art and animal rights. Quite a range. The Appendix tells you where to access some online email list catalogues.

Network News

USENET was mentioned briefly in Chapter 2. It's a worldwide conferencing system, encompassing all sorts of organizations (universities, commercial organizations, government agencies, even home computers) and supporting one service—news. USENET is a real community. People from all walks of life spend hours 'together', reading, contributing ('posting'), and responding. Each group has its regulars, its 'famous aliases'. Others come and go. Some 'lurk', while others seem to talk incessantly.

USENET is a breeding ground for free expression and thought. People are usually very frank on this network! It's a point of pride that USENET, for the most part, is an open and uncensored environment. As a result, some very explicit and candid discussions ensue, from political arguments, to religious opinions and holy wars, to explicit stories with indecent themes. Be aware of this if you're easily offended, and simply avoid the groups that focus on subjects unpalatable to you.

USENET is divided into **newsgroups**. Devoted to a certain topic, each newsgroup is made up of **articles** or **postings** that look like email messages (each has a header and a message body). There are over 12,000 different newsgroups on USENET, but not every computer or site gets all of these in its USENET **feed**. Each site can pick which newsgroups it wants to 'carry' or let its users participate in. Why wouldn't a site want to provide every single newsgroup? One reason is that the volume of daily traffic is huge (over a 100 megabytes per day), and it takes up valuable disk space. Or the site may be paying long-distance charges to transmit and receive traffic, so it participates only in a small number of groups. Another very common reason is that some of the newsgroups deal with explicit subjects that may not be appropriate to carry.

USENET newsgroups are similar to email lists, but there are a few differences. With Internet email lists, every message is sent to each person who has explicitly requested to be a participant. On USENET, every newsgroup article is received and stored on *each* participating USENET *computer*, instead of being sent to each user. Even when you're not participating in a newsgroup, all of its articles are still stored on the computer, so you have easy access to any you want. It's difficult to know how many people

asbestos longjohns n. Notional garment often donned by USENET posters just before emitting a remark they expect will elicit flamage. This is the most common of the asbestos coinages. Also asbestos underwear, asbestos overcoat, etc.

Source: *The New Hacker's Dictionary*, edited by Eric S. Raymond, with assistance and illustrations by Guy L. Steele, Jr. © 1991 Eric S. Raymond. Published by The MIT Press, Cambridge and London, 1991. Reprinted with permission.

participate or lurk in each newsgroup. Something you say might be read by as few as five people, or by as many as 100,000.

USENET Hierarchy and Newsgroup Names. Newsgroups are organized in a hierarchical structure; their names have dots in them, just like Internet domain names. The top-level (leftmost) word in the newsgroup name specifies the newsgroup's category. There are seven major USENET top-level categories, and a scattering of alternative categories, as shown below. Knowing what these categories mean can help you figure out what each newsgroup is about.

Access to USENET. As was noted at the end of Chapter 2, not everyone on the Internet has access to USENET. There's no one way to tell if you can participate, but with a little bit of sleuthing, you might have a better idea. Some universities and most individual commercial Internet providers provide access to USENET newsgroups. Many businesses carry a subset (or all) of the groups. Remember, you can (and should) always call your provider's help desk and ask.

News Readers. In order to read or post news, you need to have a news reader program. There are thousands of newsgroups, and you don't want to have to sift through every one of them. A news reader will let *you* select which newsgroups you want to participate in by allowing you to 'subscribe' to them (you don't having to send email to an administrator). The reader program will organize the newsgroups, display the articles for you to read and allow

USENET newsgroups are forums for all kinds of interests and topics.

you to post articles. Just as there are many email programs, there are many news readers. Some are user-friendly, while others use terse commands and are difficult to learn.

You'll have to get used to how your news reader works and how it displays newsgroups and articles. Some readers offer a 'threaded' function that organizes articles within a newsgroup according to discussion threads—a helpful feature if you want to follow a particular discussion within a newsgroup instead of hopping from one debate to another.

If you're not sure about your choices of news readers, check with your system administrator or news provider. If you're faced with a Unix command line prompt, try typing the name of some of the news readers mentioned in the 'Unix Survival Guide' in Chapter 6 and see if that gets you anywhere. PC and Mac owners should ask their Internet provider what user-friendly graphical applications are available to them.

Here's what a posting (or article) from the United States looks like in the *alt.fan.douglas-addams* newsgroup:

```
Xref: world alt.fan.douglas-addams:3296
Newsgroups: alt.fan.douglas-addams
Path:world!news.kei.com!sol.ctr.columbia.edu!howland.
reston.ans.net!agate!r.beggins
From: r.beggins@pro-entropy.cts.com (Richard Beggins)
Subject: Hey?
Organization: Pro-Entropy +1-305-265-9073 (DAR Sys-
tems Int'l--Miami, FL)
```

```
Date: Tue, 25 Jan 94 07:38:14 EST
Message-ID: <ap27604@pro-entropy.cts.com>
Lines: 9

What do you think about Arthur Dent's attempts to
fly. As often I try to miss the ground, I fail...

Cheers from hospital, Rich
```

Getting Started. Once you're able to access USENET news, the first thing you should do is read all the articles in the *news.announce.newusers* newsgroup. The many useful articles in this group are regularly updated and chronicle the history of USENET, explain concepts and common problems, provide a list of frequently asked questions along with the answers, give information on available news readers, explain USENET software and how to become a USENET site, and provide lists of USENET groups. This chapter cannot cover every detail you need to know, but these articles will get you up to speed. This newsgroup (*news.announce.newusers*) is not a discussion group—that is, you can't post questions or follow-up articles to it. If you have new-user questions, there is a newsgroup where you can post them, the *news.newusers.questions* group.

Posting Articles. When posting an article in a newsgroup, you're asked for some information. As when you send email, you're asked for a subject. Be descriptive, since there are many people participating and it's polite to give them a good idea of what your posting is about.

You also need to specify how far and how widely you want your article distributed. Many times you'll want to make sure that everyone in the USENET world can read it, but sometimes your article may apply to a local geographic area. For example, if you post an article asking if anyone has any tickets to the Neil Diamond concert on Friday, you probably want to restrict it to your home town of Toronto rather than sending it to Tokyo and everywhere else. It's important that you exercise good judge-

MAJOR USENET HIERARCHY CATEGORIES

Category	Explanation
comp	Computer hardware, software and protocol discussions.
misc	Topics that don't fit anywhere else, such as job hunting, investments, real estate and fitness.
news	Groups that deal with USENET software, network administration and informative documents and announcements.
rec	Recreational subjects and hobbies, such as aviation, games, music and cooking.
sci	Topics in the established sciences, such as space research, logic, mathematics and physics.
soc	Groups for socializing or discussing social issues or world culture.
talk	Lengthy debates and discussions on various current events and issues—politics, religion, the environment and so forth.

SOME ALTERNATIVE HIERARCHIES

Category	Explanation
alt	Alternative group of discussions—not carried by all USENET sites. Some are controversial; others are 'lite'. Not considered a regular part of the USENET hierarchy. Alt newsgroups generate a lot of traffic.
bionet	Topics of interest to biologists.
biz	Business-related groups.
clari	Commercial news services gateway'ed to USENET by the ClariNet Communications Corporation.
relcom	Russian-language newsgroups.

A SAMPLING OF NEWSGROUPS

rec.food.cooking	alt.internet.services	rec.humor.funny
soc.men	comp.society	news.announce.newsgroups
biz.jobs.offered	alt.exotic-music	alt.fashion
rec.motorcycles	soc.culture.French	sci.energy

Some newsgroup hierarchies are named to the geographical source of the group themselves, such as *de.comm.internet* ment, not only by specifying geographic areas, but also by posting articles only to appropriate newsgroups. For example, it's probably not the best idea to post your resume to *rec.folk-dancing*.

If you write an article that is relevant to more than one newsgroup, you can **cross-post** that article. For example, you may decide that your article posted to *rec.cooking* about how you almost burned the house down cooking dinner should also be posted to the *rec.humor* newsgroup. Be careful when cross-posting, though. Sometimes it can anger the regulars in the cross-posted newsgroups because you're essentially 'forcing' them into a conversation that originated somewhere else.

Moderators

The normal operation for most email lists and USENET newsgroups is to let everyone participate, sending or posting whatever they want. As you can imagine, this practice quite often results in what's called a low signal-to-noise ratio—lots of junk submissions that offer little or no quality to the discussion.

As a preventive measure, some email lists and newsgroups are moderated. Instead of being sent straight to the group, messages or articles are submitted to a moderator, who decides whether or not the submission has relevance to the topic at hand. The moderator may accept (or reject) each submission or may combine messages and articles to create a digest that gets posted periodically. Moderated lists and newsgroups usually contain a higher proportion of useful information, but many people don't like the idea of their postings being evaluated.

INTERACTIVE DISCUSSIONS

The types of communication that have been described so far are asynchronous—email, interest lists, and USENET newsgroups. The Internet also has interactive communication capabilities that allow one-on-one (just two people talking—typing—back and forth) or many-to-many (a bunch of people talking and listening) discussions. Since communication is happening in real time, you need an interactive connection to the Internet in order to use this feature. In other words, you can't participate in this type of communication if you're on an outernet network.

Interactive conversations aren't organized into email messages or postings; they are simply displayed on your terminal as they are received. Unless the communications program on your computer allows you to log your conversation, you won't have a permanent record of it.

Can We Talk?

One of the best-known interactive communication tools is **talk**, which allows you to set up a real-time dialogue with another person. Unlike email or news, both people must be present. Usually one person requests to 'talk' to another person by using his email address. For example, if you wanted to chat with your friend Whitey, you would use the following command to set up a dialogue:

```
talk whitey@cave.ocean.fr
```

A message will be displayed on Whitey's screen, telling him that you wish to talk to him and giving him instructions on how to reach you. If he does indeed want to talk to you, he'll issue the command **talk** *your-email-address* and a two-way interactive discussion can ensue. The talk program helps you keep 'who's typing what' straight by splitting your terminal screen in two. Whatever you type is shown in the top half, while the other person's response is shown in the lower half.

This type of communication is fun, and it can be a very useful tool. It can, however, be somewhat frustrating if you aren't a great typist, for there's a tendency to feel pressure to type as fast as you can—which, of course, introduces all sorts of interesting and creative errors. There's also the 'who talks now' problem; to resolve this you may have to resort to some radio communication techniques. For example, when you're done typing, you can type **o** for 'over', meaning that you'll wait for the other person to type in his response.

But you are not limited to one person. Conference talks are possible of you use **ytalk**, a program similar to talk but connecting you with several people on the Net. If those people also use ytalk, you have a real group chat, all participants are able to see what the others are saying. Also, people who can only 'talk' to you are able to join in, seeing only you as partner.

The talk capability, unfortunately, is not universally available. There are some implementations on certain types of computers that don't work very well, so you may run into compatibility problems. Also, some system administrators turn this capability off. You may have to just grin and accept the fact that you can't 'talk' with everyone.

Everyone Join In!

In addition to **ytalk**, the Internet has a many-to-many interactive discussion capability called **Internet Relay Chat** (IRC). This type of communication is similar to conference calls, where there are lots of people talking and listening at one time. Michael O'Brien—a.k.a. Mr. Protocol, the Miss Manners of the Internet—once said, 'In general use, it resembles a bank of . . . party chat lines.' If you're a gregarious person who likes to stay up late at night typing in your thoughts and dreams to people from all over the world, this interactive capability will definitely appeal to you (participants claim it's very addicting). In spite of its 'frivolous' appearance, IRC has proven to be a useful tool for business and education conferencing and information access, as evidenced by its ability to disseminate live reports quickly during major events, such as the Gulf War, the Soviet coup of 1993 and natural disasters.

The newsgroups on IRC, however, are called 'channels', and they are not permanently established—they are created and available only as long as people are participating in them. Anyone can create a channel and, having done so, is known as the 'operator' of that channel. Operators have special privileges—they can deny access, as well as change the mode of the channel. For example, some channels are private and deny access to curious outsiders, some are moderated (all communication goes through the operator first), while others are public and open to anyone—it's all up to the operator. Two public channels that always seem to be populated are *#Hottub* (a virtual hot tub community) and *#initgame* (a game involving initials). Channel names are prefixed by '#' or '&' characters and are not guaranteed to be very descriptive; the original purpose for a discussion may last a few minutes before shifting into a whole different topic.

Remember, when you join a channel, everything you type is shown for all channel participants to see. It is possible to con-

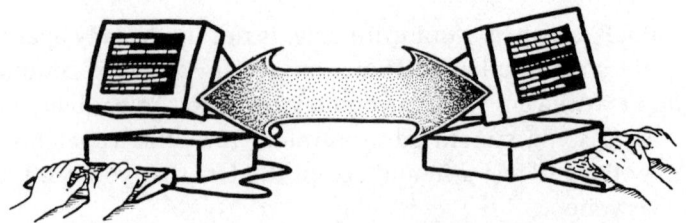

'Talk' or 'Internet Chat Relay' gives you interactive communication with other Internet users.

verse privately with people by sending a message directly to their nicknames, identifiers that IRC users register.

How It Works. You use a client IRC program on your computer, which allows you to participate in various channels (you can communicate in more than one channel at a time). Your client controls your screen; status messages, commands and your own messages are typed in the bottom two lines of the screen. The channel conversation goes on above those lines. Your client program communicates with an IRC server, which takes care of managing all the individual clients and distributing channel traffic between it and other servers. It is recommended that you use a server that's geographically close to you, but in most situations your server enables you to speak to people who are connected to other servers.

Access to IRC. Not everyone has access to IRC. To see if you do, first ask your Internet provider. If you get access through a Unix computer system, try typing **irc** and see what happens. The very first thing you should do after firing up IRC is read the help and intro files. (Start by typing **/help intro**.) Keep in mind that all IRC commands are prefaced by a slash, **/**. To get help, type **/help**. To get a list of channels, type **/list**.

For More Information. If you're interested in diving into the icy and raging IRC waters, be sure to read all the IRC documentation you can find and to make liberal use of the IRC help command. There are IRC client programs for many systems, including PCs and Macs.

Sydney Is Burning

'As I flipped through my email messages one morning, I suddenly received a new one entitled "The Sydney Bush Fires." The mail was from my Australian keypal, and he was telling me and some of his other keypals what is was like to be experiencing the bush fires that were burning all around Sydney. Forgetting all about my other messages for the time being, I quickly wrote back and arranged to go with him to the KIDLINK IRC (Internet Relay Chat). On IRC, a place where, amazingly, people can talk back and forth, I was able to ask my friend all about the disaster. It turned out he was less than ten kilometres from the fires, he could see the flame-tinged sky and smell the smoke from his window, and he was able to tell me how far the fires were from the famous Opera House and the Taronga Park Zoo. During the next several days, I communicated through email a number of times more with my Sydney friend, and the fires got even closer to his house. Ultimately, he was safe. However, all week long the information about the Sydney fires that I brought to current events in my social studies class was more up-to-date than anything in the newspapers.

'This is only one of my amazing network experiences, but it is one that illustrates how being on a computer network and having access to the Internet has changed my life in wonderful ways.'

From a winning essay, 'Networks: Where Have You Been all My Life?' by Rachel Weston, *rweston@cap.gwu.edu*, Grade 7, Georgetown Day School, Washington, D.C.

Seeing and Hearing Is Believing

In addition to interactive text-based talking, there are some interactive audio and video applications being used on the Internet. Unfortunately, these are not practical for the average user dialling in from home, but with advances in network connectivity and application development, we may not be far from extending this capability to everyone.

The MBONE. The most powerful audio and video applications are being run on the Multicast Backbone, or MBONE, for short. The MBONE is a 'virtual network' that supports the broadcasting of video and audio information. Right now, the type of people who are able to participate in MBONE audio and video conferences are 'lucky ducks' with high-powered workstations (such as a Sun Microsystems or DEC workstation), high-speed connections and quite a bit of technical prowess. This is not a general-public application, so more than likely you won't have immediate access to it—yet. Many of the participants are members of the Internet Engineering Task Force (the IETF mentioned in Chapter 2), who use it to meet online with members of various technical working groups.

The MBONE is being used to do all sorts of things. When U.S. President Clinton spoke at the University of North Carolina at Chapel Hill in honour of its 200th anniversary, he was seen by more than just North Carolinians watching local TV and cable channels. The video and audio from this event was also transmitted live over the MBONE to Internet users all over the world. Dave Hayes, a budding Internet disc jockey who happens also to work for NASA's Jet Propulsion Laboratory, broadcasts his own hundred-minute radio program called *Ecclecticity* over the Internet to MBONE participants. The program airs on Mondays and Fridays at 1:30 Pacific time, on the 'Radio Free Vat' channel. (So if you have access to the MBONE, you should catch it!)

CU-SeeMe. For those who don't have access to the high-powered equipment and fast networks that are required for MBONE participation, there is another type of video conferencing you may be able to join. Cornell University in Ithaca, New York is currently developing software called CU-SeeMe for low-end workstations. With just a Mac or PC, video capabilities (a video card and camera) and a moderately fast link (a direct link of at least 56Kbps) to the Internet, you can tap into video 'reflectors' and participate in interactive video conferences. CU-SeeMe is the enabling technology for the Global Schoolhouse, a project bringing together schoolchildren from all over the world to participate in joint learning activities.

RIPE Meeting Audio Broadcast

In Europe several RIPE (Réseau IP Européen) meetings were broadcast over the MBONE. A microphone in the meeting room sent the speakers' voices directly into the MBONE and many people who were not able to participate directly could get the information via audio broadcast over the Internet.

For more information on both the MBONE and CU-SeeMe, see the Appendix.

NETIQUETTE, ETHICS AND DIGITAL TRICKS OF THE TRADE

It's easy enough to use email and news, but there's an art to communicating effectively online. Here are some general guidelines and some advice, gentle reader, on how to behave.

Listen to Me!

If you want to make sure people 'listen' to what you have to say, don't bore and confuse them with rambling messages or postings, which tend to be skipped in favour of shorter messages that concentrate on one subject. If you've got several widely different things to say, it's probably better to organize yourself a bit and send a message on each topic separately. Some people get hundreds of messages a day, so you can't expect them to remember what was said in a previous message. Remember to include background or pertinent material that will help your audience understand the intent of your message.

Some advice on how your message or article should look: There's no hard-and-fast rule, but a good message size is a screen or two. Neatness *does* count, and spelling and correct grammar are important. Even though online conversations are informal, sloppy messages that are full of errors really stick out. Take advantage of the asynchronous nature of email and news, and spend some time making your message or posting readable.

The Live Connection

A particularly interesting use of the broadcast audio capability over the MBONE, according to Steve Casner, one of the MBONE developers, is a 'lurkers' audio channel into which people from all over the world (an average of 50 at a time) are continuously plugged. Most of the time this channel is silent, but every now and then someone will ask a question and anyone who is listening can pipe up with a response. Steve found this channel particularly useful one day when setting up some equipment by himself in an auditorium located in Washington, D.C. Since no one was around, he turned on the audio channel and asked if anyone could hear him. We understand that an answer immediately came back from someone in Australia.

Limit each line length to 70 characters or less. If you're creating messages or postings using your word processor, make sure the document is converted to 'text with line breaks', meaning that a carriage return is introduced at the end of each line. If you don't do that, your message is going to end up looking funny on the screen, and will be very difficult to read.

Try to avoid using acronyms. If you do, here are some that are well known: FYI (for your information), IMHO (in my humble opinion), BTW (by the way), ROFL (rolls on floor laughing) and RTFM (read the friendly manual).

Signing On and Off

There are accepted methods by which to begin and end messages. Depending on how official your message will be you may begin with a phrase ranging from 'Dear Mr/Ms . . .' to 'Hi folx'. If you post to newsgroups you can normally spare such a beginning. Instead of signing off messages and postings with a 'Sincerely', or 'Love', many people end with their **signature**, which is a kind of digital identifier. Signatures should be short—preferably four lines or less—and should include information such as your full name, your organization and how to reach you. You'll see all sorts of signatures—including very fancy ones, complete with pictures or cute quotes. Your signature may be included automatically by your newsreader or email program, so be careful that it doesn't appear twice. It's good to include a signature in case the addressing information in your message or article header is incorrect or not complete. This might be Whitey Shark's signature:

```
Whitey Shark,  shark@cave.ocean.fr
--------------------------------------------------------
The Dangerous White Shark, Kill & Eat Ltd, Atlantic
Ocean, Coast of France, Cave 7 - Deep Hole 1
```

Beginning Behaviour on Newsgroups and Email Lists

You want to be heard, but you don't want to be misunderstood. In addition to making your online communication readable, you need to be considerate of the folks on the other side. Here are a few tips on how to act when you begin participating in newsgroups and email lists on the Internet.

Remember that you're entering a world where there are a lot of experienced people (including technical gurus and wizards) who have been around a long time. You should treat mailing lists and newsgroups as you would any other club you join for the first time. In other words, don't get on and start blabbing without checking out the territory first. Spend some time lurking to get a feel for the nature of the group and the types of discussions. This background will help you realize what topics have already been discussed in detail and beaten into the ground. It also gives you time to observe the experienced list veterans in action; imitating the experts is definitely recommended (but you don't have to *think* like they do). And while you're silently getting up to speed, there's bound to be some other 'clueless newbie' who asks the very questions you're itching to send.

New users can't be expected to know everything about discussions that have gone on—sometimes for years. So the 'in' thing is for the 'regulars' on mailing lists and newsgroups to compile new-user questions and the answers to them in documents called **Frequently Asked Questions**, or **FAQs**. The purpose of these informative articles is to reduce the number of 'noise' postings—common questions that everyone has seen a

The Global Schoolhouse

Don't you wish you were a kid sometimes? The Internet is stretching its tentacles to the classroom, and children are finding that their playground is the whole world, not just the climbing frame and games pitch in the field behind the school. One project, called The Global Schoolhouse, is not only promoting the Internet for education but it's also giving it eyes! Participating Global Schoolhouse classes are holding video conferences over the Internet using low-cost equipment. The enabling software is CU-SeeMe, developed by Cornell University and freely available over the Internet. With CU-SeeMe, a Mac, an inexpensive video card, a video camera (almost any kind will do) and an Internet connection, these children are able to reach out and see other children, scientists and researchers. The first pilot in spring 1993, involved four classes in California, Virginia, Tennessee and London. After reading *Earth in the Balance* by Al Gore, the children performed watershed pollution studies in their own cities. They used email to collaborate on results, and at the end of the project held a video conference to present their findings.

million times. Not every group or list has a FAQ, but the ones that do publish them regularly (usually once a month). There are now hundreds of FAQs available, on a variety of subjects, from junk mail to supermodels to crossword puzzles. These documents detail resources, facts and opinions from people all over the world and can make for very interesting reading.

See the Appendix for information on how to obtain some useful FAQs.

Your Invisible Audience

Online communication is informal. It's much less intimidating to type your thoughts and fire them off to thousands of people than it is to stand up and say something, live, in front of the same group. But because you can't see all these people, it's easy to become careless, forgetting to include necessary background information or not thinking about your intended audience. It's also easy to think that because email doesn't use the formal conventions we're all used to in letters on paper or in face-to-face meetings, it is an unrestrained free-for-all. To deal with this, the Net has acquired its own conventions and etiquette.

One problem is that electronic conversations are missing body language and voice intonation, crucial components of effective communication. Take these elements away and people are forced to fill in the blanks when a typed online message doesn't come across quite right. For some reason, people become much more sensitive when they're online, and they tend to blow things entirely out of proportion—for example, taking a couple of sentences originally meant to be humourous or sarcastic entirely the wrong way. It's even worse if you've had a bad day and you've decided that 'no one likes you' (we've all had those moments); in this frame of mind, you're much more susceptible to misunderstanding messages. Once that happens, everything can go downhill quickly. Instead of asking for clarification ('You were kidding, weren't you?') or just ignoring it, many people—forgetting that they're dealing with another human being on the other end—decide to defend themselves and tell the originator of the offending message exactly what they think of him. This outcome is what's known in the business as a **flame**. If both sides begin insulting each other, it's called a **flame war** (kind of like fighting fire with fire). These digital battles often erupt in 'public' and can sometimes be very entertaining to the lurkers.

Friendly Advice

To avoid being involved in a flame war with someone in an electronic public square or a misunderstanding in regular one-on-one communication, follow this advice.

Showing Emotion. First and foremost, always be polite and considerate of the people on the other side. Because you're missing the important visual and aural cues that add nuance to direct conversation, you need to learn how to show emotion online—not an easy task. Probably the most common trick to show emotion is :-). That's a sideways smiley face (turn your head 90 degrees to the left) used to indicate humour or sarcasm. Since

Retorts Courteous :-) and Valiant Reproofs :-(

SHAKESPER, an international electronic conference for scholars, instructors, students and fans of William Shakespeare, prides itself on the quality and courtesy of its spontaneous informal discussions. Flame wars are not a feature here. But things got a little heated when one of the SHAKESPEReans compared email to Elizabethan masques, calling both 'thin' communication media in which the expression of subtle emotions like irony can be difficult. This observation brought on an extended discussion of email, during which a number of participants threatened to return to fountain pens.

One hapless respondent seemed to recommend the use of 'emoticons' for emotional expression ('If people wish to communicate with a limited set of characters, they find a way to do so').

'Irony and far subtler nuances have flourished in printed discourse for centuries without recourse to special typographical symbols or graphical heighteners', one of the professors flew back.

Another quoted *The Chicago Manual of Style:* 'Skillfully prepared for, an ironic meaning seldom eludes the reader

(Continued)

there's no smiley face on the keyboard, you have to 'roll your own', using a colon, a hyphen and a right-end parenthesis. You'll also see variations on the smiley. Sometimes people use a semicolon to indicate winking: ;-). Or a sad face will look like this: :-(. There's quite an art to the smiley face, and there are hundreds of variations.

Upper case is used for shouting, so don't use it unless you want to make a point. For example, if someone wanted to indicate that she was excited or mad, SHE'D SURE AS HECK LET YOU KNOW THAT!!!! Or, she could let you know what she was REALLY thinking by using caps in appropriate places. You can also introduce some online intonation by the use of asterisks in even though quotation marks [or smilies] are not used' (6.68).

The shelling got so intense that it brought on the following concession from the emoticon camp: 'I assume, given temperaments and opinions expressed recently on this list, no emoticons are necessary. I'd like to take this opportunity to beg forgiveness for my silliness in using them in the past. How foolish it was of me to think that some inane little graphic could possibly help me to express myself better. How immature I was to ever possibly imagine that a few strokes of my keyboard, rendering such pale little ASCII graphics, could replace or enhance my pitiful words. I most humbly ask my august colleagues on this list who were subjected to my use of these ridiculous characters in the past to please, please forgive me'.

This led to a certain amount of mutual congratulation about SHAKESPER's culture of thoughtfulness and civility, after which Professor Jim Schaefer of Georgetown University brought the discussion to a halt with this comment: 'Here we are discussing the means of discussing Shakespeare. Is this a post-modern dialogue? Have we had fun yet?'

SHAKESPER is a LISTSERV list (*SHAKESPER@utoronto.bitnet*) maintained by the University of Toronto. (LISTSERV and its conventions are discussed elsewhere.)

certain places. For example, 'This *is* what I meant!' places emphasis on *is*.

Terse Responses. Terse responses can sound rude. For example, responding to someone's question with only a single sentence—'No, you can't do that!'—might make him feel as if he's inconvenienced you, that you can't be bothered to explain *why* he can't do something. If he asked you 'live', in person, you'd probably explain. You don't have to be verbose, but a few extra sentences will go a long way to ensure that you don't hurt someone's feelings.

On the other end, if you receive a short message that leaves you wondering, 'What did I do to deserve this?', don't lose too much sleep over it. Perhaps the sender was in a big hurry and didn't have time to explain everything fully.

What may be worse than a terse response is no response at all. Don't expect an immediate response to your email or news queries. People tend to get bogged down in unread and unanswered electronic correspondence. You might get an answer in five minutes—but it also might take five days, or *weeks*. Just because you don't hear from someone immediately does not mean she or he thinks your message was unimportant.

Always Point a Loaded Mailer or News Reader at the Ground. Just as you shouldn't drive when you're angry or upset, you shouldn't send responses to email and news articles when you're mad at someone. If someone has 'ticked you off' and you're bound and determined to respond to a message or posting, go ahead and type your response—but don't mail it for at least a day. A delay may seem frustrating, but chances are that when you come back later to read your response, you'll be glad you didn't send it. And you should realize that many times people will say things just to wind you up. The thing these folks want most to see is an emotional, tear-stained response from you. Don't give them that pleasure!

You should also watch what you say in everyday situations. A good rule is never to send anything that you wouldn't mind seeing on the front page of a major newspaper. Online correspondence can be easily archived, retrieved at a later date and sent out to a large number of people. Avoid saying anything insulting about someone or disclosing confidential information. Private, sensitive email messages, or even public flames, could come back to haunt you someday; in fact, they may 'follow you around' for the rest of your life.

The security and privacy, or lack thereof, of corporate—and even personal—email has caused quite a stir lately, and you've probably got a few concerns about the security of *your* mail. It's best to resign yourself to the fact that email on its own is not very secure. Once you transmit an email message, its privacy depends on the security of the destination system, over which you basically have no control. Chapter 5 discusses computer and network security further.

Internet Ethics

As noted, you can't depend on email being secure. About the only thing you can hope for is that people will behave themselves and not snoop around in others' accounts, reading private correspondence. You should be careful not to violate copyrights by transmitting another person's work verbatim without permission. Additionally, everyone is under a moral and ethical obligation to respect other people's property and wishes. A common courtesy is not to forward private email to anyone without the permission of the author. For example, you should be careful when you reply to a message sent to you personally—you may want to 'cc' other people in your reply. Keep in mind, however, that the sender of the original message may not want his or her words copied to other people.

The Need for Self-Restraint. Because it is so easy to transmit communication and information, you may be tempted, on occasion, to broadcast your message to the world. You should realize, however, that even though for the most part you are free to post and email anything, you are expected not to abuse this privilege by being inconsiderate. This means, be selective in choosing newsgroups and email lists to receive your submissions. There are many recorded cases where a zealous inter-prophet has broadcast his 'end of the world' (or related) message to every newsgroup and email list he could find. While it may appear that little damage is done—it's only electronic information, right?—there are many people and organizations located on the 'outskirts' (rural areas and foreign countries) who end up footing the bill for the extra traffic or online time such a message may incur. This situation also applies to your individual correspondence with people. It's worth finding out what the recipient's situation local connectivity situation is before you blast him or her with a large email message or file.

Advertising. In 'reality space', we're constantly being bombarded with advertisements, subtle or obnoxious, everywhere we go. We're used to it, and we don't think anything about TV and radio programmes being interrupted by them. On the Internet, however, direct advertising is considered by most to be rude

and invasive. There are several reasons for this. The original users of the Internet community, the researchers and academics,
disdain self-promotional activity, preferring to review and promote products and information in a scholarly fashion. The second reason has to do with the NSFNET AUP, which once forbade
blatant advertising and commercial activity on U.S. Government-
funded networks. The AUP has been relaxed somewhat since the
proliferation of commercial Internet networks, but its legacy lives
on. A third aspect is the large number of messages landing in
most people's inboxes, making it hard for them to keep track of
what is really important, and if they find the time to read your
advertisement, they might also take the time to make an angry
and very unpleasant response.

Just be aware that you're playing with fire if you initiate a
direct email campaign, and you'll probably be flamed for quite
a while (more likely doing more harm than good to your reputation). There are still lots of ways to get your company's message
across through more passive channels (such as providing a public
information service such as a WWW server, mentioned in Chapter 4).

These suggested guidelines may lead you to believe that the
Internet is a strictly ruled environment populated by humourless
and overworked people. Not so! Many people you will encounter
on the Net are helpful, friendly and the type you'd like to have as
partners or friends. The netiquette described in this chapter has
built up over the years, created and policed by the netizens. This
section cannot cover every aspect of polite and ethical behaviour,
so in unfamiliar situations you should rely on common sense and
good judgement.

Now that you know how to use the Internet to communicate,
you'll soon be adept at email and conferencing, LISTSERVs and
chat. And no doubt you're ready to move on to explore some of
the wondrous realms of information that have been alluded to.
Stay tuned. The very next chapter looks at the information resources on the Internet, and shows you how to use Internet tools
to tap into the world's online library of libraries.

Chapter 4

FINDING INFORMATION

*G*et *ready to switch gears* on the Infobahn! Instead of communicating with people, we're going digging for information. What is available on the Internet is as varied as life itself. Almost anything you can think of is there for the taking—graphics, software, books, library catalogues, bulletin boards, data, sounds, movies, journals, newsletters, newspapers and magazines. There are many thousands of independent databases, archives and online services available via the Internet, making it essentially a huge virtual library and shopping arcade.

Unfortunately, this electronic library is not as well organized as a real library. There isn't just *one* catalogue where you can check to find what's available or where things are located. However, graphical interfaces and user-friendly tools have entered the scene, and can help you chart a course through what at first may appear to be a vast and unnavigable info-jungle.

Of course, not *everything* is online yet; for instance, the Internet is still a long way from offering access to the latest best-selling novel. But the amount and diversity of information available online is increasing so rapidly that today you *can* find quite a bit of what you are looking for. The Internet landscape is constantly changing, and enumerating its resources is next to impossible. The first edition of this book reported an impressive number of free public offerings, most of which were found in the academic and research domains. Since then, an increasing number of commercial organizations have started offering free online catalogues, manuals, brochures, services and software.

'Libraries are the last democratic educational institution . . .
the most important and democratic source of information . . .
and the last refuge of those without modems.'

—Gloria Steinem, speech at the American Library Association in July 1992.

Additionally, more and more commercial providers of info-
goods are popping up all over the Net. For example, Dialog Information Services, Inc., provides online newspaper and professional articles, the *Official Airline Guide,* financial services and
pharmaceutical directories—all accessible to subscribers. The
Lexis (for legal research) and Nexis (for business, financial and
general news) databases from Mead Data Central are also accessible. ClariNet Communications Corporation transmits Associated Press (AP) and Reuters news feeds. The Online BookStore
(OBS) sells books, and many virtual malls have recently opened
their doors. The Virtual Inc provides a mall of about 800 companies offering products from hardware and tools to holiday trips or
flowers for the one we love. Several organizations have established 'commercenets' in the U.S. as well as in Europe.

There are too many nifty and useful information resources to
list. What this chapter will do is help you take advantage of the
Internet by engaging it as an external brain, a vast storehouse of
information resources. Already there are applications that utilize
distributed hypertext—linking related resources and allowing
users to travel a never-ending web of information.

We are only beginning to realize the vastness of this online
future and naturally, the transition from a paper-based information environment to online illumination will be rocky; there are
fundamental issues we must face and processes that must be
redefined.

What are the implications of having such widespread, ready
access to timely information? Access to information is considered
an advantage, a weapon. Businesses and governments have been
built and destroyed based on the information they had available
to them. Today, people talk of equitable access to information,
and the U.S. government is working to ensure universal—afford-

The Internet Jukebox

The 6 August, 1994 issue of *Billboard* magazine was headlined 'U.K. Bands Attack Convention Thru Internet', thereby announcing the launch of the first of the long-awaited digital delivery systems for home entertainment services. Cerberus Sound+Vision, based in Denmark Street, London (the original "Tin Pan Alley") created the Cerberus Digital Jukebox. This is a server on the Internet that stores a database of music (and eventually video) tracks from both signed and unsigned artists. Internet users with the freely distributed Cerberus Digital Player software can buy credit with Cerberus, which allows them to download encrypted and compressed CD-quality music tracks for a few pennies each and play them through either PC loudspeakers or a normal hi-fi system. The reaction of the mainstream music industry to this upstart has been either to attempt to stop it or to buy it. At present Cerberus remains resolutely independent, with an arrangement that enables bands to distribute their recordings at a fraction of the cost of producing music on a hardware medium such as CD.

Source: *Billboard*, 6 August 1994; *Financial Times*, 26 October 1994.

able and accessible—services for Americans on its National Information Infrastructure.

The world is on its way to becoming everyone's information oyster and, therefore, the ways we learn and do business will probably change. The people who will succeed in tomorrow's world will be those who can learn, discern and deal with issues rapidly and intelligently using information tools. This requires a fundamental change in the way we operate our businesses and schools.

There are some things to keep in mind while accessing information over the Internet. In reality, there's no guarantee that what you're hearing or reading is one hundred percent correct. It's the same on the Internet. However, on the Internet you can obtain information from a variety of sources to cross-check and form your own opinions.

CAN YOU GET THERE FROM HERE?

Reading this chapter may tantalize and frustrate those who have only limited access to the Internet. You may be able to reach all of these resources, or only some of them. If you're on an outernet network, you're limited to using email servers—where they exist—to retrieve files and access services. Technical, economic and political barriers are factors that can limit Internet access, but—fortunately for us— nothing in life today changes faster! Your system or provider may add Internet services or connections tomorrow or next month. So experiment and find out what you can and can't get at. If you *really* need access to a particular resource, your system gurus or provider may be able to offer you another path. Once you know what's available, you may find that you need better access. If so, shop around for a connection that offers what you need. Chapter 7 tells you about Internet connection options.

As for the validity and accuracy of documents, keep in mind the plausible situation in which a document has been archived, downloaded, annotated, edited and saved by a friend before being emailed to you. Unless the document contains complete attribution, checking its source and authenticity might very well be a nightmare.

The following pages will walk you through the most basic Internet information access-and-retrieval tools: remote login and file transfer. It's useful to know about these applications and how they work, but with the proliferation of graphical and menu front ends, you may not have many opportunities to pull them out of your info-toolbox. The new applications on the block are painting the Internet neighbourhood in bright colours, essentially giving it a face-lift. The latter half of this chapter explains how to get started with information discovery-and-retrieval applications such as archie, Gopher, WAIS and WWW.

USING ONLINE RESOURCES AND SERVICES

There are several classes of info-tools described in this chapter. All of these tools require that you have a direct connection to the Internet—meaning, you're not on an outernet. Also—and this is part of the Internet standard disclaimer—the tools may operate differently on your system, so be sure to read local documentation and any instructions shown on the screen. In some cases, you have to type the commands; in others, you may use a straightforward menu system; in others, you may be clicking icons. The examples used in this chapter will, for the most part, be from a command-level perspective, showing the commands (most of them in lowercase) as you would type them on many computers. If you understand these basics, it shouldn't be hard to use an icon-based system.

The first info-tool class includes the very basic, low-level, 'vanilla' devices you can use to access just about anything. They're called **remote login** and **file transfer**.

The second class is known as information discovery and retrieval tools. These present archives and databases in a user-friendly format, and let you search or peruse them. These tools mentioned in this chapter are archie, Gopher, WAIS and WWW.

The third class can be considered not as a tool, really, but as a tool shop. This is the interface species, the applications that present the Net as a graphical environment, using icons, which when selected will call up appropriate tools and select the right resources. One such application is Mosaic, and it's explained at the end of this chapter.

Something to keep in mind is that the services explained in this chapter will most likely not be located on your own computer. You're not transmitting and receiving communication as you were in the last chapter; you (or your applications) are going out and actively getting information from other places all over the globe. The explanations here refer to the location of a desired service as the remote computer. A remote computer isn't necessarily thousands of miles away. It could be in the same room; it could be four countries away. The point is, on the Internet, it doesn't matter where it is—and, in many cases, you do not need to know where it is.

Let Me In!

Despite system differences, you will usually need to know a few specific pieces of information, such as the name of the computer or host that you want to connect to, perhaps a login id, and a password. Some computer systems require that you know the magic word to 'be let in' to an account, and usually 'please' won't work. What's an **account**? It's like your own room in a hotel. You have a key that lets you into your room (the account), where all your treasured possessions (files) are stored. On a computer, the key is most often a combination of a unique id and a secret password. The id (also known as a username or userid) lets the computer know who you are, and the password (which only you should know) proves it's really you.

If you live in Amsterdam, it's unlikely that you're going to have an account on a computer in Tokyo, unless you have some type of special arrangement with an organization there. But many people do have accounts on remote systems, for various reasons.

Public Services

If you don't have any accounts on other systems, you may be wondering what you can use these tools for. You will have occasion to use them—more than you may realize at first. Lots of organizations are providing services, such as public information archives and databases. To use them, you don't need a personal account on the computers where they reside. (If you do need an account, you're usually given an opportunity to apply for one.) All you need to know is the login id or name of the service, and that's usually easily available or very well known. Most of these services don't require passwords or, if they do, they either publish them, accept anything as a password, or request that you type in your email address or some other information that lets them track who's using their resources.

A word on the hospitality of people and organizations providing publicly accessible services, file transfer sites, databases and other resources. Many of these services are made available by volunteers, so act politely and try not to hog resources. Sometimes it's requested that you use a service after working hours; so you should respect that rule, keeping in mind the time zone as well.

Different Environments

When you are accessing remote services, you are connecting to another environment that may look very different from that which you're used to using on your own system. It should be obvious by now, but there isn't just one way to do things in the Internet world. Different organizations, different computers and different operating systems all provide different services. Each remote system and service is going to have its particular look and feel.

The interface—the face that the other computer presents to you—will probably be different from the one you're familiar with. The words may even be in a foreign language. Don't worry; the public interfaces to these systems are pretty robust, so you won't harm anything if you don't know what you're doing and make a few mistakes. Keep in mind that things change on computers, too. Information is added and deleted. Interfaces change. Most of these online services don't come with manuals, so you'll need to read the instructions and use the help screens that are shown when you sign on. It doesn't hurt to make a few notes. A contact name is sometimes listed with the description of the service or on one of the initial login screens; if you have problems, you can email or call. Remember that you're accessing another computer, so your own system gurus may not be able to assist you.

Error Messages

Occasionally you'll get an error message or just not be able to get to that computer. One or more things may be wrong. First—and most likely—is that you misspelled or incorrectly typed the name of the computer, in which case you'll get a message such as *unknown host*. If that happens, check to be sure you have the right hostname. If you're sure you have the right name, then it's possible that this computer simply doesn't exist anymore.

If you know that the computer exists and that you have the correct name, and you still get an error message, you can try something else. Remember from Chapter 2 that the DNS allows you to use computer names instead of IP addresses. It could be that your computer is having a hard time figuring out what the remote computer's IP address is. If this is the case, and you do know the IP address, you can always try substituting it for the computer name.

If you have the right computer name, and the remote computer doesn't respond after you initiate a connection using an information tool, there may be problems with the network or the

Bienvenidos a Mexico!

Sometimes the benefits of networking come in subtle packages. The Bush School in Seattle, Washington, is one of the first schools in the world to give Internet accounts to all the students, not just the teachers. Fred Dust, the school's Headmaster, relates how the Internet plays a very important role in learning, professional development and parental involvement at his school. 'All the teachers, students and parents are encouraged to participate,' he says. 'The results have been tremendously positive.' For example, two ninth-graders were experimenting one day with online library access; not content with the local libraries, they connected to a catalogue in Mexico. To their surprise, the interface greeted them in Spanish. 'That floored them,' said Dust. 'They'd lived their lives in English-speaking Washington State, had taken classes in Spanish, but hadn't realized it was actually *used* somewhere. They also realized their entrance into other countries wouldn't be blocked by the technology, but by language barriers. It was a very powerful discovery that they made on their own. This experience couldn't have been duplicated in a traditional classroom setting'.

remote computer may be 'down'—that is, not working or available. Some noncommercial Internet sites have become so popular that they have to restrict outside access during their working hours in order to allow their own people to have some machine time available. The time zone a site is in will, of course, determine at which hours of the day or night you may or may not be allowed a connection. Just try again later. If the problem persists, contact your network provider or system administrator for more clues.

ACCESSING INTERACTIVE SERVICES

Remote login is a basic tool that lets you 'fly' electronically all over the world, reaching your destination in a fraction of a second. This section will tell you how to connect to other computers and services using remote login.

How It Works

Remote login on the Internet is a lot like using your modem to dial into another computer, but it's usually much faster and you don't actually have to dial a phone number. The name of the protocol that enables remote login is **Telnet**, which is also the name of the command on many systems to allow you to login to other computers.

When using Telnet to login to a computer, just issue the *telnet* command followed by a space and the name of the computer. (You can also issue the *telnet* command without the computer name, at which point you'll be in command mode. When you see a `telnet>` prompt, you can type commands or **help** for more information.) For example, if you want to check out an online book order service called Book Stacks Unlimited, Inc type the following:

```
telnet books.com
```

The Telnet program will make a connection to the *books.com* system. In this particular example, you'll be asked to type in your full name, pick a password and specify your contact information (email and address). You can then use the menu system to search and order books (over 240,000 titles are offered) and participate in a book discussion group.

Now, when you telnet to most other systems, you are usually greeted by a computerized 'Who goes there?' routine. The typical prompt is `Login:` or `Username:`, at which point you type your login id or username followed by the <RETURN> key. If you already have a username, type it in; you'll then be prompted for your password. When you supply the password, don't worry that it doesn't appear on the screen. It is not shown because your password is supposed to be secret, and you don't want anybody who might be looking over your shoulder to see what it is.

In some cases when you connect to a resource, you'll have to specify an additional identifier called a **port number**. There can be many services running on a single computer; the port identifier serves to keep them separate. When a port number is required, you usually don't have to type in a username or password. Let's test-drive this command:

telnet madlab.sprl.umich.edu 3000

Here it was necessary to specify the port number, *3000*, because it identifies a specific program. Resource guides always
include the port numbers with the instructions for accessing resources, so if you don't see one, don't worry about it. In this case,
you're connecting to the Weather Underground, a service provided by the University of Michigan's College of Engineering.
The Weather Underground has a menu system that's almost
easier to use than your cash point machine. There's something
for everyone, such as local weather reports, snow ski reports for
some parts of the country, earthquake reports for other parts and
hurricane reports.

```
The Login Screen for the Weather Underground

sport% telnet madlab.sprl.umich.edu 3000
Trying...
Connected to madlab.sprl.umich.edu
Escape character is '^]'.
-------------------------------------------------------
*                University of Michigan              *
*                WEATHER UNDERGROUND                 *
-------------------------------------------------------
*   College of Engineering, University of Michigan   *
* Department of Atmospheric, Oceanic, and Space Sciences *
*             Ann Arbor, Michigan 48109-2143         *
*          comments: sdm@madlab.sprl.umich.edu       *
*   With help from: The National Science Foundation  *
*               supported Unidata Project            *
*   University Corporation for Atmospheric Research   *
*             Boulder, Colorado 80307-3000           *
*                                                    *
*     This service is for educational and research   *
*                   purposes only.                   *
* Commercial users should contact our data provider  *
*   Alden Electronics, 508-366-8851 to acquire their  *
*                  own data feed.                    *
-------------------------------------------------------
*  NOTE:----------> New users, please select option  *
*              "H" on the main menu:                 *
*         H) Help and information for new users      *
-------------------------------------------------------
Press Return for menu, or enter 3 letter forecast
city code:
```

Sometimes when you login to another system, you'll be asked about your terminal type. In most cases, you can say you're emulating a 'VT100' (or something similar) terminal, and you'll do just fine. Some resources, such as online library catalogues, are running on IBM mainframes, however, so you might have to use a different version of Telnet called *tn3270* (if it exists on your system) in order to emulate an IBM 3270 terminal. It works similarly, though the keys may not correspond exactly to what you're used to; just substitute *tn3270* for *telnet*.

Let Me Outta Here!

Why is it so hard to say good-bye? Sometimes the biggest problem new users have using publicly available services is getting out of them without shutting down the computer or turning off the modem. When you're remotely logged in to another computer, everything you type is being sent to the remote system for execution. There are two ways to exit a system. One way is simply to logout of the service. Unfortunately, there's no standard 'let me go' command. The best advice is to read carefully any instructions that show up when you login to a system. If the screen doesn't tell you anything, try one of these commands: *exit, quit, logout, leave, bye, goodbye, ciao, disconnect, CTRL-D*.

If you still can't exit, then you can terminate the session by signalling your *local* Telnet program that you wish to quit. Using a special 'escape' character or command allows you to temporarily suspend your Telnet session, and you're brought back to reality to a Telnet prompt (usually `telnet>`) on your home system. The escape character can vary, but on many systems it's a *CTRL-]*. (Hold down the control key and at the same time press the ']' key.) On some systems, *CTRL-^* is used. You can then quit the Telnet session by typing **quit** at the Telnet prompt.

ONLINE RESOURCES

The Weather Underground is fun, but it's just the tip of the iceberg! There's much, much more. Here's an idea of the types of resources that are accessible via remote login and how to try some of them out.

Online Library Catalogues

Some of the most common and most often mentioned Internet resources are the online library catalogues. At least 500 catalogues are accessible via the Internet, mostly at academic organizations all over the world. Most don't allow you to look at or transfer entire online books; they just let you review bibliographic records. You can peruse a certain library's collection, verify a citation or reference, or see if a book is checked out or if it's available through the interlibrary loan system. Online library catalogues, by the way, are usually open all day and all night!

Some online catalogues offer more than just bibliographic records. For example, to explore the UHCARL Library System at the University of Hawaii, Manoa, type:

telnet starmaster.uhcc.hawaii.edu

At the 'enter class' prompt, type **lib**. Select **5** for VT100 emulation. Wander through the menus. (See if *this* book is in the database!) Items of interest include an index of Hawaiian sheet music and the 1993 edition of the *Hawaii Data Book*.

Some online library catalogues even offer access to online encyclopaedias. Not every service offered in the menus may be available to outside users. Some, such as online encyclopaedias, may be limited to registered users because of licensing restrictions.

Other Sites Accessible Via Remote Login

In addition to online library catalogues and commercial services, there are a lot of different types of services you can access via remote login. For example, bulletin board systems (BBSs) on the Internet are a lot like the electronic bulletin boards that you can dial into using a modem. Most BBSs offer a menu of services. Some supply conferencing capabilities, while others provide 'read-only' information, similar to regular bulletin boards at a library, where information is tacked up for everyone to read and taken down when it's no longer relevant.

TRANSFERRING INFORMATION

Imagine that you're creating an important report at your personal workstation. You want to print it out, but you don't have a

plokta /*plok'ta*/ (Acronym for 'Press Lots Of Keys To Abort')
v. To press random keys in an attempt to get some response
from the system. One might plokta when the abort procedure
for a program is not known, or when trying to figure out if
the system is just sluggish or really hung. Plokta can also be
used while trying to figure out any unknown key sequence
for a particular operation. Someone going into *plokta mode*
usually places both hands flat on the keyboard and presses
down, hoping for some useful response.

Source: *The New Hacker's Dictionary*, edited by Eric S. Raymond, with assistance
and illustrations by Guy L. Steele, Jr. © 1991 Eric S. Raymond. Published by The
MIT Press, Cambridge and London, 1991. Reprinted with permission.

printer nearby. So you copy the document onto a floppy, put on
your running shoes, and dash down the hall to load the floppy at
the nearest workstation-printer site. This process is known as **file
transfer**, because the report is being transferred to another computer. If both computers were on the Internet, you could have
transferred this file in a matter of seconds using the file transfer
capability. Instead of sending the file through the slower 'Sneaker-
Net', you could have sent it over the electronic highway. In
short, the file transfer capability gives you the ability to copy files
from one computer to another.

What Is a File?

A file can be anything. It can be a document you create in your
PC's word processor. It can be a spreadsheet or a software program. It can be a picture, or even music. Or it can be ASCII text,
which is plain vanilla text with no formatting codes such as boldface or underlining.

Many of the documents are just text (and readable by humans) no matter what computer or software you're using. You
should be aware, however, that some of the files you transfer
won't mean anything to the computer system you're using. A
word processor document—one that was prepared by Microsoft
Word, for example—has special typesetting codes within the
document that signal the program to 'make this word bold' or

'use the Times font'. Obviously, this file won't be useful if you don't own the Microsoft Word application.

Similarly, a file can be a software application. Not all software will 'run' or work on every computer. In fact, it's safe to say that there isn't one piece of software that will work on every type of computer. A Mac program won't run directly on a PC, and vice versa. Similarly, a program created for the VMS operating system won't run on a Unix system. (VMS and Unix are operating systems, just as DOS is an operating system for PCs.)

File Transfer Clarified

Many people get file transfer and remote login confused—an easy enough thing to do. Both applications allow you to connect to other computers and obtain information, but file transfer is a more specific and straightforward tool. Its main mission is to transfer files between computers. You're not actually interactively querying another computer's database or using a service to find out any information.

There are also similarities and differences between file transfer and email. Email is used for transferring personal messages, although you can send and receive information in the form of files, too. You wouldn't use file transfer to deliver personal messages, but if you and another person need to transfer a file, such as a text document, back and forth, then email will work just fine. Indeed, in most cases it is probably preferable, because you don't want to give another person your username and password. Two warnings, however. Some computers cannot handle extremely long email messages. If your file is very large, you may need to send it in smaller sections. Some email systems can also throw extra characters into your text, but file transfer guarantees integrity.

If the file is a nontext file, such as a software program, then it's almost always better to transfer it by using the Internet file transfer tool. As mentioned in Chapter 3, you can send nontext files, such as software and graphics, if your email application (and the receiving end) supports MIME, or if you have the necessary tools such as BinHex to encode for transmission and decode upon reception. Since the latter process may require several extra steps, it probably is simpler to use file transfer rather than email.

From Russia with Byte

Worried about gainful employment for all those Russian scientists and computer types, now that they're not doing arms development? Dave Hughes was looking for a way to develop a universal graphics/telecommunication package for education—and to make it inexpensive enough for schools to buy. He could find no funding in the United States, so he hooked up with some Russian computer scientists and hired them to write the software. The Russians get a very capitalistic piece of potential sales and are paid in hard currency. So what's the Internet connection? Hughes and friends are in the United States; the programmers live in Moscow. They've never even met; everything—software standards, technical documentation, general articles, sample software, code models—travels via the Internet.

Source: Derived from a posting by Dave Hughes on the Consortium for School Networking Discussion Forum List *COSNDISC@bitnic.bitnet.*

How File Transfer Works

Using the file transfer capability on the Internet is fairly straightforward. The protocol is called File Transfer Protocol (FTP). On many systems, the actual program that you will use is called *ftp*, which stands for file transfer program. FTP allows you to connect to another computer and perform certain actions, such as listing the files in a directory and copying files back and forth between both systems.

To start a session, type **ftp** *host-name*. (Or you can also use the **ftp** command by itself, at which time you'll be put into the command interpreter, which waits for more instructions from you. The **open** *host-name* command will establish, or open, a transfer connection.) You should be prompted for your username and password on the remote system, just as in the Telnet process. Once you've identified yourself to the remote system, you'll most likely see a prompt that looks like this: ftp>.

When you use FTP, be sure to check local system documentation for more information. It will tell you about the many other

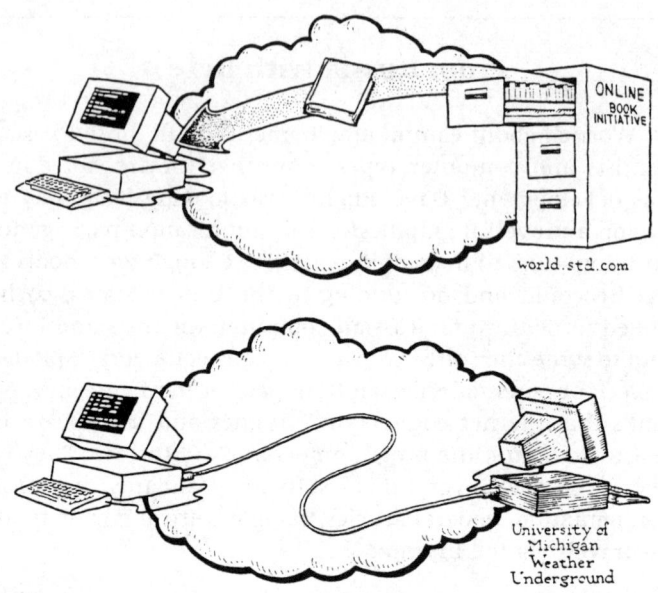

File transfer (above) lets you move files between computers. Remote login
(below) lets you interact with another computer's services.

commands you can use and things you can do, as well as any
system-specific characteristics you should know about. Keep in
mind that most of the following commands will tell you information about and perform actions on the *remote* system. For example, you can find out what files are in the remote directory
using the command **dir** (for 'directory') or **ls** (for 'list'). You can
change to another directory where other files are stored using
the command **cd** *directory-name* ('change directory'). To go back
up the directory ladder to the parent directory, use the **cdup**
command. If you don't know which directory you're in, the
pwd ('print working directory') command will tell you.

If the changing directories part of this confuses you, then you
need to understand that directories in computers are organized
similarly to folders in a filing cabinet. A directory is basically an
electronic folder with files and perhaps other folders in it, and
when you change directories, you're just opening up a new

folder. Once you're 'in' the right directory on the remote system, you can do several things, two of which are *getting* a file (or files) and *putting* a file (or files). To download or transfer a file from the remote system to your local computer, use the **get** *filename* command. To upload or put a local file on the remote system, use the **put** *filename* command. You can always get help by typing **help** (for a list of commands), or **help** *command*. In fact, you should probably check out the help screens on any system when you are using it for the first time. When you finish transferring files, you can close the connection and exit by typing either **bye** or **quit**.

Many of the public archive sites run the Unix operating system, so if you're familiar with that, then the listing **dir** produces will make sense. If you're not, it may help to know that the Unix file system is a hierarchical directory structure similar to that of a DOS or Mac computer. (Hierarchical means that you start at the top, also known as the root, and work your way down through various directories.) Also, Unix is case-sensitive, so if a filename is shown in lowercase, then you must type it in lowercase. (A good rule is to *always* type the instructions or filename exactly as shown.) Chapter 6 ('Unix on the Internet: A Survival Guide') will tell you a bit about Unix commands and applications. Following is a sample listing of a directory on an anonymous FTP host that runs Unix:

```
-rw-r--r--  1 tracy  ftp      198 Apr 10 13:16 README
dr-xr-xr-x  2 root   bin      512 Apr  1  1991 bin
dr-xr-xr-x  2 root   bin      512 Apr  1  1991 etc
-rw-r--r--  1 tracy  ftp    88349 Aug  2 15:26 glossary
dr-xrwxr-x 14 ftp    ftp      512 Jul 23 09:10 pub
```

In this example, the filenames are on the far right. On the far left are the permission and file type specifications. The letter *d* in the first column indicates that the entry is a directory, so *bin, etc* and *pub* are directories. The file creation date and time are easy to spot: *README* was created or modified on April 10 at 1:16 p.m. Another thing you should notice is the number immediately to the left of the date—the size of the file in bytes. The glossary file is 88,349 bytes, which is fairly large. Because it's so easy to transfer files, you may find that you can fill up your disk space quickly, so you'll need to implement a good file management system. Remember to delete the files you don't need and to compress the ones you want to keep. (See below for a list of file formats and compression tools.)

Publicly Accessible Files

The transfer of publicly available information is one of the most widespread uses of the file transfer capability on the Internet. Many of the organizations connected to the Internet provide openly accessible file transfer sites with information that anyone can obtain (or *get*). Files are stored in 'open' or public areas of computers, and you can access them by using the file transfer program to connect to those systems. A file that is 'available via anonymous FTP' is publicly available, and you can connect to a public archive computer and use the file transfer program to copy it to your own system.

Remember that you need a login name and password to be allowed into a computer. For publicly accessible files, the login name is **anonymous** or **ftp** and the password can be anything, although it's a good idea to type your email address. (Sometimes **guest** is the specific password required.) Once you master spelling *anonymous*, you can roam around the public storage areas on computers on the Internet just as you explore public libraries.

Not every computer on the Internet makes public file storage areas available, but there are thousands of systems that offer gigabytes and gigabytes of 'published' information. (One recent count put the number of publicly available files at well over 2.2 million.) These sites are making available electronic books, public domain software and graphic images—lots of amusing, useful and interesting stuff. Check the Appendix for instructions on obtaining a list of anonymous FTP sites.

Navigating around different computer public storage areas takes some practice. As mentioned before, there are different kinds of computers out there, and some present their electronic folders somewhat differently. Many systems provide README files that explain what files are available or anything you might need to know about the collection of files. You simply transfer the README file: **get README**. (There's no standard name for an information file; they may be called *00README*, or *readme*,

READ.me, INFO, INDEX. You can usually tell what file will provide information when you get a directory listing.)

Let's transfer a short story of Stephen King, 'Umney's Last Case', which was released on the Internet by the Online Book-Store (OBS) and shown at the Frankfurt International Book Fair in 1993 by EUnet before it was available on paper. The file is available in many places throughout Europe (where it was electronically published) and in our example you can obtain it from the server *ftp.Germany.EU.net* via anonymous FTP. It is located in the directory */pub/books/king* with the filename *king-us.txt.Z* in English and *king-ger.txt.Z* in German language. Just pick up the file with the language you prefer.

Please note that both the files are text files (extension *.txt*), but they are also compressed files (.Z). You therefore have to use binary transfer mode and decompress after transmission on your own computer to be able to read them. Not all filenames have an extension that specifies file type, but many do. See the 'Common File Formats on the Internet' table for a listing of the more common ones.

The example below will not walk you through executing a directory listing (using the *dir* command), but remember that you can use that command to see what other files are available. If you wish to rename the file as you're transferring it to your system, the command is **get** *remote-file new-file-name*. Here's what you'd see on your screen (the commands you would type on many systems are shown in bold):

```
sport>ftp ftp.germany.EU.net
Connected to ftp.germany.EU.net.
220-
220- Welcome to the anonymous FTP service of the
220- German EUnet Backbone, which is also the
220- official X11R5 server for Germany. EMail contact
220- address for this archive is <archive-
220- admin@Germany.EU.net>.
220-
220-
220- Other EUnet information services are available:
220- gopher://gopher.Germany.EU.net:70/  #
220- http://www.Germany.EU.net:80/
220-
220- If your FTP client crashes or hangs shortly
```

```
220- after login, try using a dash (-) as the first
220- character of your password. This will turn off
220- the informational messages which may be
220- confusing your ftp client.
220-
220- FSP access to this server is avail. on port 2001.
220-
220- Directories:
220- /pub:  public archive
220- /shop: commercial software and data
220- /ITR:  Internet Talk Radio (EUnet customers only!)
220-
220- ** Login as "anonymous" with your e-mail
220- address as password.
220- **
220- ** FOR ACCESS TO THE INTERNET SHOP, YOU MAY
220- ALSO LOGIN AS "shopuser"
220- ** WITH PASSWORD "shopuser". (No access to
220- public archive in that case!)
220-
220 simpson FTP server (Version wu-2.4(1) Wed Apr 20
15:28:24 MET DST 1994) ready.
Name (ftp.germany.EU.net:infoadm):anonymous
331 Guest login ok, send your complete e-mail
address as password.
Password:Stephan.Deutsch@Germany.EU.net
230 Guest login ok, access restrictions apply.
Remote system type is UNIX.
Using binary mode to transfer files.
ftp> cd pub/books/king
250-
250-                  UMNEY'S LAST CASE
250-                  UMNEYS LETZTER FALL
250-
250-                  by/von Stephen King
250-
250-This electronic document is for online personal
250-use only and not for reformatting, resale or
250-distribution, by electronic means or otherwise,
250-without written permission from Editorial Inc./
250-Online BookStore (OBS), PO Box 267, Rockport,
250-Mass., 01966, U.S. Don't print it out; for
250-printed books, check your local library,
250-bookstore, or order from Viking/Penguin
250-(ordering information provided in the document
250-itself).
```

Connecting Europe since 1982

offers readers of *The European Internet Companion* one month of service FREE OF CHARGE for an individual dialup IP account. Contact your local EUnet National Service Provider for this special offer.

EUnet is Europe's largest commercial Internet service provider, operating in 30 countries across Europe and North Africa. National, European and global—EUnet's infrastructure and support provide your best opportunity for quality service, reliability and enterprise advantage. When contacting the EUnet office nearest you to redeem this special offer, please indicate that you have purchased *The European Internet Companion*. Questions about our other national networks should be addressed to EUnet Communications Services BV, Singel 540, 1017 AZ Amsterdam, The Netherlands (Tel +31 20 623 3803; Fax +31 20 622 4657; Email *info@EU.net*).

EUnet Austria
Email: info@Austria.EU.net
Tel: +43 1 3174969
Fax: +43 1 3106926

EUnet Belgium
Email: info@Belgium.EU.net
Tel: +32 16 23 60 99
Fax: +32 16 23 20 79

EUnet Czech Republic
Email: info@Czechia.EU.net
Tel: +42 2 24 31 03 37
Fax: +42 2 24 31 06 46

EUnet Denmark
Email: info@Denmark.EU.net
Tel: +45 39 17 99 00
Fax: +45 39 17 98 97

EUnet Germany
Email: info@Germany.EU.net
Tel: +49 231972 00
Fax: +49 231972 1111

EUnet Great Britain
Email: info@Britain.EU.net
Tel: +44 227 266466
Fax: +44 227 266477

EUnet Ireland
Email: info@Ireland.EU.net
Tel: +353 1 6719361
Fax: +353 1 679 8039

EUnet Italy
Email: info@Italy.EU.net
Tel: +39 2 2700 2528
Fax: +39 2 2700 1322

EUnet Netherlands
Email: info@Netherlands.EU.net
Tel: +31 20 663 9366
Fax: +31 20 665 5311

EUnet Norway
Email: info@Norway.EU.net
Tel: +47 22 95 83 27
Fax: +47 22 60 44 27

EUnet Portugal
Email: info@Portugal.EU.net
Tel: +351 1 294 28 44
Fax: +351 1 295 77 86

EUnet Slovakia
Email: info@Slovakia.EU.net
Tel: +42 7 377 434, +42 7 725 306
Fax: +42 7 377 433, +42 7 728 462

EUnet Slovenia
Email: info@Slovenia.EU.net
Tel: +386 611405 183
Fax: +386 611405 381

EUnet Spain
Email: info@Spain.EU.net
Tel: +34 1 413 48 56
Fax: +34 1 413 49 01

EUnet Switzerland
Email: info@Switzerland.EU.net
Tel: +41 1 29145 80
Fax: +41 1 29146 42

This offer is available up to and including 31st December 1996.

```
250-
250 CWD command successful.
ftp> get king-us.txt.Z
200 PORT command successful.
150 Opening BINARY mode data connection for king-
us.txt.Z (50045 bytes).
226 Transfer complete.
50045 bytes received in 0.064 seconds (7.6e+02 Kbytes/s)
ftp> quit
221 Goodbye.
```

After connecting to this computer, one of the first messages you get before the ftp> prompt is 'Using binary mode to transfer files'. This means that the system is assuming you are transferring nontext files—images, software or compressed files, for example. If you know you're transferring a text file, then before initiating the transfer set the transfer type to 'ascii' by typing the command **ascii**. If you don't do this, your file may appear funky because the line terminators might not transfer correctly.

Non-text Information

To summarize, if you're planning on transferring nontext, then you need to do a **binary transfer**. Files that have been **compressed** are binary files, as are software programs. A compressed file is basically 'dehydrated'—or squeezed—to conserve disk space and also to make the transfer time faster. As was noted above, some systems automatically assume you're doing a binary transfer, but if not, you can set this mode easily by typing **binary** <RETURN> before you type **get** or **put** to transfer a file. This tells the system that you're moving a compressed, or nontext, file. Typing **ascii** will put you back in text mode.

Obtaining Software

Need some software? Software archives are all over the Internet. The FUNET Public Domain archive server in Finland is a great place to start, with a boatload of public domain and shareware software. There's so much on this system that it's advisable to obtain any README files in each directory to learn about what's available before you go exploring. If you want to check out this system, type the **ftp ftp.funet.fi** command, login as **anony-**

guiltware /gilt'weir/ n. 1. A piece of freeware decorated with a message telling one how long and hard the author worked on it and intimating that one is a no-good freeloader if one does not immediately send the poor suffering martyr gobs of money. 2. Shareware that works.

Source: *The New Hacker's Dictionary*, edited by Eric S. Raymond, with assistance and illustrations by Guy L. Steele, Jr. © 1991 Eric S. Raymond. Published by The MIT Press, Cambridge and London, 1991. Reprinted with permission.

mous, and use your email address as a password. (Don't forget to specify *binary* transfer for software!) Before you stock up on software, read the section on viruses in Chapter 5. And check the Appendix for some other places to find software.

File Formats

As mentioned earlier, certain files work only on certain computers, so it's good to have a little knowledge of the types of files, how to know which is which, and what programs, if any, you'll need to use the files.

Mac programs are sometimes in the BinHex (ASCII) format. Once downloaded and un-BinHexed, the files will most likely have to be uncompressed. Because PC files and programs are usually in compressed format, they will almost always have to be uncompressed with a utility like PKZIP or StuffIt after being downloaded.

The table below shows some of the more common file types you'll see—sounds, graphics and compressed—the programs they work with, and how you should transfer (ASCII or binary mode) each of them.

A document available via anonymous FTP explains most file compression, archiving and text-binary formats, and tells where you can get software to convert these various formats. This regularly updated document is maintained by David Lemson, and can be obtained from *ftp.cso.uiuc.edu*, in the directory *doc/pcnet*, filename *compression*.

Common File Formats on the Internet

File Program Name	File Type	Computer	Transfer Method	Ext
MacBinary	binary	Mac	binary	.bin
Compact Pro	compressed	Mac	binary	.cpt
StuffIt	compressed	Mac	binary	.sit
BinHex 4.0	encoded	Mac	ASCII	.hqx
BinHex 5.0	encoded	Mac	binary	.hqx
self-extracting	Mac application	Mac	binary	.sea
Quicktime	video	Mac/PC	binary	.qt
ARC, PKPAK	compressed	PC	binary	.arc
ARJ	compressed	PC	binary	.arj
LHArc	compressed	PC	binary	.arj
PAK	compressed	PC	binary	.pak
Soundblaster	sound	PC	binary	.voc
WAVE	sound	PC	binary	.wav
PKZIP/InfoZIP	compressed	PC	binary	.zip
zoo	compressed	PC	binary	.zoo
NeXT audio file	sound	Unix	binary	.snd
compress & uncompress	compressed	Unix	binary	.Z
GNU Zip Archiver	compressed	Unix	binary	.gz
tar	archive	Unix	binary	.tar
X-Bitmap	image	Unix (X)	binary	.xbm
Sun Ulaw	audio	Unix/any	binary	.au
Sun raster	file image	Unix (X)	binary	.rs
PostScript	page description	Any	ASCII or binary	.ps
GIF	graphics	Any	binary	.gif
text	text	Any	ASCII	.txt
uuencode & uudecode	encoded	Any	ASCII	.uu/.uue
JPEG	image compression	Any	binary	.jpg/.jpeg
TIFF	image	Any	binary	.tif
MPEG	video compression	Any	binary	.mpg/.mpeg

Obtaining Information Via Electronic Mail

If you don't have direct access to the Internet, are you forever cut off from publicly available files? Take heart—there are other ways to get files. If you are in a situation in which you can't interactively use FTP, you might want to check out the alternatives explained in this section.

Using what's called an *info-server,* or an *email-server* or an *archive-server,* you can get publicly accessible files by just sending an email message with a command (such as **send info**). One command that should always work is **help**. The message is sent to a server that processes the order and emails the requested files back to you within a few minutes or, usually, by the next day. That's all there is to it.

Many anonymous FTP sites also provide an email service for access to their own files. Some computers, however, will act as general purpose email/FTP translation servers. This means that the files don't have to exist on those computers—you can send orders for *any* publicly available files, no matter what computer they're on. These are known as FTP-by-email servers; they transfer the files from the computers they reside on, and then email them to you.

One FTP-by-email server is *ftpmail@pa.dec.com.* Send an email message to that address, with a one-line message in the body: **help**. (Don't worry about the Subject—anything will do.) You will be sent a help file telling you what commands to use to obtain files. Another server is BITFTP, named because it processes file requests from BITNET users. If you're on BITNET, send email (command **help**, initially) to *BITFTP@PUCC* or *bitftp@pucc.princeton.edu.* You should receive a help file explaining how to use BITFTP. The Appendix lists some other FTP-by-email servers.

FINDING RESOURCES AND FILES

So many resources and public archives are available that it's impossible to cover everything, and people all over the world are constantly cooking up interesting new offerings. There are *lots* of resource directories, guides, lists of public FTP sites and lists of online library catalogues that can help show you the way to important resources. Usually they're maintained by volunteers and

Faster Than Braille Mail

Like a lot of undergraduates these days, Wanda Willis (not her real name) roams the Internet for research and recreation. From the terminal in her dorm room at Indiana State University, she uses all the standard tools and utilities— email, FTP, Gopher, news and IRC. The Internet doesn't know that she's blind.

Willis, a computer science major, uses voice-synthesizing hardware to read the output from her screen. The ASCII text she brings home from the Net is easier to scan and search than the Braille and cassette sources she uses offline in her studies, and the USENET news is far more timely. Logging in to Genie's forum on disability issues allows her to communicate effortlessly with other handicapped Internauts, including the deaf, whose signing she can't interpret in real life.

She bumps against the limits of her system only when she crosses a language barrier—a MUD game in Stuttgart made her voice synthesizer crazy—or encounters ASCII art. A rose is not a rose on her terminal—it's a maze of audible punctuation marks. Otherwise, she sails along like any other student on the Net. 'When I'm home on vacation', she reports, 'I really miss it!'

made available without cost via anonymous FTP, posted regularly to certain mailing lists and newsgroups, or in hard-copy form for a nominal price. The Appendix lists the more popular guides. Sometimes, however, you have to resort to learning about new resources through mailing lists and USENET postings, or by word of mouth. Or you may read a newsletter article about the Internet and find out about a new server. This is true discovery—which is fun—but it makes you feel as though you're missing out if you aren't reading email or news in the right places or if you're not talking to the right people. (Does this sound like real life?)

Uniform Resource Locators

As our lives seem to become increasingly complex, finding key pieces of information, both in your office filing cabinet and on your computer's hard drive, can be difficult, especially around tax time. You've probably been heard to mutter (more than once, perhaps every day), 'I need a new system'.

As the Internet has matured, the number of different applications and resources have grown up too, and the need for a new resource naming system has become apparent. Pick up any documentation or guide describing the great Internet resources you can access, and chances are you'll see a lot of different ways of describing *how* to find that information. A new naming methodology for locating information has surfaced and, as of this writing, is currently still developing. However, you will probably see it here and there, and the chances that it will be adopted universally are very good.

The naming system is called Uniform Resource Locators (URL), and it applies not only to 'stuff' that can be accessed via current information retrieval-and-discovery tools, but to any applications that are developed in the future. The URL naming system can be used by people when referring to a particular resource (in an email message, resource guide or book), and by computers when giving directions to an application on how and where to access a resource. As with anything in the computer and networking industry, the URL system can get quite complicated. This section explains some of the more common ways you'll see it used. The *basic* anatomy of a URL is as follows.

First Part. The first identifier you see refers to the type of application used to access the information, for example, FTP, Gopher, WAIS and so on. (See below for an explanation of these tools.) This identifier is always followed by a colon.

Second Part. For Internet applications, the URL designation begins with a double slash, '//', and then specifies information needed to find and access the host where the resource resides. This includes a user login name and password (if needed), the domain name of the host and a port number (if needed). Usually, what follows the double slashes is just the hostname.

You'll know if a port number is referenced because following the hostname there will be a colon and then a number. That number is the port number. If you don't see one, you don't have to worry about it.

Third Part. Once you've accessed the host, the resource needs to be located on that host. This part describes the 'path' of the information.

Here's an example of a URL:

```
ftp://nysernet.org/pub/resources/guides/
                                    surfing.2.0.3.txt
```

This describes an FTP site, *nysernet.org*, and the directory path */pub/resources/surfing.2.0.3.txt*. To retrieve this file (an article called 'Surfing the Net'), use ftp to connect to the host:

ftp nysernet.org

Then change directories:

cd /pub/resources/guides

And then get the file:

get surfing.2.0.3.txt

Here's another URL:

```
gopher://rugcis.rug.nl:70/
```

This is the URL describing a Gopher server for the Netherlands (Gopher is described below). In this example, a port number is specified: *70.* In this case, 70 happens to be the default port number for the Gopher application, so you usually don't have to type it in. But if you did, here's how you could access this resource:

gopher rugcis.rug.nl 70

URLs can also describe USENET newsgroups. Here's a USENET URL:

```
news://rec.arts.marching.drumcorps
```

Keep in mind that the preceding description is only meant to get you started in learning how to understand a URL, if you come across one. The URL system is very flexible, so there are many ways to use it. See the Appendix for pointers to the URL standards documentation.

Information Discovery-and-Retrieval Tools

Online lists and guides are useful for reading about interesting on-line services, but there are so many resources and information archives available that it's hard to keep these guides up to date. They can also be difficult to search if you've got something particular in mind that you want to know about. If you subscribe to a resource announcement email list, like *net-happenings@is.internic.net* (staffed by a very famous dedicated volunteer, 'Mr. Re-Post Man' himself, Gleason Sackman), you may start scribbling names and numbers all over the place. Most people starting out use the 'Post-It Database System', sticking those little yellow memos all over their computer monitors. Save yourself the effort, because there's no way you can keep up with all the new and great stuff that's made available every day. There is a better way.

What you should spend your time on is learning about the electronic tools (the second class of info-tools mentioned earlier) that are available to you—tools that help you search and browse documents, retrieve information on certain subjects, and locate interesting resources. In 1993 there was an explosion of access and interest in powerful tools with names like archie, WAIS, Gopher, Veronica and WWW. Most of them are responsible for generating the phenomenal growth rates in network traffic; for example, the traffic for the WWW in 1993 increased by 341,634%. (So if you get caught in an Internet traffic jam, you know whom to blame.)

Each of these applications provides a single interface into the hundreds of disparate services and databases on the Internet, offering easier ways to search or browse them. In other words, you don't have to remember computer names, port numbers, or directory structures, or learn lots of new interfaces to hundreds of different computers. These applications can even establish links and relationships between themselves and other services, cross-referencing and helping you find information more easily. Unfortunately, though, you'll still be forced to play confusion roulette every now and then to figure out which application is needed to find a resource.

Clients and Servers

To comprehend how these advanced applications work, you need to understand a fundamental networking concept—the client/server model. This is a very powerful networking concept, and it's used all over the Internet for more than these applications. In general, **clients** are applications that run on your own computer, taking advantage of its special features. A graphical client, for instance, will allow you to use your mouse instead of typing in commands. A client program hides many of the network details from you, including computer names, ports and commands, and it obtains its information from servers. **Servers** are programs running on computers that are reachable via the network. They know where the data and documents are, and they take care of servicing client queries.

Unfortunately, the client/server model requires a *direct* network connection to the Internet. If you're sitting at home with just a microcomputer, modem and terminal emulation software, you probably won't be able to partake of these powerful applications right away. However, there are ways to turn your PC or Mac into a directly connected computer even though you're dialled-in, simply by using some special software. This type of connection (described in Chapter 7) uses protocols called SLIP (Serial Line Internet Protocol) and PPP (Point-to-Point Protocol) that must be supported by your Internet provider. If all you've got is terminal emulation software (such as Kermit or PRO-COMM), you can still use these applications through **terminal clients** and **telnet clients**; in other words, you either remotely login to public terminal-based interfaces, or you use a client application that's not resident on your own computer (perhaps on the computer into which you've dialled). They're not as friendly and easy to use as their graphical client counterparts, but at least you'll still have access to these powerful servers, and can get an idea of what they do.

One more thing: because there are so many different ways to access resources, you need to take an inventory of your local situation and what is available to you. Once you're on the Net, you'll hear people casually say something like, 'Point your Gopher client at *gopher.Germany.EU.net*'. You should first take note of the method of access (in this case, Gopher), and the destination (in this case, *gopher.Germany.EU.net*). Most of the time, people will not give you explicit instructions when telling you about a great resource (such as, type **gopher.Germany.EU.net**, or select 'Another Gopher' from the file menu and type **gopher.Germany.EU.net** in response to the prompt), because

Client programs hide network details from you. Server programs
find most Internet resources and deliver them to your computer.

there are just too many ways to get there. Once you understand
how to use the applications on your own system, an instruction
like the one quoted above should be enough to get you going.
The following explanations will help you understand what's
available for your situation; you need to follow up and read suggested help files to learn the specifics.

Gopher

By far the easiest tool for novices is **Gopher**. You're just going to
love Gopher, because it's simple, it's fun, you don't have to get
dressed up to use it and it gets you places fast. Just one Gopher
session will fly you to a hospital in Melbourne, the Minnesota
State Legislature, the Exploratorium in San Francisco, the Wel-
lington City Council and Chulalongkorn University in Bangkok.
And if you're not up to it, you don't have to go places. You can
browse and download magazines, such as *Wired, The Economist,
Inc* and *Financial World Magazine*.

    The name gopher can mean several things. In the traditional
sense, it is a 'gopher' for information. You can also think of it as a
furry animal that runs out and sniffs around 'Gopherspace' for

you. The name actually came from its birthplace, the University of Minnesota, whose mascot is the gopher.

So get ready, 'cause you're about to go gophering! Gopher organizes access to Internet resources using a uniform interface—in a nutshell, it's a menu system. It provides smooth passage into other Gopher servers, allowing you to browse and search documents, and links you to resources and databases, such as USENET news, online library catalogues and Campus-Wide Information Servers (explained below). You may not know it, but while you're 'sniffing' around Gopherspace, you're actually doing things like transferring files, changing directories, telnetting to computers and querying servers (including archie and WAIS, which are explained below) all over the world.

The way it works is, organizations can bring up their own Gopher servers and menus, and make available any information they want. It's really easy for any Internet-connected organization to bring up a Gopher server. When this book was first written in the summer of 1992, there were around 100 Gophers. As of today, there are as many as 25,000 Gophers poking their heads out of the ground. The estimated growth rate for Gopher traffic in 1993 was 997%! Most of the participating Gopher servers are tied together by Gopher links in their menus, so by connecting to one organization's Gopher, you can usually 'break away' and burrow into other Gopher holes across the world.

How to Use It. Gopher has a hierarchical menu system. When you initiate a Gopher session (with a client program), you can either connect to a default Gopher server or specify a particular server. Either way, you'll be accessing some organization's top-level menu. You travel Gopherspace by either typing the corresponding menu item number, using your arrow keys to position a menu arrow, or clicking on an icon. This will lead you to another menu, another computer (via Telnet), the document you seek (which may be text, an image or a sound file, for example), or a searchable database. Once you figure out your local Gopher situation, you should familiarize yourself with all the commands and options available to you; be sure to read all the help messages on your screen. For example, when a Gopher menu item leads you to a Telnet session, it will warn you that you're 'leaving Gopher'. Be sure to read the instructions on your screen (if there are any) that explain how to login and how to use the system. During a Gopher session, you may burrow down very deep into menu after menu before you find what you're looking for. At this point, you can either quit or work your way back up through the menus until you get back to where you started.

Accessing Gopher. There are lots of different ways to access Gopher. One is by using a public Telnet Gopher client. To do this, you simply telnet to one of the public Gopher computers and login. This is not the best way to use Gopher, because these public clients are often incredibly busy; but if you do use this method, choose a host that's geographically close to you. Below is a list of computers you can telnet to, login as **gopher** (usually), and then use their menu system.

Some Public Gopher Sites Accessible Via Telnet

Geographical Area	Hostname	Login Id
North America	consultant.micro.umn.edu	gopher
North America	ux1.cso.uiuc.edu	gopher
North America	gopher.msu.edu	gopher
North America	panda.uiowa.edu	panda
Europe	gopher.ebone.net	gopher
Sweden	gopher.sunet.se	gopher
Australia	info.anu.edu.au	info
South America	tolten.puc.cl	gopher
Ecuador	ecnet.ec	gopher
Japan	gan.ncc.go.jp	gopher

All these Gophers are accessible by Telnet. For example, type **telnet gopher. sunet.se** and login as **gopher** to access the Swedish Gopher.

The second way is by using a Gopher client on your own computer. If you're on a Unix system, for example, try typing **gopher** at the Unix prompt and see what happens. There are easy-to-use graphical clients available for most computer systems, PCs, Macs, Unix (X Window, emacs) and so on, but they need to be directly connected to the Internet in order to work. The Appendix lists places where you can download free Gopher client programs for your computer.

Terminal Gopher Systems. If you're accessing Gopher via a terminal client (not a graphical client), here are some useful instructions. First, take a look at the sample Gopher menu below. As you can see, each item has a '/' following it. That means each of those selections will actually take you to another menu. Other symbols:

<TEL>	Telnet session
/	Another directory
<?>	A keyword search

Terminal Gopher Navigating. By using your arrow keys, you can navigate Gopher quite well. The up and down arrows position your cursor arrow; the right arrow selects the item; the left arrow takes you back up to the previous menu. (You can also go back up a level by typing **u** for 'up'.) You can skip forward and backward through the screens using the following commands:

Next Screen: >, +, Pgdwn, space
Previous Screen: <, -, Pgup, b

Other commands include **h** for 'help' and = to display technical and location information about the entry (useful when you use Veronica—discussed below). You can also save files to your hard disk by typing **s**. For a list of other commands, type **?**.

Here's a sample Gopher menu for the Internet Wiretap (*wiretap.spies.com*):

```
         Internet Gopher Information Client v1.11

                     Internet Wiretap

->   1. About the Internet Wiretap/
     2. Clinton Press Releases/
     3. Electronic Books at Wiretap/
     4. GAO Transition Reports/
     5. Government Docs (US & World)/
     6. North American Free Trade Agreement/
     7. Usenet alt.etext Archives/
     8. Usenet ba.internet Archives/
     9. Various ETEXT Resources on the Internet/
    10. Video Game Archive/
    11. Waffle BBS Software/
    12. Wiretap Online Library/
    13. Worldwide Gopher and WAIS Servers/

Press ? for Help, q to Quit, u to go up a menu      Page: 1/1
```

Where to Start. To get an idea of the extent of Gopherspace, select 'Other Gopher and Information Servers' (or something close to that) if it's available on your top menu. You should see a menu item called 'All the Gopher Servers in the World'. Choosing this will give you an alphabetical list of every registered Gopher server in the world.

In the above Wiretap example, to get to 'All the Gopher Servers in the World', you would select number 13, 'Worldwide Gopher and WAIS Servers'. Choosing that will give you another menu, with the top selection 'All'. This is the selection that shows you the alphabetical list of all Gopher servers. So you see, the street signs are not standardized, but by carefully reading each menu for clues, it's easy to cruise Gopherspace.

If you browse this list of every Gopher server, you'll see a lot of university entries. Gophers are native to the university environment; the system was invented as a way to provide campus-wide information systems (CWIS). Today Gopher CWISs are serving as digital kiosks that provide campus-specific information, such as event calendars, phone and email directories, newsletters, restaurant guides, local weather, available jobs, athletic and cultural events and course catalogues. While much of the information may not be of interest to outsiders, some of the services do provide links to useful databases and online library catalogues. Also, these systems may be a good place to look for email addresses.

Try visiting the Earlham College Gopher, based in Richmond, Indiana (*gopher.earlham.edu*). Or Gothenburg University in Gothenburg, Sweden (*gopher.gu.se*). Or Griffith University in the Brisbane–Gold Coast corridor of Australia (*griffin.itc.gu.edu.au*).

Even though there are a lot of university Gophers, more and more companies are realizing the advantages of providing online access to information about their products and services. For example, many publishers are making their book catalogues available online. And you can even make purchases online using Gopher! All you need, of course, is a credit card for those easy and convenient monthly instalments. But just think, no waiting in long queues at the shop or suffering those high-pressure pitches on infomercials! Of course you'll soon be able to use one of the digital 'electronic cash' systems currently being tried on the Net. These can even manage to extract value directly from your account or cashcard without giving you the breathing space until your next credit card bill!

If the long list of 'All the Gopher Servers in the World' overwhelms you, check out the other menus that organize Gophers geographically (by continent, country, state or city) or by subject. If you've been following the examples in this book, you've probably seen these menu items.

Navigation Paths. Many resource guides list ways to find a document hidden deep down in Gopher menus. A common way to represent this is to list all menu items separated by slashes, '/'. Using the Wiretap example above, let's say a friend found an article she wanted you to see. She might send you email telling you how to find it using this notation:

Wiretap Online Library/Music/Various Top 100 Lists/ Worst 100 Singles of Last 25 Years

She could just tell you the menu item numbers (12, 11, 4, 7), which would be shorter and easier, but Gopher menus can change easily—items added and deleted at a moment's notice. So it's better to list out the complete path.

With these directions, you can read someone's personal list of the 'Worst 100 Singles of the Last 25 Years', and then have an intense, emotional discussion with your friend about *why* 'Kung Fu Fighting' should *not* be on that list.

GOPHERS FOR U.S. GOVERNMENT WATCHDOGS

Agency/Document	Gopher Host
World Constitutions	wiretap.spies.com path: Government Docs (US & World)/ World Constitutions
U.S. Central Intelligence Agency	wiretap.spies.com path: Electronic Books/CIA:World Fact Book
U.S. Commerce Department	gopher.esa.doc.gov
U.S. Smithsonian Institution	nmnhgoph.si.edu path: National Museum of Natural History
U.S. and World Politics	sunsite.unc.edu path: Worlds of SunSITE/U.S. and World Politics

Bookmarks. Once you've gone gophering and lost yourself in Gopherspace a few times, you'll appreciate this next feature. Gopher allows you to tag places of interest to you, and assemble all of them in one easy-access menu. To do this, you simply mark an entry with a **bookmark** and it gets added to your bookmark list. So instead of bumbling around and looking lost, remember to use the bookmark feature!

Here's how you tag entries using a terminal gopher client. Suppose you are browsing the Metaverse Gopher (*metaverse.com*), and you decide to bookmark the *woodstock* menu (information about the 1994 Woodstock music festival). Position the arrow on the 'woodstock' entry and type **a** (for 'add'). The 'woodstock' item will be added to your bookmark list. To access your bookmark list (a Gopher menu), just type **v**. (To leave the bookmark list, type **u** or the left arrow.)

You can also add entire menus to your bookmark list by typing an **A** (uppercase 'A'). If you typed **A** in this example, the entire Metaverse Gopher menu would be added to the list.

It's easy to delete bookmarks. First, call up your bookmark menu by typing **v**. Then position the arrow on the item you wish to delete and type **d**.

Veronica

Going gophering can become an addictive hobby, and it's an engaging way to find out all sorts of interesting things you don't really *need* to know. But what if you need to find an idea for a game to play at your next family reunion, and you don't have time to go burrowing through every Gopher site in the world? You can rest easy because there's a device nestled within reach of most Gopher menus called **Veronica**. Veronica was developed by the University of Nevada; it stands for Very Easy Rodent-Oriented Net-wide Index to Computerized Archives. (How convenient that this acronym happens to spell Veronica, *n'est-ce pas?*)

What Veronica does is let you search for an item from every Gopher menu in the world. All you've got to do is supply it with a keyword (or several words), and it will compile a single Gopher menu of items containing that word (or words). This is quite handy, as you have everything available to you at once, instead of having to sift through mountains of menus. From your results, item 1 may be from a Gopher server in Chile, while item 2 might be found in Hong Kong. You can find out where selections were obtained by positioning the arrow to the desired item and typing = if you're using a terminal gopher client.

Accessing Veronica. Veronica is 'built into' Gopher, so at this time, you don't need a special client program to access it. It's usually available as a menu item on most Gophers. There's no standard name for it, but try selecting the following items to find it: at the top-level Gopher menu, select 'Other Gopher and Information Servers'. That should produce a menu that provides choices of other Gophers indexed by geographical region. There should be a selection called 'Search Titles in Gopherspace Using Veronica'. When you select that, you should have several selections to choose from. (Be sure to select the items that begin with 'Search gopherspace at'.) In the Wiretap example, Veronica can be found via this path: *Worldwide Gopher and WAIS Servers/Veronica.*

Veronica is a very popular tool, and during peak times you may get a 'busy signal' from the Veronica servers. If this happens, just try again later, perhaps in the evening or early in the morning. Rush hours on the Internet are usually during work hours; however, as people are always working somewhere in the world, that doesn't help much. But remember, even though you may be playing around on the Internet during your lunch break, you may be accessing a Veronica server in some part of the world when it's 3 a.m.! Also, a Veronica search may return a menu of 213 items, 50 of which are exactly the same. That's because many sites 'mirror' Gopher menus. Veronica doesn't care—it dutifully tells you about each one. There's also no indication (on the menu) whether they're all the same or, if not, which is more up-to-date. So you'll just have to do it the hard way and check them all or act on faith.

For More Information. For general searches, using Veronica is pretty straightforward. If you want to learn more about the inner workings or how to compose more involved search queries, read the Veronica FAQ document and 'How to Compose Veronica Queries' selections available on the Veronica menu.

Jughead

Veronica is great when you want to do a survey of all of Gopher-space. But, as mentioned before, Veronica servers are frequently too busy to help you. Here's where Jughead comes in. **Jughead**, or 'Jonzy's Universal Gopher Hierarchy Excavation and Display' (isn't that amazing!), searches only a local part of Gopherspace, rather than all of it. Many organizations provide Jughead menu items for their own Gopher servers, so if you want to confine your searching to a local area, use Jughead (if it exists on that Gopher). Jughead can be found (and used) in the same way as Veronica on a Gopher menu. There's no standard place or name for a Jughead menu item, but you can spot most of them because they contain the word 'Jughead'. Here's a sample Jughead menu item for the University of Texas at Austin Gopherspace:

```
Jughead: Search menus in University of Texas at
                        Austin gopherspace <?>
```

Selecting this item will allow you to search for a keyword from the menu items of the University of Texas at Austin Gopher.

Archie

Archie (derived from the word *archive*) is an online file-finding utility originally developed at the McGill University School of Computer Science in Montreal. If you've ever looked high and low for a file on your microcomputer's hard disk, you'll understand the usefulness of this tool. About 1,500 (and growing) known public sites are providing access to files via anonymous FTP. Trying to figure out where a particular document or archive is located on the Internet is like looking for the proverbial needle in a digital haystack.

The way it works is simple. The archie system maintains a database of all the names of files stored at known public archive sites. A user can search this database by using a client program, by remotely logging in to an archie server computer using Telnet, or by sending email (with commands) to the server. Quite a few server computers are scattered throughout the world and users are requested to pick the one that's closest to them. All archie servers exchange their new data with one another on a regular

PUBLIC ARCHIE SERVERS

You can query these servers several ways. The best way is to use an archie client program and specify the nearest server. For example, if you live in Spain, use the archie.rediris.es server.

If you don't have an archie client, you can telnet into most of these, and login as **archie** to use the service. Again, use the one closest to you. Once you're on, type **help** to get a list of commands. If you want to start searching for a file, simply type **prog** *filename* where *filename* is the name of the file you're searching for. Archie will 'think' for a while and then produce a list of every place that has a file by that name. You can then have this list sent to you via email by typing **mail** *your-email-address*. When you're done searching, just type **exit** to get back to home base.

Country/State	Archie Server Name
ANS server, NY, USA	*archie.ans.net*
Rutgers, NJ, USA	*archie.rutgers.edu*
AT&T, NY, USA	*archie.internic.net*
SURAnet, MD, USA	*archie.sura.net*
U. of Nebraska, NE, USA	*archie.unl.edu*
Australia	*archie.au*
Austria	*archie.edvz.uni-linz.ac.at*
Austria	*archie.univie.ac.at*
Canada	*archie.uqam.ca*
Finland	*archie.funet.fi*
Germany	*archie.th-darmstadt.de*
Italy	*archie.unipi.it*
Japan	*archie.kuis.kyoto-u.ac.jp*
Japan	*archie.wide.ad.jp*
Korea	*archie.kr*
Korea	*archie.sogang.ac.kr*
New Zealand	*archie.nz*
Spain	*archie.rediris.es*
Sweden	*archie.luth.se*
Switzerland	*archie.switch.ch*
Taiwan	*archie.ncu.edu.tw*
United Kingdom	*archie.doc.ic.ac.uk*

basis. So you are sure to get the information you need by asking your local server. If you don't have an archie client program, you can login to a public archie server. Be aware that, just as with Gopher, this is not the recommended way to use archie.

Here's an example using a Unix client archie. Suppose that you're giving a big speech, and you're looking for a good opening joke to break the ice. A great starting point is to search archie for any files with the word 'jokes' in their titles. All you have to do is type **archie jokes**. Your client will search a default server and return the results to you. If you want to specify another server, do it with the **-h** option (server host). For example, to switch to the German server, type **archie -h archie.darmstadt.de**.

If your Internet access is limited and you can't telnet to an archie server, you can access archie via email. Basically, you send commands in an email message to an archie server, and the results are emailed back to you. To test this out, send a message to *archie@nearest-archie-server* (see table below), with the command **help** in the body of the message. A description of the basic commands will be sent to you. You can then use the 'FTP-by-Email Servers' described earlier to obtain the files you want.

Wide Area Information Servers

Archie will tell you *where* a file is, based on a name that you give it, but it can't help you search for information based on what's *in* the file. That's a job for an application called **Wide Area Information Servers** (**WAIS**, pronounced 'ways'). WAIS was conceived by Brewster Kahle in the late 1980s, and was developed by Dow Jones, Thinking Machines, Apple Computer and KPMG Peat Marwick as a joint project. Since then, Brewster has formed a company called WAIS, Inc. which is now developing WAIS as an information tool for corporations. But many WAIS databases and applications are still freely available on the Internet.

WAIS allows you to search for information in databases located on server computers. How does it work? Think of WAIS as a sort of electronic reference librarian. When you ask it where you can get information on a certain subject, it searches databases and returns documents it thinks will help you. Now, the servers don't actually *understand* your question; they simply look for documents that contain the words and phrases you used. The documents can be pictures and sound as well as text. The nifty thing about WAIS is that once you find some articles that fit the bill, you can ask WAIS to find more documents with those characteristics. WAIS tries to 'listen' to the feedback you give it before continuing its search. If you're using a WAIS client, you can save your questions and ask WAIS to continue searching at regular intervals for updates to it, or only when you specifically ask for something.

The WAIS system is very powerful and covers a lot of territory. At least 600 databases (with more being made available all the time) are on server computers all over the world. Here's just a small sampling of the information you have access to: poetry, sheet music indexes, science fiction reviews, journalism periodicals and organic gardening. There are also archives of many mailing lists and USENET newsgroups searchable by WAIS.

As is the case for archie and Gopher applications, you can either access WAIS by using a client program running on your system or by remotely logging into a public client. There are client applications available for Unix systems, called **swais** and **waisearch** (**xwais** for X Window systems).

You can try out a simple WAIS terminal interface by remotely logging in to *sunsite.unc.edu*; login as **swais**. When you login, you will be asked for your terminal type; in most cases, you'll be emulating a VT100 terminal. Although this interface is very powerful, it's not very user-friendly. There are other options; graphical clients are available for PCs and Macs. The Appendix lists where to obtain these and provides information on how to become a WAIS expert. In the meantime, you may have an occasion or two to search WAIS databases accessible via a Gopher or the WWW interface (explained below).

WorldWideWeb

WorldWideWeb (**WWW** or **W³**) is a browsing-and-searching system originally developed by the European Laboratory for Particle Physics (also known as CERN). It allows you to explore a seemingly unlimited worldwide digital 'web' of information. The WWW is built upon the concept of hypertext and hypermedia, which stretches independent but interrelated documents and pictures into a three-dimensional cyberspacious world.

Almost every piece of WWW information you look at provides you with pointers, or hooks, into other documents on related subjects. And these documents aren't just text—they can also be sound and images—so the WWW is really a hypermedia information retrieval system.

The Web is a continuous construction project for distributed information; tens of thousands of people are adding knowledge to it daily by bringing up their own **web servers**, which provide content and links, or bridges, between documents. Servers are also referred to as **pages** or **home pages**; for example, you may hear someone say, 'Visit the Dr. Fun home page located at SunSITE'. At the time of this writing, there were thousands of web servers, and the number is growing every day.

The Web lets you embark on digital journeys, travelling information links by simply clicking (or selecting) highlighted words or phrases. Once you make a selection, a hyperlink is followed to the destination, a related document, which may also contain links to other documents (and so on). WWW does more than just let you browse—it also allows you to search for key words in certain documents.

This system is very similar to the way our brains work. The Web lets you locate information of interest to you, in a way mimicking your thought processes. We don't think or learn in a linear fashion; most of our thought processes can be pretty random at times. For example, while you're driving to work the song on the radio reminds you of a party you were at several months ago, and then you start thinking of Joe, whom you saw at that party. You haven't seen Joe in a long time and you decide to give him a call. A simple song on the radio led you to Joe's doorstep. So who knows what the Web will lead you to?

The WWW operates using some special protocols that you'll probably see from time to time when you're 'webbing' it. One of these is **HTTP**, which stands for **HyperText Transfer Protocol**. This protocol simply allows very quick network file transfer, and it's used in WWW browsers (explained below) as a faster alternative to FTP. **HTML**, or **HyperText Markup Language** is a very simple language used for basic formatting and presentation of hypermedia documents. Many of the WWW browsers use it to specify the format of the document, where the hypertext links go, where images and sounds go, and so on.

Is There a Swimming Pool in the Kremlin?

A group of reference librarians at a major university library (which shall remain nameless) were a bit sceptical when a WAIS terminal was installed at their reference desk. Not that they were computerphobic—they just felt they were already masters of the best research tools available. So someone posed the question, 'Is there a swimming pool in the Kremlin?' Well, in this post-glasnost era, we should certainly be able to find out.

The reference librarians scurried off to their favourite research mines—some to the card catalogue, some to Dialog, some to the periodical indexes. The WAIS wizard worked quietly at his terminal; within ten minutes, he'd found several citations and one whole article about a retired member of the Red Guard who swam every day, just outside the Kremlin walls. More than half an hour after he'd finished, the librarians straggled back. A few had struck out, a couple had a few cold leads, and one had, with a lot more work, located the same article in about quadruple the time it took on WAIS. Think they were convinced?

You should know about HTML because you may want to publish some information on your own server someday. It's a really simple language that you use to describe how you want a document to look on the screen.

Accessing WWW. There are a number of ways to plunge into the WWW. The programs that provide an interface to the WWW are also known as **browsers.** Just like all the client programs discussed above, browsers come in two flavours: terminal (text-based) and graphical. Your options depend on how you're connected to the Internet. If you're dialling in and using a slow modem, it's best to stick to the terminal clients; two well-known ones are the CERN LineMode Browser and Lynx. If you've got a high-speed dedicated or SLIP/PPP connection, you can probably use powerful graphical client applications, such as Mosaic, Cello

---

The Multilingual Internet

In February 1995, the U.S. magazine *Business Week* wrote that "Industry pundits are billing 1995 as the year that Europeans go online. . . . Market researchers are predicting some 500,000 Europeans going online this year, with as many as 15 million by 2000." To answer the reading needs of that vastly increasing, multilingual Internet audience, the Online Bookstore (OBS) started its BookFinder service in 1994. Using the Internet to connect readers from around the world to book professionals—people, not database catalogs—who can address individual reading needs by searching out and finding in-print books in any of 236 languages, the OBS is supplementing its core business of online publishing by using the Internet as a communications medium and a marketplace. Collaborating with well-established, multilanguage bookstores on two continents, the OBS seeks to satisfy readers' literate habits worldwide, demonstrating how the Internet can preserve and enhance the rich diversity of the world's cultures by enabling the dissemination of literature and languages electronically.

Source: http://marketplace.com/obs/top.htm.

---

and TKWWW. The CERN browser, Lynx and Mosaic are explained in this chapter. If you're interested in learning more about other browsers, you should explore the Web itself for information. Try the URL *http://info.cern.ch/hypertext/www* as a start, or obtain the WWW FAQ. (For more information, see the Appendix).

Public Telnet Clients. If you don't have a WWW client program installed on your computer, there are public browsers you can access via Telnet. You can try connecting to the granddaddy of them all, the WWW server located at CERN in Geneva, Switzerland. Just type **telnet info.cern.ch** (this is a really popular site, so you may have problems getting through). Another one that's publicly available is located at the University of Kansas in the United States. Type **telnet ukanaix.cc.ukans.edu** and login as **kufacts**. Or you can try one located at the Hebrew University of Jerusalem, Israel: **telnet vms.huji.ac.il**, login as **www**. (The WWW FAQ lists some other public sites.)

The public telnet clients are good for evaluating the WWW, but they're heavily visited sites, so it's recommended you access and use a local client browser. To find out what's available on your system, ask your Internet provider.

CERN's LineMode Browser. This application is a very basic interface to the WWW for those users without graphical client capabilities. If it's available on your system, you simply type **www** and a home (startup) document will be shown on your screen. You'll see numbers scattered throughout the document; these specify the links. To select a link, type the corresponding number.

At the bottom of the screen is a status line that tells you what type of document you're looking at—if there's a number range (for instance, 1–15 equals 15 links), it means a hypertext document with links to other documents. If there are a lot of links in the document, you'll have to page through each screen to see all of them (since they can't all fit on the same screen). So if you press <RETURN> (perhaps several times, if there are several screens), you'll see the rest of them. A **help** command lists all of the commands and a brief explanation. The last command option, **quit**, allows you to leave.

The very first thing you should do, of course, is type **help** to get a list of commands. There are some keywords that will help you navigate; for example, you can type **home** to return to the home (startup) screen, and **back** will put your browser in reverse, navigating backward on your Web path. If you follow a bunch of links (by typing their corresponding numbers), and get yourself deeper into the Web, you can then back up to each link you referenced by typing **back**.

The other commands, **top**, **up** and **bottom**, help you navigate when you're looking at a document with a large number of links (150, for instance). At any time you can type **up** to look at the previous screen, <RETURN> to look at the next screen, **top** to return to the beginning of the document, and **bottom** to jump to the end.

You will definitely want to learn how to jump to other Web servers when you hear about them. The command to do that is **go** *URL*, where *URL* specifies the desired server. For example, if you want to peruse *Wired* magazine's web server, type **go http://www.wired.com**.

Lynx. A widely recommended WWW browser is called Lynx, and it's available on Unix and VMS systems. Lynx differs from the CERN browser in that it's a full screen-oriented application—you can use your arrow keys to position your 'pointer' on the different links in the document.

If Lynx is available on your system, you can start it up by typing **lynx** at the command prompt. You'll see a screen with text, a 'home page', containing words and phrases that stand out (boldfaced or highlighted) from the rest of the text. Each of these phrases provides a hyperlink to another document, which may contain more links (and so on).

The three lines at the bottom of the screen contain helpful instructions. Here's a summary of some of the commands:

H)	Help	G)	Go to URL
O)	Options	M)	Go to Main (Initial) Screen
P)	Print	Q)	Quit

You can navigate the WWW Lynx application by using your arrow keys—the up and down arrows position your cursor on a link, and the right arrow (or return key) selects that link. To return to previous links (backing up the hierarchy), simply use the left arrow key.

If you find a URL for a great Web server that you'd like to test-drive, you can jump directly to that also. Using the *Wired* magazine example above, you would type **go http://www.wired.com**.

Mosaic

The terminal client browsers will give you an idea of what's available on the Web, but keep in mind when you're using these that you don't have access to sounds, images and movies, only to text-based documents. There are other ways to access the WWW besides a text-based terminal browser. Weighing in on the client mega scale is the Mosaic hypermedia distributed-information-discovery-and-retrieval browser, developed by the National Center for Supercomputing Applications (NCSA) in Champaign, Illinois. The Mosaic client is a graphical interface to the WWW of information, and is one of the best applications to make the Internet scene. An Internet Jack-of-all-trades, Mosaic also has hooks and gateways into Gopher, USENET, WAIS, archie and other front ends. It does just what its name implies—that is, show the Internet as a world made up of colourful, varied and interesting pieces of information, including text, images, sound and movies. Taking a Mosaic journey is a real trip—you can indulge all sorts of online whims and curiosities. While Mosaic is the granddaddy of graphical WWW browsers, its features have now been replicated and, in some cases, surpassed by other software, most notably by the Netscape WWW client (originally called Mosaic Netscape but recently renamed). Most graphical browsers, however, work in a sufficiently similar manner that a description of one gives a reasonable guide to them all.

Many people confuse browsers like Mosaic with the WWW and vice versa. They are two separate but related entities; just remember that the WWW is a global hypertext world of information, whereas Mosaic provides an *interface* into this world (as well as into the other applications mentioned above).

When you fire up Mosaic, it presents you with a startup screen, also known as a **home page.** Think of it as your front door to the WWW. As is the case for LineMode Browser and Lynx, this home page is actually downloaded from a server that is located somewhere on the Internet. If this is your first time, your home page may be downloaded from NCSA. Be sure to select the 'demo document' to check out recommended must-see items. Keep in mind that your Mosaic client program can be customized; you can change your front door to open anywhere on the Internet. To begin your search, all you have to do is point and click on underlined (or highlighted) words and phrases. Every time you do this, a related document (which can be text, sound or pictures) is downloaded and presented to you. Mosaic provides a 'bread crumbs' feature, known as a **hotlist** (similar to Gopher bookmarks), that you can use to find the places you're interested in quickly without having to go searching through layers and layers of the Web every time you fire up the application. Mosaic will also let you specify a URL to visit directly—a useful feature when someone announces the availability of a new resource (look for a menu item that lets you 'Open URL').

During a Web session, it's likely that you will jump around quite a bit from resource to resource. Mosaic keeps track of where you've been in a particular session, so you can easily navigate backward and forward. Look for arrow buttons on your screen that, when selected, will help you retrace your steps. There's also a menu that lists all the places you've been. To go back home, simply click on the 'home' icon or select 'home' from the menu. When you quit a session, all of these history features will be lost, so be sure to add the most interesting places to your hotlist.

What's New, Mosaic? Groping your way around the WWW can be akin to getting dropped off in a strange city with no directions or maps. There are several resources that can help you find what you want in Webspace. A popular one is the 'What's New with NCSA Mosaic' page, a regularly updated source of announcements of new Web servers and the latest WWW developments at NCSA. This server is available via the NCSA Home Page (the default home page for many Mosaic applications), or by jumping directly to *http://www.ncsa.uiuc.edu/SDG/Software/Mosaic/ Docs/whats-new.html.*

If you need to find a specific resource, you should check out the Internet Resource Meta-Index page, accessible via the NCSA home page, or by jumping directly to *http://www.ncsa.uiuc.edu/SDG/ Software/Mosaic/MetaIndex.html.* Included in this page are pointers to subject catalogues (for WWW, Gopher, WAIS and Telnet) and searchable indexes of WWW servers.

Unfortunately, Mosaic is one of those 'power user' applications. In other words, if your Internet access is obtained by a PC or Mac and a dialup line, you may not have the patience to sit around while it inhales the huge image, sound and movie files off the net for your viewing and listening enjoyment. If you've got a really fast modem (14.4 or 28.8Kbps) and you're using SLIP or PPP (see Chapter 7 for more information), you can participate, but it's pretty slow, and it's easy to start imagining the application huffing and puffing while it's lifting large documents off the

'WAY COOL' WWW SERVERS

- Dr. Fun, a cartoon in the style of 'The Far Side'
  http://sunsite.unc.edu/Dave/drfun.html
- The NASDAQ Financial Executive Journal
  http://www.law.cornell.edu/usr2/wwwtext/nasdaq/nasdtoc.html
- Global Real Estate Guide
  http://www.gems.com/realestate
- The Online BookStore
  http://marketplace.com
- The Cisco Education Archive (CEARCH)
  http://sunsite.unc.edu/cisco/edu-arch.html

Net. Your Mosaic application has an option that lets you turn off automatic image download feature—in this case, you'll just download text without any graphics, which is much faster, especially for dialup SLIP/PPP links.

In order to hear and see everything, Mosaic requires a lot of 'pieces/parts'—meaning, you need 'external' (to Mosaic) viewer and player applications installed on your workstation to see and hear what's out there. And if that isn't enough, your workstation needs a pretty big engine, ample disk space and a lot of memory. Assembling and installing all these parts, if they're not already available on your workstation, will take a while and might cause you some frustration.

Don't let all this negative stuff deter you, though, because Mosaic and its competitors are the 'killer apps' (*app*, meaning application), a portent of Internet interfaces to come. You may not be able to take advantage of it now, but you'll definitely be seeing and hearing more about it in the future. Many businesses are using it to provide easy access to their company product information and services or to provide commercial information services. Mosaic has become so popular right now that it's being blamed for traffic jams and bottlenecks on the Internet. This is due, in part, to the existing network infrastructure, which in some places is not 'broad' enough to carry the data flows without causing some backup. One way to solve this problem is by building faster and faster communication highways (similar to adding more lanes). Developers of WWW browsers such as Mosaic are also doing their part to make the clients more efficient by bundling requests over the network—a sort of digital car-pooling solution.

Mosaic Clients. If you do have all the right stuff and want to test-drive Mosaic, you can download the client applications via anonymous FTP from the *ftp.ncsa.uiuc.edu* host in the *Mosaic* directory. Clients are available for Unix workstations running the X Window system, Apple Macintoshes and PCs running Microsoft Windows. (There are also many other archives that make Mosaic available. If you have problems accessing the above server, ask around.)

If you're interested in publishing (serving) information that other people can access, introductory documents are available on this very subject via the WWW. Just follow the Web to learn more about the Web. To get started, check out the WWW Initiative Page: *http://info.cern.ch/hypertext/WWW/TheProject.html.* To learn more about publishing your own info, start with the WWW and HTML Developer's JumpStation: *http://oneworld.wa.com/htmldev /devpage/dev-page.html.*

As you roam the Internet, you'll definitely get the sense that there's a culture and a shared history—things that people just 'know'. So that you don't feel left out, Chapter 5 gives the flavour of Internet culture, reviews some of what's gone on before you made the scene, shares some 'insider' information about security, and tells you where in the network world you can go to get help.

Chapter 5

INTERNET IN-THE-KNOW GUIDE

*N**ow that you've learned* what you can do on the Internet and a bit about how it works, it's time to cover a few 'Advanced Internet Topics'. The Internet is more than just how-to. It has its own culture, its own myths and legends. There are fantasy games on the Internet that become a world unto themselves for many of the players. You should know, too, about the organizations dedicated to the Internet and to network users. And there are some niceties—such as directory services and advanced methods for finding email addresses—that you can master if you're willing. Technical necessities, like computer security, are a must. A 'Finding More Help' section gives some direction for times when you need additional information or help with an Internet problem.

Put a few million people together anywhere, even in electronic cyberspace, and they'll develop some kind of culture—a fabric of shared experiences, shared recreation, shared fears, shared rules of behaviour—that makes them all feel part of a community. The Internet's formal and informal codes of conduct were discussed in Chapter 3. Now it's time to learn about some of the less tangible aspects of the Internet culture, the Net legends and the notable—and notorious—subculture of network games.

LEGENDS ON THE INTERNET

Probably everyone knows at least one story that qualifies as an 'urban legend'—a story that, while it may have started with a grain of truth, has been embroidered and retold until it has passed into the realm of myth. It's an interesting phenomenon that these

---

What Does It Take for a Troll to Get Drunk?

Terry Pratchett, author of the famous Discworld novels, is an Internet regular. He joined his own fan newsgroup on the USENET news system *alt.fan.pratchett* to get to know what they were thinking about his books. (Maybe the tons of sold printed paper was not signal enough that they like his work. :-) Anyhow, his fans discuss the content of his books (including the ongoing fate of Rincewind, the most incapable wizard of the Universe) and ideas about his figures and characters. Realizing the potential for humour, Pratchett participates in these discussions. Sometimes he raises questions such as 'What does it take for a Troll (who is made mostly of stone) to get drunk?' You can imagine the answers he gets.

---

stories get spread so far and so fast—and so often. Urban legends never die—they all just seem to end up on the Internet! You won't be on the Internet long before you start seeing references to these legends. Experienced Internet users have seen some of these old chestnuts come around regularly for years.

The following stories document the most well known of the bunch. You will probably be exposed to these, or variations on the theme. Be 'street-wise' and wary of any posting promising fame and fortune or asking you to forward a message far and wide. Check the source before you act.

The Infamous Modem Tax

The U.S. Federal Communications Commission (FCC) Modem Tax Scare is a classic example of an Internet legend that refuses to die. Several years ago, a proposal surfaced in Washington to put a telecommunications tax on modems. The tax was quickly quashed in a congressional committee, and it was not—repeat, *not*—under reconsideration at the time this book was published. But you wouldn't know that from some users of the Internet. The scare resurfaces continually on the networks, riling new users at the prospect that their new-found electronic freedom is about to be taxed. The story just keeps on rolling. Before the first

An April Fool's joke by Piet Beertema of CWI in Amsterdam actually took on a life of its own. It began with Beertema's fictitious announcement on April 1, 1984 of the first Internet-connected VAX (a VAX is a mainframe computer) in the Kremlin. Called 'kremvax', it supposedly was authorized by Konstantin Chernenko, the leader of the Soviet Union during that period. This incident occurred while the Cold War was going on, and it reportedly was investigated by the Soviet secret police—who naturally found no evidence of dire plots. Only six years later, the first genuine site in Moscow, *demos.su*, joined USENET. Eventually the domain's gateway site was named "kremvax", thus turning fiction into truth.

Source: An online version of *The New Hacker's Dictionary*, by Eric S. Raymond, and, of course, Piet Beertema himself.

edition of this book was published (November 1992), people reported modem tax sightings, and they still do.

The FCC story is essentially innocuous, although its constant recycling through the Internet wastes people's time, as well as network resources. It has also created a 'cry wolf' situation, and if another modem tax ever *is* proposed, it will certainly be harder to mobilize the opposition. Imagine the damage, though, of a malicious rumour or flat-out lie, broadcast around the world again and again. After you imagine it, promise you'll think twice before you forward anything, and check the facts before you do.

Get-Well Cards Gone Amok

Back in the mid-eighties, a British seven-year-old named Craig Shergold was diagnosed as having an inoperable brain tumour. Craig wanted to set the Guinness record for receiving the most get-well cards, and his efforts got worldwide publicity, from mimeographed sheets to email pleas.

Craig is in his late teens now, and he's doing just fine; his brain tumour was successfully treated. He did set the Guinness record for get-well cards in 1989, and has received more than thirty million cards to date. That's the good news.

Following the Internet to the Letter

Jayne Levin is an independent businesswoman who has successfully substituted Internet know-how for start-up capital to fund her own newsletter.

She uses the Internet for interviews, production, reviews, marketing and sales. After one year, her newsletter has been very successful, and she expects it to be profitable after the first year of publication.

'I decided to launch *The Internet Letter* after exploring and writing about the Internet for a year, feeding my intellectual curiosity and seeing its power to help companies cut communications costs, gather corporate intelligence, and leverage scant resources.

'As a start-up company, I didn't have much money . . . and no staff. I knew I had to conserve funds to make this venture work. The Internet offered invaluable resources, including desktop publishing software that was much less expensive than similar software sold at a computer store.

(Continued)

Incredibly, however, the Craig Shergold story keeps circulating on the Internet, as fresh as the day it started. Sometimes it mutates into requests for postcards or business cards, but otherwise the story is the same. The hospital where Craig was treated is still being buried with cards. The Shergolds and the hospital, among others, have sent out pleas to stop them, but the story has taken on a life of its own, and the cards keep rolling in. In short, the situation has taken on a nightmarish quality for all involved. The hospital and post office, which have to cope with all the mail, sell some of it to stamp collectors and paper recyclers. Guinness has discontinued the category to prevent anything like this from happening again.

So, if you see a plea on the network for cards for a little boy who's dying with a brain tumour, pass it up. And pass the word that Craig Shergold is doing just fine. No more cards, *please!*

'With an Internet account that cost only $15 a month, I greatly reduced long-distance phone bills, conducting interviews online. I also cut my research costs by accessing CARL (Colorado Association of Research Libraries) through the Internet. CARL, a free database service, provides abstracts (sometimes full text) on articles that have appeared in national dailies and other publications.

'The Internet also provided a vehicle to distribute and sell my newsletter. I announced the availability of the premiere issue, including subscription information, on several Internet mailing lists. Within hours, information about my newsletter was forwarded to other mailing lists and people around the world. I was contacted, via email, by a person in the former Soviet Union who asked for permission to translate the newsletter into Russian. I received requests for trial subscriptions from people in Turkey, India, Brazil, Cuba, Singapore and Israel, and others used the electronic subscription coupon to sign up as charter subscribers.'

Source: Jayne Levin, Editor and Publisher. *Net Week, Inc.*

How to Win Enemies and Influence People Against You

The promise of easy and fast money is one that few people can resist. Combine some ambitious entrepreneurs with the broadcast capability of the Internet and there's bound to be trouble. Enter the latest class of chain letters, the *make money fast* genre. This type is basically a digital pyramid scheme on fast forward. If you don't want to *lose your friends* or *lose your Internet access,* just say no to chain letters and pyramid messages in general. Chain letters violate every known acceptable policy. So don't send them.

Speaking of things not to send—everyone hates junk mail, but Internet users hate it even more. In fact, they're fighting back with a vengeance. You may be tempted to take advantage of the Internet for your business marketing programs, but consider the

The Food Is Better in the Virtual Dorm, or, Finding the Quad on a Penta Chip

A simple multi-user role-playing game in cyberspace called Multi User Dungeons (MUDs) may turn out to be the key to an entirely new approach to education. Recent Internet explorers playing MUDs saw new applications for these interactive, virtual worlds that were far from the Dungeons and Dragons and Star Trek realms of the early MUDs and their derivatives.

In an attempt to incorporate education and 'distance learning' into the virtual environment, MIT's MicroMUSE (Multi User Simulated Environment) University laid the foundation for educational uses of a technology once viewed cynically as a time-wasting and resource-gobbling game.

Over the last two years, virtual colleges have begun to appear. Unlike traditional online, email-based distance learning classes, virtual colleges provide micro-worlds that enhance the subject matter being presented and provide environments in which students and faculty interact in real time. Typical of these new environments are DeanzaMUSE at De Anza College in Cupertino, California, and MariMUSE at Phoenix Community College in Phoenix, Arizona.

DeanzaMUSE is a precise replication of the 'real' De

(Continued)

consequences before broadcasting commercial product and service advertisements; literally thousands of angry people will bombard your email box and tie up your phone to tell you how much they don't appreciate your doing that. A widely publicized case involved a lawyer in Arizona who sent a description of his services to over 2,000 USENET newsgroups. He received over 30,000 email messages, and it's probably safe to say that none of them are fit to print in this book.

Just because the current models of advertising and direct mail don't work doesn't mean that you can't use the Internet to promote your products. It's perfectly acceptable to provide a database or archive with details of your offerings that people can

Anza College. Students and faculty easily navigate this virtual environment based on their familiarity with the actual college. At the same time, the VR (virtual reality) campus serves as a metaphor for navigating the information resources of the Internet. For example, the DeanzaMUSE campus planetarium has specialized links to astronomy resources around the world, the Euphrat Gallery features exhibits of images drawn from a variety of sources, and biosciences classrooms access data from similar programs at major universities and research centres. DeanzaMUSE has recently expanded to include links with local high schools, Cupertino City Hall, corporate neighbours and several local businesses.

Phoenix College offers a credit course through its language arts division taught entirely on MariMUSE. Students and faculty log on to the Internet from their homes, offices or classrooms and attend regularly scheduled classes. Depending upon the course being offered, class might be held on the deck of a Viking ship, at a street corner in New York City or in a quiet study in sixteenth-century England. With nearly two years of experience in the newly emerging field of virtual instruction, MariMUSE instructors are doing pioneering work in the development of instructional tools and techniques.

Virtual colleges may provide an entirely new and highly cost-effective environment in which to explore education in the twenty-first century.

peruse when *they* want to. There are books and journals that explain this new fine art of doing business in cyberspace; some recommended ones are listed in the Appendix.

GAMES

Just about every computer user has at least one game tucked away somewhere—the kind you play surreptitiously when the boss isn't watching or when you've got a bad case of writer's block. The Internet is no exception. There are shareware and freeware games you can download for your own computer, as well as game newsgroup discussions and email lists. Games are played on the Internet, too. There's the Trivia USENET Newsgroup, whose participants have passed the stage of naming all the seven dwarfs and moved on to higher-order thinking—naming all the characters in sitcoms from long ago (*Gilligan's Island, The Brady Bunch, Laverne & Shirley*). Try the Weekly Trivia Contest on the USENET newsgroup *rec.games.trivia*.

As you might imagine, the 'big' games on the Internet tend to match the network itself in scale and complexity, and they are a world and culture unto themselves. Generally, the games—with names like Galactic Bloodshed, Empire, Multi-User Dungeons (MUDs), and MUD-Object-Oriented (MOOs)—are adventure, role-playing games or simulations. Devotees call them 'text-based virtual reality adventures'. The games can feature fantasy combat, booby traps and magic. Players interact in real time and can change the 'world' in the game as they play it by creating environments, rules and characters.

All the games demand an intense learning process to figure out all the characters and game idiosyncrasies, not to mention the rules. They can be extremely addictive—small-time players may spend no less than an hour or so a day. Some people literally spend all of their waking hours in the game. Many of the game players seem to feel the need to leave their mark on the game, and generations of game variations have evolved. Empire, for example, a military simulation written by Peter Langston, has five or six multi-player spinoffs and a single-player version. According to *The Hacker's Dictionary*, all of the empire games 'are notoriously addictive'.

In most games, new players take on a persona and then participate *in* the game. To quote from the FAQ document for MUDs, 'You can walk around, chat with other characters, explore dangerous monster-infested areas, solve puzzles, and even create your very own rooms, descriptions and items. You can also get lost or confused if you jump right in.' If these games sound interesting, check out the USENET newsgroups under the hierarchy *rec.games.muds* or *alt.mud*. Read the postings there and then study the FAQ documents for 'your' games.

SECURITY ISSUES

Computer security is a major issue no matter where you go, what type of computer you use or whether or not your computer

mudhead n. Commonly used to refer to a MUD player who sleeps, breathes and eats MUD. Mudheads have been known to fail their degrees, drop out, etc., with the consolation, however, that they made wizard level. When encountered in person, all a mudhead will talk about is two topics: the tactic, character or wizard that is supposedly always unfairly stopping him/her from becoming a wizard or beating a favourite MUD, and the MUD he or she is writing or going to write because all existing MUDs are so dreadful! See also wannabee.

Source: *The New Hacker's Dictionary*, edited by Eric S. Raymond, with assistance and illustrations by Guy L. Steele, Jr. © 1991 Eric S. Raymond. Published by The MIT Press, Cambridge and London, 1991. Reprinted with permission.

is connected to a network. No doubt you've heard stories about break-ins on the Internet and would like to know what you should be concerned about. You might be wondering, 'Can people read my email? Can they login to my computer? Will my computer get a virus?' This section will provide some insight into security on the Internet and the answers to those questions.

First of all, you should realize that despite its U.S. military origins, the Internet is not a classified network. The ARPANET was a network research experiment, so there was a lot of collaboration, with information being transferred between machines and researchers. Collaboration is difficult if computers are locked up tight. Besides, the ARPANET was a small community, and users left their doors unlocked, just as trusting people in small towns do. Today, the Internet is a massive cooperative with tens of thousands of networks—several orders of magnitude larger than the ARPANET—all 'tied' together. And because there's still a lot of research being conducted, it's still considered an open, 'sharing' network. That doesn't mean, however, that security is not an issue. Sensitive information is stored on computers on the Internet and is therefore vulnerable to attack from intruders.

To further complicate matters, the Internet has spread its tentacles worldwide. Any computer directly connected to any network is potentially at risk if proper precautions are not taken.

Security is a major concern for commercial services on the Internet. What's the point of putting valuable information for sale online if people are just going to break into your 'shop' and steal the goods? Paying for goods and services raises another issue: ensuring that any transaction or credit card details you transmit are secure and can't be copied. These aren't insuperable problems and, with the incentive of a marketplace worth billions, a lot of very bright people and companies are designing and testing systems that allow fast, convenient and secure ordering and payment on the Net.

What's not so secure about the Internet? Basically, the computers—different computers running different operating systems, each with its own characteristics, bugs, misconfigured software and so forth. The security of each computer is the responsibility of a system administrator. When a new computer arrives at an organization, all the factory-set passwords and network configurations need to be changed; if they're not, the host will be an easy target for break-ins and outside attacks. Surprisingly, many system administrators don't bother to seal well-known security holes, or they may not know about them. Since all parts must work together to make the entire Internet secure, it's probably best to assume that things just aren't and act accordingly. If you follow a few simple rules, you'll probably be okay. Well-publicized compromises in security have happened and will continue to happen. Fortunately, when they do, lessons are learned, 'holes' or weaknesses get fixed, problems are highlighted and the Internet takes another step toward becoming more secure.

Breaking Down Account Doors

The term 'hacker' seems now to describe any denizen of the night or fourteen-year-old out on an electronic joyride. Actually, a more accurate term for these computer hooligans is **cracker**. **Hacker** in the computer world is a term of respect—hackers are basically nuts about computers and like to learn systems inside and out. Real hackers aren't angels, but they don't get their kicks from breaking into other people's systems to exploit holes and snoop in someone else's information. Most break-ins are accomplished by incredible patience and 'brute force'. There isn't anything magical about those who do it. 'Cookbook' recipes, giving step-by-step instructions on how to break into certain systems, have even been published over the network.

What Can You Do?

As a user of the Internet, you can't do much about fixing security problems if the computer you're getting Internet access from is not your own. There is, however, something very important that you can and must do. You can stop an intruder in his or her tracks simply by being responsible about the password(s) you use.

Most levels of service on the Internet require some type of authentication to prove it's really you accessing the service. Most of the time, this involves a user identification and a password to allow access. Your userid is usually well known (you give it out so people can send you email, for example), so the only way you can protect yourself is with a secret password. Your password is the key to the locked door of your account or your electronic mail service. Most common security problems can be prevented simply by being careful with your password.

If an 'undesirable' gets your password and uses it to enter your account uninvited, worse things can happen than just your files being looked at, modified or deleted. Crackers have posted articles to newsgroups or mailing lists from an account they shouldn't be using. You may find that, without your knowledge, 'you' made an insulting, politically incorrect statement that infuriated everyone who read it. No matter how many follow-up apology messages you send to rectify the situation, damage will have been done. A lot of people may not get your real message, and many who do won't believe you.

Never give anyone your password. But if you do have a valid reason for giving someone your password so he or she can obtain some information or perform some action, change the password as soon as that is done. If you get an account on another system, such as a public database or bulletin board, do not use the same password that you use on your local system. You have no way of knowing where it is stored or how private passwords on other systems are. Don't write your password down and leave the paper in an obvious place, such as in the desk drawer next to your computer. Some computers tell you upon login when you were last seen on that account. You should check to make sure it agrees with when *you* were really last logged in to that computer. If there's a discrepancy, call your system administrator.

'Don't Try This at Home . . .'

You can't point-and-click on CompuServe to make toast in Cairo, but way out on the frontiers of Internet development, the cognoscenti are whipping up elegant hacks to do just that.

TGV, Inc., a networking software company in Santa Cruz, California, first got involved in networking home appliances at a chance meeting between then TGV technical support manager Stuart Vance and Simon Hackett of the University of Adelaide. In December 1989, when Vance was in Adelaide for a networking conference, he discovered in conversation with Hackett a mutual love of perverse (interesting) computer and networking applications. Hackett had been developing control hardware and software for multimedia applications. They decided that it would be easy to extend control across a network, using the TCP/IP network management protocol SNMP (Simple Network Management Protocol).

Upon returning home, Vance managed to persuade TGV management to fund Hackett's development of a custom controller to interface to a Pioneer Stereo system. <techspeak on> Pioneer components have a 'remote in' jack in the back, allowing them to be controlled by TTL signalling. The custom controller Hackett developed included a 68,000-based microprocessor, a chip to generate TTL signals and a serial inter-

(Continued)

Copying the scams in which callers try to get your credit card number over the phone, some potential intruders call or send email claiming to be a system administrator. This person will tell you that, for various reasons, you need to change the password for your account to something he tells you. Be careful of anyone claiming to be a system administrator. If you're not sure, get a telephone number and call back or try to see him in person.

How to Pick a Password

An easily guessed password is one of the most common causes of security problems. If you don't know how to change your pass-face. Engineers at TGV wrote a small IP stack for the micro-processor, and Hackett and Vance ported the Epilogue Technology SNMP agent to run on the controller. Additionally, they developed (but never quite completed) a home electronics SNMP Management Information Base for selecting input (CD, tuner, cassette deck, phonograph), volume, tuner band and frequency and other standard stereo features. <techspeak off> The world's first network-manageable stereo system debuted at INTEROP 90.

The stereo system project led to further collaboration between TGV and Hackett, including:

- one of two independent implementations of an SNMP-manageable Sunbeam toaster;
- an SNMP-manageable Sony 60-disc CD jukebox;
- and the Interphone, a scheme for audio communication over TCP/IP.

Hackett has since founded Internode Systems, a networking company in Australia, and continues to work with Vance on connecting unconventional (and conventional) devices to the Internet and making them do interesting things.

Perhaps Hackett and Vance were influenced by comedian Stephen Wright, who told the following story: 'In my house, there's a light switch that doesn't do anything. Every so often, I flick it on and off just to check. Yesterday, I got a call from a woman in Germany. She said, "Cut it out".'

word, put it at the top of your list of things to learn. Passwords should never be based on your own name—not even your name spelled backwards. They should also not be easily guessed, such as your husband's or wife's name, girlfriend's or boyfriend's name, the dog's name, your car registration, the street where you live, your birthday—you get the picture. Passwords also should not be dictionary words. Crackers often use online dictionaries and programs to guess words by 'brute force'. For example, the most well-known password-cracking program is 'crack', which simply takes your encrypted password and compares it with its dictionary, but also checks it against your username, family names and so forth. It will recognize the words forward and backward, lower and upper case.

So what *can* passwords be? There's nothing left to pick, right? Well, be creative. Take your favourite saying—'Take a long walk off a short pier'—and use the first letters from each word, 'TalwoasP'. (It's recommended that the word be at least six characters long.) This way the password is not a word, but it's easy to remember and hard to guess. You can also combine words, such as 'baby-cakes'. It's also a good idea to mix some numbers with the letters and throw in some punctuation for pizzazz, but never make your password all numbers.

Can People Read My Email?

Can they read it? Yes, they can. That doesn't mean that there is always someone out there reading your email. With millions of people on the Internet, individual messages most likely get lost in the crowd. But you need to realize that once email leaves your system, it may sit on another computer hundreds or thousands of miles away, and you have no control over who has access to it. What if that computer has a liberal security policy, or is full of security holes? The best thing to do is to realize that your email is not going to be secure, and to avoid transmitting sensitive material, as already recommended in Chapter 3. Even if no one reads your email while it's in transit, the recipient could forward the message on to whomever he or she pleases.

It is physically possible to 'tap' networks, just like tapping telephone lines. And if someone is able to do that, he or she can read anything going across those wires. But all hope is not lost—there are ways to make your email more secure. One way is to encrypt it before it leaves your computer. **Encrypt** means simply that it's encoded into something that no one else can read without the proper key. Upon receipt, the message must be decrypted on the recipient's machine. There are no *automatic* mechanisms available on the Internet right now to encrypt email, but if you have the necessary software on your computer, you can do it.

An increasing number of people are interested in the privacy of their correspondence, and a number of programs and solutions are popping up to assist them. An Internet standard called **Privacy Enhanced Mail** (PEM) will take some of the worry out of sending 'naked' email. PEM provides for, among other things, encryption and authentication services. (Authentication ensures that it's really *you* who's sending the message.) PEM implementations are, unfortunately, not in widespread use yet, but they've begun to proliferate, and may be coming soon to an email application near you. Another encryption program in use on the Internet is called **Pretty Good Privacy** (PGP), and it's used a lot outside the United States. If you're interested in learning more about PEM and PGP, check the 'Security' section in the Appendix.

Viruses

Should you lose much sleep over viruses on the Internet? Well, no, and yes. Your computer can't get a virus from using email or telnetting around to other computers. If you're just transferring text files, then you shouldn't worry; they're not going to reach out and 'grab' your computer and do something to it. Well, actually, there *have* been cases where this has happened, but it's very rare. During the Christmas season several years ago, a seemingly innocuous text-art picture of a Christmas tree was mailed to unsuspecting users on an IBM network. When the picture, which contained special codes, was printed on the screen, it also took the opportunity to spread the cheer, duplicating and sending itself to the recipient's closest friends. (This type of activity can effectively grind a network to a halt.)

Even though it's happened in the past, you don't need to spend as much time worrying about viruses or worms in text files as you do in other types of files. In order to avoid catching a virus, a good general rule is to be wary of all public domain and shareware software (available via anonymous FTP, Gopher and other tools). If you remember that you have to do a *binary* file transfer to get this software, then be aware that you're transferring something that could possibly carry a virus. To guard against problems, there are several things you should do. First, always keep backups (copies) of all your work. Second, to guard against viruses from the Internet and elsewhere, be sure that you have the best available virus-detection software installed on your computer. And keep it updated—new viruses appear all of the time.

Where there's a problem, a solution is usually near at hand, and security advice is readily available on the Internet. The Computer Emergency Response Team (CERT), now officially referred to as the CERT Coordination Center, focuses on the security needs of the research community. Based at Carnegie-Mellon University, CERT has an anonymous FTP archive of security advisories, tips, tools, articles, suggested references and so on. The computer name is *cert.org*. Start by reading the CERT FAQ, available on the CERT archive as *pub/cert_faq*. There's also a LISTSERV called *VIRUS-L*, a moderated, digested mail forum for discussing computer virus issues. The USENET newsgroup *comp.virus* has the same postings as *VIRUS-L*, only in a slightly different, non-digested format. The VIRUS-L FAQ document answers questions on how to get the latest free/shareware antivirus programs. It's available on the CERT public archive in the directory *pub/virus-l*, filename *FAQ.virus-l*. See the 'Security' section in the Appendix for the CERT contact information.

Firewalls

The fact that the Internet is going commercial leads to a new level of solving the security problems on the network. If you run a company doing business in a competitive environment, you certainly have to store and to transmit data you don't want to be public. To make intrusions as difficult as possible, you can install a **firewall**. As intimated by its name, the firewall shields you from intruders by burning down all the attempts to get into your system. Firewalls are often complicated schemes and not easy to install, but there are professional companies around who can build them for you.

A number of computer manufacturers are now producing equipment specifically intended for connection to the Internet and preconfigured to make the business of setting up an Internet server or client as painless as possible. This equipment usually comes with the option of firewall security built in, which makes setup by mere mortals not only possible but practicable.

INTERNET ORGANIZATIONS

The Internet has spawned a number of organizations and interest groups over the years with many different missions and purposes. Some are special interest groups; some are task groups responsible for certain aspects of the Internet. One organization that may be of interest, and that provides direction and information for the entire Internet, is the Electronic Frontier Foundation (EFF).

The EFF

The EFF's concerns extend beyond the networks to cover all of the social and policy issues that arise as we integrate computers and networks into our culture. The EFF was founded in 1990 to 'help civilize the electronic frontier; to make it truly useful and beneficial to everyone, not just an elite; and to do this in a way that is in keeping with our society's highest traditions of the free and open flow of information and communication'. The catalyst for EFF's founding was the heavy-handed investigation of supposed 'computer crimes' by U.S. Secret Service agents who, as the stories go, hardly knew a disk drive from a discus. In addition to practically bankrupting a couple of innocent small businesses, the investigations rode roughshod over the free speech and privacy rights of electronic communications. EFF's most famous founder, Mitch Kapor, developer of Lotus 1-2-3 and current president of ON Technology, led the charge in finding funding and hiring defence lawyers. The EFF has continued to represent computer network users in debates on public policy covering privacy, law enforcement procedures for computer crime, network development and more.

Local Groups

The latest trend is to establish local interest groups devoted to the Internet or to the WWW. For starters, there are Internet user groups in Austin, Texas and in Baltimore, Maryland. Many computer user groups associated with universities and community colleges are covering Internet topics and providing training. User groups are popping up all over the world; if there isn't one in your area, start one! If you're interested in finding out what's available near you, inquire on a local USENET newsgroup (for example, *de.general*, if you're in Germany), or post a query on *alt.internet.services*, a newsgroup devoted to discussions about general Internet services.

HELP! GETTING MORE INFORMATION

As it was so well put in the FAQ on MUDs, 'What if I'm completely confused and am casting about for a rope in a vast, churning wilderness of chaos and utter incomprehension?' If you're confused, have questions, and don't know where to turn, here are a few survival tips. First of all, realize that you're not alone, and that we all started off feeling dazed and bewildered. Everyone's digital digestive system is different; sometimes it takes a while to get the drift of all of this. Remember, even Net veterans don't know everything! (In fact, the bigger the Internet gets, the less we know.) There is no way you can ever know about or visit everything on the Internet, not even if you studied and gophered all day and night for the rest of your life. The Internet is bigger than you can imagine.

Knowing this, relax a bit and take a load off while reading this section. The biggest hurdle is figuring out exactly what your problem is. The kinds of things that stump people include working out what they can do from their system (what applications they can use, what levels of services are available to them and so on); how to use the applications; how to diagnose problems once they do figure out the applications; and, after they've learned those ropes, finding the resources that will help them.

Think Globally, Ask 'Locally'

If you've got a problem that needs solving or a question that needs answering, the very first thing you should do is start close to home when you look for help. Consultants who understand the applications running on your system or network will be able to give you the best assistance. The Internet's flexibility in being able to connect so many different types of computers has been one of the reasons why it has been so successful. But it's also a reason why the Internet is so 'difficult'. Each type of computer runs different TCP/IP implementations, graphical user interfaces and client applications, and this makes documenting or providing answers for every situation next to impossible. There are an infinite number of combinations that anyone can be using at any one time. So your best hope is your local help desk, which is probably accessible by email or phone. Now, understand that 'local' refers to your own Internet provider's help facility, which may not be geographically near you. Be as specific as possible when you do ask for help. Write down error messages exactly as you see them on the screen (including all numbers and punctuation), and try to recall the chain of events that got you into trouble.

If you're getting network access through work or college, there most likely is a local consulting office or help desk in the computer centre that can give you information about applications and available services, such as documentation, manuals and online help. Many help desks offer their own online Gopher systems that provide easy-to-use interfaces to steer you in the right direction, help you learn about your local network and the Internet, and provide links into other systems.

If you are getting (or planning to get) your Internet access through a commercial provider, you'll need to look to the provider for help. Ask about support before you sign up. (Chapter 7 includes information about the types of connections and applications that are available.) Most Internet providers offer hotline services or even publish extensive information materials about how to use the Internet and how to solve communication problems. Look out for beginners' guides and handbooks or ask your provider for information about literature, USENET newsgroups and FAQs.

Network information centres (NICs) offer information about the Internet and about their networks and services. Your network provider isn't required to have a NIC, but if it does, check out what it has to offer. NICs are springing up all around the Internet; many nationwide backbones have them, as well as most of the mid-level and regional networks. These organizations vary in size and services. Many provide online guides, newsletters and tutorials. Others offer seminars and classes. This may be more information than you'll ever need, but it's useful to familiarize yourself with what's available.

Another Source for Help: InterNIC

As the Internet continues to grow and evolve into the Global Information Infrastructure, user and information services have become a more important part of network operation. Recognizing this, the U.S. National Science Foundation funds a NIC to serve Internet users around the world. It's known as the Inter-NIC, and it offers three different types of services: information, registration, and directory and database. Most top-level domains, such as *uk* for the United Kingdom, *de* for Germany, *at* for Austria, *ch* for Switzerland and so on have network information centres that work together with the InterNIC. For Europe in general, the RIPE NCC (Network Coordination Centre) in Amsterdam located at the CWI is providing these services for you. If, for instance, you are looking for an Internet provider near you, you can make a telephone call to the RIPE NCC or send email or a fax and ask for help. They will, in turn, contact your local provider, who will send you information. As you can see, the Internet is working for you even before you subscribe to it.

RIPE NCC CONTACT INFORMATION:

RIPE Network Coordination Centre
Kruislaan 409
NL-1098 SJ Amsterdam
The Netherlands
Tel: +31-20-592-5065
Fax: +31-20-592-5090
Email: *ncc@ripe.net*

RIPE NCC INTERACTIVE INFORMATION SERVICE

Information about RIPE and RIPE NCC services can also be obtained using the Interactive Information Service. This menu-driven service allows browsing through the RIPE document store, reading documents and sending them by email. It can be reached by telnetting to *info.ripe.net*. The service is also available via the public X.25 networks at 0204129004331.

ACCESS TO THE RIPE DOCUMENT STORE

All RIPE documents and Internet RFCs are available via anonymous file transfer (FTP) from host *ftp.ripe.net*. The same documents are also available via a gopher server at *gopher.ripe.net* and a WAIS server at *wais.ripe.net*. Access via WWW server at *http://www.ripe/*

FINDING EMAIL ADDRESSES: THE SEQUEL

Finding email addresses was briefly mentioned in Chapter 3. Now that you know more about using Telnet, FTP, email, Gopher and WAIS, here are a few more advanced methods for tracking down email addresses. Literally millions of people can be reached via email. And, as you've seen, the Internet is growing by leaps and bounds, with more computers and people being added every minute. People are getting 'on', but are having a hard time locating the people with whom they wish to communicate.

Unfortunately, there is no *one* way to find email addresses. You simply need to be an electronic detective. There isn't a central database, nor is there a distributed database directory system for you to query. If you are willing and have some time, you can 'feel' your way around the Internet and you'll probably find someone's email address, or at least get close. Some of the more common methods are mentioned here.

Directory services on the Internet are classified as two basic types: **white pages** and **yellow pages**. White and yellow pages get their names from the corresponding pages in a printed phone book. In other words, white pages refer to directories of people, and yellow pages refer to directories of resources.

Providing comprehensive directory service information is difficult for several reasons. First, many people have more than one address, and those addresses can often change. For example, you may have a CompuServe address, an Internet address from a commercial Internet service and a BITNET address from a local university. Each of these addresses has a slightly different format, and is part of a different organization's directory system. To compound matters, computer names can change; therefore, your email address may change. Privacy and security are other issues; you may wish for your CompuServe address to remain private, but be willing to publicize the others. Some organizations don't wish to release their entire directories of contact information. And others just don't have directory information compiled yet, owing to lack of staff or other reasons.

Network Information Servers and Tools

Some well-known services and methods for finding email addresses are discussed below. Basically, you have to know a lot about people you're trying to reach in order to query a database or service to reach them. It helps if you know where they're located, what organization they work for, what university they attend, or what network provider they're getting access from. If you have that information, try to find an online directory for that particular organization. Don't worry if these databases aren't always very intuitive or understandable. They may contain the answer you're looking for, but the bumping and tripping you'll go through just to search them will take you longer than calling (by phone) the person you're trying to reach. Most of these databases are provided by universities, but more and more companies are making their directories available online.

Directory Services Standards. The three most common directory standards in use right now at various organizations are WHOIS (yes, that's *who is!*), X.500 and CSO. These databases can be accessed a number of ways, but they're all available via—you guessed it—Gopher.

The Gopher Directory Way. Look for a menu item on your local Gopher called 'Phone Books' or 'Directory Services'. If you've got that, you can play around with each of the services through the menu system. If you don't see one on your own Gopher menu, the University of Minnesota has an extensive menu of all of these directory services. Point your Gopher at *gopher.tc.umn.edu* and select the 'Phone Books' entry. You should see menu items for 'Phone Books at Other Institutions' (another menu that includes CSO, X.500 and WHOIS) and for 'Internet-wide Email Address Searches', which is a menu for Netfind (explained below) and a USENET database of email addresses.

WHOIS. Many computers have a **whois** client program available on their systems. If you have this available, and you're on a Unix operating system, you can type **whois -h** *host-name person-name*. The whois client is available for other systems, and may require a slightly different command format. To find Adam Curry, who is registered at the InterNIC, type the following if you're on a Unix system:

```
whois -h whois.internic.net "Curry, Adam"
```

As mentioned in Chapter 2, you can also query the InterNIC WHOIS database to find out the contact for a country. To find the contact for Denmark, you would type:

whois -h whois.internic.net "domain DK"

Here, DK is the two-letter country code for Denmark. Since there are two entries that match DK, the WHOIS database returns a one-line summary of each:

```
DKnet / EUnet DK (DK2-DOM)                          DK.NET
Denmark (Kingdom of) top-level domain (DK-DOM)          DK
```

The second one is the entry we want. To find out more information, send another WHOIS query, this time specifying the **handle** or the string in parentheses:

whois -h whois.internic.net DK-DOM

This will return information on the Denmark Network Information Centre.

The InterNIC's server is considered the 'official' WHOIS database, so someone who just mentions the WHOIS database is probably referring to the InterNIC's. However, the InterNIC probably won't have information on the person you are seeking. To access other WHOIS databases, just substitute the *whois.internet.net* part with other WHOIS servers. A list of WHOIS servers can be retrieved via anonymous FTP: *ftp://sipb.mit.edu/pub/whois/whois-servers.list*. If you seek a person in Europe, it may be better to ask the RIPE NCC WHOIS server to help. To do so using a Unix system, issue the command **whois -h whois.ripe.net** *person-name*.

An easy way to access all the WHOIS servers without FTP'ing the list is via Gopher. Point your gopher at *sipb.mit.edu*. At this menu, select 'Internet whois servers/'. You'll then get a menu of over 180 items. Instead of Adam Curry, let's look for the famous Piet Beertema, who works on the CWI in the Netherlands (you remember the *kremvax* joke). He works and lives in Europe, so contacting the RIPE NCC WHOIS server seems reasonable. Using the Gopher menu-searching feature, you'll find it under 'Reseau IP Europeens'. Selecting this, you will see 'Words to Search For'; type **Beertema**. At this point, you'll be given two choices—you should choose the 'Commit to search for . . .' item. After indicating that you want to see the information even if it might be a binary file (Gopher sometimes tends to complicate things), you will get information about Piet and how to reach him. But please, don't send him mail if you do not have to; he is heavily loaded with work all the time.

X.500. Committees, working groups and standards bodies have wrestled with the directory problem, and they are working on a directory services standard called **X.500**. But don't hold your breath waiting for a complete worldwide X.500 directory system any time soon. It's true, however, that many organizations are making their internal directories available via the X.500 database format. There are a lot of different ways to access X.500 servers, but the easiest way to start is through Gopher (mentioned above).

CSO. CSO actually stands for Computing Services Organization, which was the group at the University of Illinois at Urbana-Champaign who developed this electronic directory service. There are a lot of other universities and organizations that have set up CSO servers containing information about employees, students or faculty. If you're just starting out, check out all the CSO directories through Gopher using the instructions above. There are also client and server applications, respectively known as 'ph' (for phone) and 'qi' (query interpreter). So you may be able to type **ph** on your own computer to look up people's names.

Netfind. Netfind is an intelligent directory 'clearinghouse' service. It doesn't actually store names and addresses; rather, it tries to provide a 'one-stop shopping' service that knows which directory services, databases or computers to contact, based on the keywords (login name, first and last name, organization) that you supply. You can query Netfind through Telnet: **telnet bruno.cs.colorado.edu**, login **netfind**. You can also access Netfind through many Gopher menus (look for 'Netfind' in the directory menus).

Knowledge Information Service. KIS is based on the concept of a **knowbot**—a knowledge robot that knows how to navigate networks in search of information. KIS queries a number of directory services to help you find directory assistance information. You can access this service using Telnet: **telnet info.cnri. reston.va.us 185**. You'll be asked for your email address (for the guest book). The first thing you should do is type **help** to learn about the possible commands, but you can also get started by typing **query** *name*, where *name* is the person you're searching for. To find out which directory services KIS is searching, type **services**.

Other Methods

Finger. A program called **finger** is available on many computers directly connected to the Internet, and many people use it to find information about users on other computers. It's simple to use: type **finger** *name@hostname*. When you use finger, you have to know what computer the user is on. You do not, however, always have to know the exact login name of the user. You can usually use any part of the person's name, and finger will return essential data on all the users with that name on that computer. The type of information finger returns (depending on how much is available) includes the name, login name, office and location, phone number and so on. Many organizations make their entire online directory available and searchable using finger. Usually these are located on 'official' or well-known computers. You can also use finger to find out about all the users logged in to a computer at any one time. To do this locally, just type **finger**. Or to check for all the users at a remote system, you can type **finger@** *remote-hostname*. Unfortunately, finger isn't available on all computers, or it may be disabled for security reasons, so you can't depend on it to provide all the answers. One of the more obvious security reasons is that many people don't want others to know where they are or when they were on the computer last.

As an aside, some organizations use finger to provide frequently updated information, such as the weather or daily headlines. These include *NASA Daily News*, which you can get by issuing the command **finger nasanews@space.mit.edu**, and up-to-date earthquake reports, available by issuing the command **finger quake@gldfs.cr.usgs.gov**.

USENET Addresses. USENET has an address database of all the people who have posted articles to USENET, which has proved very useful. To use this service, send email to *mail-server@ rtfm.mit.edu,* and type the command **send usenet-addresses/** *name* in the body of the message; *name* should be the name or names you're looking for. The search is 'fuzzy'—meaning, you don't have to put the exact name, but can use several words you think might be in the address. For more information, send the command **send usenet-addresses/help**. This USENET database is also searchable via WAIS; the WAIS database is called *usenet- addresses.*

WorldWideWeb Search Engines. You can also locate people by using "search engines" available through the WWW. Try out the URL *http://cuiwww.unige.ch/meta-index.html* .

Directory Projects. A number of enterprising individuals are taking it upon themselves to provide directory services for the world. Next time you're at the bookstore browsing in the Internet section (probably an entire wall of books by now), look for the massively huge books that list people's email addresses. While these books can be useful, you should be somewhat wary of **shovel-ware** compilations—those that contain huge data- bases of addresses scooped up from various sources around the Internet and printed out. It is nice sometimes to have all this in- formation in one place, but you can save money by just learning how to query the regularly updated sources.

NetPages. An interesting project to pay attention to is a direc- tory service called NetPages, maintained and published by Aldea Communications. NetPages is a white and yellow pages directory (it looks just like your telephone directory) that's available both in hard-copy and online formats. The white pages contain email listings, and the yellow pages list advertisements and business contact information. The NetPages prints listings only for people who have registered themselves, which means the information is very accurate. It costs nothing to list yourself, and it's really easy, too. Just send email to *np-add@aldea.com,* and include the follow- ing information:

We'll Make You a Star!

Jean Armour Polly and Jane Dunlap Smith see each other every day. Jean works in Liverpool, New York, while Jane hangs her hat in Chapel Hill, North Carolina. How do they do that? They use CU-SeeMe, video-conferencing software developed by Cornell University, to keep their virtual friendship alive. Both keep video cameras rolling non-stop during working hours, and beam their images over the Internet to a 'reflector' that re-transmits incoming video streams to viewers who have 'tapped' into it. They go about their day and, from time to time, other people, friends and co-workers 'pop in' to chat with them. Through it all, they've become quite famous; their faces have been shown coast-to-coast and overseas during demonstrations to large seminars and TV news broadcasts. Don't they get nervous having 'big brothers' all over the world? 'You get used to it', shrugged Jean. 'After several days, you don't even notice the camera anymore'.

This gives new meaning to 'see you on the Internet'.

Your name:
Your email address:
Business or personal account?
Company name:
Your title:
City:
State, Country:

The NetPages directory is free (but you have to pay for postage and handling if it's snail-mailed), and it is published two times a year. You can subscribe to a NetPages announcement list to keep updated about availability; just send a message to *np-list@aldea. com*, and ask to be subscribed to the email list or the hard-copy list (include address information). For more information, send a message to *netpages@aldea.com*, or call +1 619-943-0101.

SLED. Another project is the Stable Large Email Database (SLED), which describes itself as 'the place online users advertise

When you log on to the White House site in the United States, you are logging on to the busiest Web site on the planet—in fact, three times busier than the next most popular Web site. The White House WorldWideWeb server is:

http://www.whitehouse.gov

their existence'. SLED also registers people and provides a directory service. However, there's a nominal charge to be included in the database and an ongoing maintenance fee. There are several reasons for this: to verify the registration data (by comparing your personal cheque against the information you submit), and to offset the cost of providing the service. To get more information about SLED, send email to *sled@drebes.com* with the subject **info**.

You're making great progress—you're almost an official cyber-sleuth by now! The next challenge—ahem, opportunity— is learning the ups and downs of Unix, an operating system that's very prevalent on the Internet. It has been said, 'In Unix, no one can hear you scream', but the next chapter will calm your fears somewhat and show you that UNIX is not so bad. In fact, it's actually pretty easy to use once you know how to hold your mouth right. So stay put, get out your thinking cap, and get ready for Unix! Because, as they say, it's not just for techies anymore.

Chapter 6

UNIX ON THE INTERNET: A SURVIVAL GUIDE

nce you're a regular on the Internet, you'll notice that many computers run the UNIX (Unix) operating system. Developed by American Telephone and Telegraph Company, Unix is still popular among researchers and computer science departments, partly because some of the first versions of TCP/IP were distributed free with one version of Unix known as the Berkeley Software Distribution (BSD). Many computer companies sell their machines with Unix and TCP/IP bundled in, which makes it a more popular combination than some of the other computers and operating systems, for which TCP/IP support has to be ordered separately.

You don't have to be a Unix expert to use the Internet, but it doesn't hurt to know some of the basic commands. Unix—fairly or unfairly—has achieved a reputation for being unfriendly. If you're using the Internet, however, sooner or later you'll have to deal with Unix face-to-face, so included in this chapter are some explanations of the more common idiosyncrasies and applications you may encounter when using Unix on the Internet. Knowing how to navigate through directories and use some of the basic Unix commands will make you a more powerful Internet user.

Be aware that this chapter will give you only the barest of tools to get you started and help you accomplish what you need to do. There are many different ways to do things on a Unix operating system, and these instructions offer just one way. You should also know that there are different flavours of Unix. Most of the commands here will work for whatever version you're using. If they don't, you should use the help facility (explained below), or call your local help desk to find out what the proper command or sequence of commands is. If you're interested in going beyond what's discussed here, be sure to check out the Appendix for more Unix resources.

LOGGING IN

Let's start with the basics: getting access to your Unix account. You'll need a userid and password. Typically, the login looks like this:

```
login:
```

At this point, type your userid. The next prompt is for your password:

```
Passwd:
```

When you type your password, it will not (and should not) display on the screen.

Important! Be sure to type your userid and password *exactly* as they've been given to you, preserving upper- and lowercase. Unix differentiates between the two, so if you've got the caps-lock key on, you'll probably have some problems. Later on, you'll see lots of commands and filenames, mostly written in lowercase. A good rule is always to type whatever you're told to *exactly* as shown.

GETTING HELP

Unix may not always offer a lot of help outright, but it does have a help facility called **man**, which stands for 'manual pages'. If you ever need help with a command, type **man** *command* where *command* is the name of the command. For example, to learn more about man, type **man man**. If you want to know which other commands are relevant to the one you're interested in, use **whatis** *command* to ask the *whatis* database. On some Unix systems (the less well administered) a *whatis* database is not available. In this case, simply ask your system administrator for help. Another useful command is **apropos**, try **man apropos** to find out what is does.

hacker (originally, someone who makes furniture with an axe) n. 1. A person who enjoys exploring the details of programmable systems and how to stretch their capabilities, as opposed to most users, who prefer to learn only the minimum necessary. 2. One who programs enthusiastically (even obsessively) or who enjoys programming rather than just theorizing about programming. 3. A person capable of appreciating hack value. 4. A person who is good at programming quickly. 5. An expert at a particular program, or one who frequently does work using it or on it; as in 'a Unix hacker.' (Definitions 1 through 5 are correlated, and people who fit them congregate.) 6. An expert or enthusiast of any kind. One might be an astronomy hacker, for example. 7. One who enjoys the intellectual challenge of creatively overcoming or circumventing limitations. 8. [deprecated] A malicious meddler who tries to discover sensitive information by poking around. Hence *password hacker, network hacker.* See cracker.

It is better to be described as a hacker by others than to describe oneself that way. Hackers consider themselves something of an elite (a meritocracy based on ability), though one to which new members are gladly welcome. There is thus a certain ego satisfaction to be had in identifying yourself as a hacker (but if you claim to be one and are not, you'll quickly be labelled bogus).

Source: *The New Hacker's Dictionary*, edited by Eric S. Raymond, with assistance and illustrations by Guy L. Steele, Jr. © 1991 Eric S. Raymond. Published by The MIT Press, Cambridge and London, 1991. Reprinted with permission.

More and Less

The *man* command uses another Unix program called **more** that lets you page through files—meaning it shows you one screen of the file at a time instead of letting it fly off the screen. To advance to the next page, simply hit the space bar once (typing <RETURN> will only advance the file by one line). If you want to quit looking at the file, type **q**. Finally, to get a summary of 'more' commands, type **h** for help. On several systems, following the motto 'less is more', a program called **less** is installed to give you further functionality and ease of use.

Other Things to Know

Many of the applications and commands mentioned below refer to **control commands**. This means that you need to use your control key in conjunction with a command letter. The control key is usually represented in documentation and helpfiles by 'CTRL' or '^'. When either of these precedes a letter, you should hold down the CTRL key and, at the same time, press the command letter. For example, if you see ^G, ^g, or *CTRL-G* written in documentation, you should hold down the control key while pressing the 'g' key (it's a lowercase 'g').

THE UNIX FILE SYSTEM

The Unix file system—the way files are organized on the computer's hard disk—is hierarchical, similar to the DOS file system. (In fact, DOS is similar to Unix, for Unix came first.) If you understand how the DOS file system works, then it shouldn't take you long to find your way around Unix systems. Since a good number of the public file archive sites are computers running the Unix operating system, learning your way up and down a Unix directory (as was discussed in Chapter 4) will come in pretty handy.

As a user on a Unix/Internet system, you have your own space on the file system. When you login, you're placed in your 'home' directory, which is like your own personal filing cabinet. Everyone on the Unix system gets his or her own home filing cabinet. You can organize this filing cabinet any way you want— it can be very structured, neat and tidy, or it can be extremely messy and unorganized. If you like some order to your life, then you'll be happy to know that you can create directories that house files or other directories. A directory can be compared to a manila folder, which you can use to organize and store papers (files) and other folders (directories). The ability to create subdirectories within directories makes Unix a hierarchical file system. If you looked at it from the top, it looks like a tree.

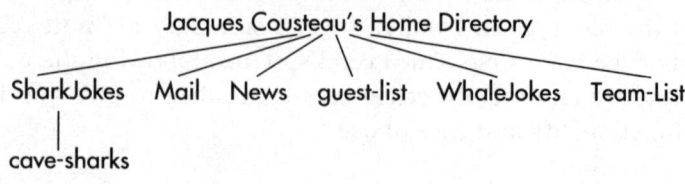

Miles of Files, Directories and Commands

Once you start surfing the Internet, you'll be pulling down articles, books and software, among other things, from all over the place. You'll also probably be creating quite a few files, using either the Unix editors mentioned below, or by uploading them from your own PC or Mac (if you're dialled-in to the Unix system). You'll also probably want to save the email messages you receive. Because there are so many different types of files and so many ways to create them, you should definitely have an organized system for storing them.

First of all, to see which files you have in your home directory, you can use the **ls** command to list them. If you type **ls** with no arguments, it will list your current directory (which, if you've just logged in, is your home directory). To list your Mail directory, you would type **ls Mail**. You can add options to the **ls** command to show you more about the files and directories. There are lots of options, but a common one is **-l**, which triggers a 'long' listing. When you type **ls -l**, you'll see several columns of information that specify permissions, links, owner, group, size in bytes and the time of the last modification for each file.

Here's a sample listing of Jacques Cousteau's home directory after he types **ls -l** to get a long listing:

```
cbs-host> ls -l
total [*****]
drwx-w--w-  4 cousteau  bbc   1536  Feb 13, 14:34  ./
drwxr-xr-x  8 root      bbc  29184  Feb 10, 19:34  ../
drw------   1 cousteau  bbc   3449  Feb 13, 10:49  Mail/
-rw-r--r--  1 cousteau  bbc   9383  Jan 17, 11:03  SharkJokes
drwxr-xr-x  2 cousteau  bbc   1024  Feb 12, 10:39  News/
-rw-r--r--  1 cousteau  bbc    792  Feb 6,  17:51  Guest-list
-rw------   1 cousteau  bbc   5097  Jan 29, 13.59  WhaleJokes
-rw-r--r--  1 cousteau  bbc   5039  Jan 1,  10:59  Team-List
```

The top two files indicate directories: '.' is the current directory, and '..' is the parent directory.

Your listing may not have as many columns as in this example. Here, the first column lists permissions. It also indicates whether the file is a regular file or a directory. If the first character is a 'd', it's a directory. In this example, there are four directories: current (.), parent (..), Mail and News. Skip to the third column, which indicates the owner of each file. Here, 'cousteau' owns most of the files. The column after that is the group ownership. Cousteau belongs to the 'bbc' group. The next column indicates size in bytes. Sometimes you need to know the size of a file, especially if you're running out of disk space on your account. The next columns specify the date and time of the last modifications of the file. And finally, you'll see the file name.

Note that some of the filenames in this example have a '/' after the name. The '/' also indicates that the 'file' is actually a directory.

When you login, your current directory is your home directory. You can change your current (or default) directory with the **cd** command. Suppose that you want to change to the *News* directory. You would type **cd News**. Now every command you type that doesn't explicitly list a directory will, by default, be performed in the *News* directory.

Again, another warning about case sensitivity. (The reason this is mentioned so much here is because it's such a common problem.) You need to type commands and names exactly as they appear in resource guides, email and news. If the output of a **ls** command shows a file called **SharkJokes**, and you want to look at that file, you need to type the name *exactly* as shown; **sharkJokes** or **Sharkjokes** simply will not work. This may seem a little tedious, so you might want to use the copy and paste functions of your workstation, if they're available.

There are several commands to view files; one of the most common ones, already explained above, is **more**. To look at the file mentioned above, type:

```
more SharkJokes
```

This program lets you page through a file. To continue to the next page, simply hit the space bar. To stop looking at the file, type **q** for quit. For a list of more commands, type **h** for help.

If you decide you don't want to keep the *SharkJokes* file anymore, use the remove file command, **rm**. In this case, you would type:

```
rm SharkJokes
```

You have to be very careful with the **rm** command. If you remove a file on a Unix system it is gone; there is no way to get it back. If you have removed a file and you really need it back, ask your system administrator if he is dumping the files of your Unix system every night and if you can get the file from a stored copy.

Or, if you want to rename the file, you can use the move command, **mv**. For example:

> **mv SharkJokes SJ**

This would rename the file 'SJ'.

If you forget where you are—what directory you're in—type the 'print working directory' command, **pwd**. It will show you the pathname of your current working directory. You'll see a string of words separated by slashes—for example: '*/home/tracy/ IC-files*'. In this particular case, the username is *tracy*, and her current working directory is *IC-files*. When *tracy* logs in, her default home directory is */home/tracy*.

If Tracy wants to go back to her home directory, she can issue one of two commands in this example. She can type **cd**, which by itself automatically puts her back in her home directory (*/home/ tracy*) no matter where she is. Or she can type **cd ..** which will change her current directory to the parent of the one she's currently in (up one level). Remember these two 'change directory' commands in case you find yourself deep in your directory tree.

Back to the Jacques Cousteau example. If he decides to organize his joke files a bit, he could create a directory called *jokes*. To do this, he types:

> **mkdir jokes**

The next thing he should do is move the two joke files he has in his home directory to the jokes directory. To do this, he'll type the following commands:

> **mv SharkJokes jokes**
> **mv WhaleJokes jokes**

He is using the 'rename' command to move the files, but they do keep their original names in the jokes directory. To change directories to the jokes directory, Jacques will type:

> **cd jokes**

Now his current directory is */home/cousteau/jokes*. If he types **ls**, he'll see 'SharkJokes WhaleJokes'.

He can then edit or look at the two files in that directory. If he decides to change back to the parent directory, he types **cd ..**, and he'll be one level above (*/home/cousteau*).

If he decides later on to remove the jokes directory, he needs to use the 'rm -r' command:

rm -r jokes

This will recursively delete every file in the *jokes* directory, and the *jokes* directory entry as well. Your system may be thoughtful enough to prompt you before each file is deleted, but don't count on it. Whatever the case, be careful if you decide to use this command!

These instructions are the bare minimum, but they should get you started moving, removing, renaming and looking at files and directories.

Creating Files

Perhaps one of the reasons Unix doesn't have a good reputation for being 'user-friendly' is the choices of editors. They're not that hard to use—it's just that in most cases you can't use your mouse to point, click and insert text. The three most common editors available to you are **vi, PICO** and **emacs** (which has, since Version 19, a friendly Windows-based interface allowing you to pull down menus and do mouse clicking). Or, you can create a file on your PC or Mac, and upload it (transfer it from your PC or Mac to the Unix system). The following section provides very brief survival guides for each of these.

Uploading Files to the Unix System. If you decide to heck with learning another editor, and you'd rather upload files you created with your easy-to-use word processor on your PC, here's what you need to do. This section assumes you're dialled-in to the Unix system using a communications package like Kermit, PROCOMM or WhiteKnight. Most of these packages come with the Kermit file transfer protocol (which is different from the Kermit communications package—confusing, yes). This section demonstrates how to transfer using Kermit. There may be other protocols available to you, such as Zmodem. Ask around if Kermit won't work for you.

Most likely the files you've created on your home computer are not text files. For example, a word-processed file is not a text file because there are a lot of codes and symbols in it known only to your word processor program. You should decide before you start transferring the file whether you need to do a binary or a text transfer. This is similar to what was described for the FTP program in Chapter 4. You can also convert a word-processed file to a text file by saving it as 'text with line breaks' or 'text with no line breaks'.

To transfer a text file from your own computer to the Unix computer, initiate Kermit on the Unix system by typing **kermit -r**; the '-r' option means that the Unix system is going to receive the file. You should then 'escape' back to your PC or Mac and initiate the sending process on your home computer by specifying what file you're sending, either through the menu system (choose 'Send file') or by typing a command (for example, **send file1.txt**). Unfortunately, there are so many communications packages that it is impossible to tell you here what to do in your particular situation. You should refer to your communications manual for the specifics. If everything goes according to plan, your text file should transfer nicely, and then it will be 'on' the Unix system. You can then email it, post it on USENET news, or just look at it from time to time.

If you decide to transfer a binary file, such as software or a word-processed document, you can do that too. On the Unix side, type **kermit -ir**. Here the 'i' option indicates that the Unix system is prepared to receive a binary file. You need to specify on your PC or Mac that you're going to send a binary file also. This may be set through a menu or a command. Again, if everything goes according to plan, you should have successfully transferred your binary file to the Unix system.

A word of warning: Unfortunately, most PC-based programs define ASCII in a different way and add characters to it that will disappear if you do not use the binary transfer mode. Unix programs might also interpret the files in a different way than your PC editor. To be sure of the transfer, you can use the "rich text format" or a MIME application for creating the file on your PC. Most modern Unix applications will understand those formats.

Vi. Vi is a VIsual, display-oriented, interactive text editor, and it's very hard for newbies to figure out on their own. It's not the beginner's fault, mind you. Vi is not very helpful or intuitive at all.

Here's your basic survival guide. The first thing you should know is that it's pronounced vee eye', not 'vie'. To create or edit an existing file, you type **vi** *filename*, where *filename* is the name of the file you want to create or modify.

When you fire up vi, you'll recognize a vi session because your screen doesn't contain much explanatory information, just the text in the file or, if the file is empty, a bunch of ~'s in the first column of every line. There are two vi modes you should know about: **command mode** and **insert mode**.

Upon initiating a vi session, you'll automatically be put into command mode. This means that most of the keys you type are interpreted as commands to vi. If you're creating a file, use the 'insert' command, or **i**. (There are other single letters that will also put you into insert mode, such as **a, o** and **O**.)

When you type **i**, it won't show up on your screen, but you will instantly be put into insert mode. (There are no status messages to indicate which mode you're in.) Now everything you type goes into vi's temporary editing buffer. When you're finished typing, press your <ESC> key one time to return to command mode. (If the <ESC> key doesn't work, try holding down the <control> or <alt> key and typing a '['. This is written as ^[.)

Here's a way to tell if you're in command mode or insert mode. If you <ESC> while you're already in command mode, your terminal will beep or flash at you. So just hit the <ESC> key a couple of times to reorient yourself in command mode, and proceed from there.

You can move around and position your cursor by using the arrow keys. These may work when you're in insert mode, but most of the time you use them in command mode. You can also use the letters 'h, j, k, l' (in command mode only) to move left, down, up, and right, respectively.

To delete characters when you're in command mode, position the cursor over the character to be deleted and type **x**. To

SUMMARY OF VI COMMANDS

Command Mode

Insert Commands:

i	insert before the cursor
a	insert after the cursor
o	'open' or start inserting in the line below the cursor
O	'open' or start inserting in the line above the cursor

Delete Commands:

dd	delete the current line
dw	delete word
x	delete the character under the cursor

Exiting Commands:

:w	write or save file
:q!	quit without saving changes
:wq	write (save) changes and quit
ZZ	write changes and quit (shortcut)

Other:

:r *filename*	include *filename* in buffer
ESC	returns to Command Mode

delete a word, position the cursor at the beginning of the word and type **dw** (for 'delete word'). To delete an entire line, type **dd**.

It's possible to include other files in a vi session. Suppose that you've typed a lot of stuff, and you want to add the contents of another file to it. Make sure you're in command mode first, then position the cursor where you want the file insertion to begin. Type:

```
:r filename
```

where *filename* is the name of the file. Notice that when you type a colon in command mode, the cursor automatically positions itself at the bottom of the screen. That's so you can type additional information required by the command.

A common predicament that newbies find themselves in is getting stuck in this "colon mode". If you find yourself in this situation, just type **vi** and <RETURN>.

Finding out how to leave vi is the biggest question most newbies have right after they start it up. To quit, type **:q**. To write and quit, type **:wq**. To quit without saving changes, type **:q!**. A shortcut command to writing changes and quitting is to type **ZZ** without a colon (which is just *really* obvious!).

PICO. PICO stands for 'PIne COmposer', and it's the default editor used with the email application PINE, which is described below. PICO is a full-screen editor, and it's very popular among new users. If you shudder when you hear vi mentioned, see if PICO is available.

To edit a file with PICO, simply type **pico** *filename*. Your screen will split into several parts. The top line is a status line, the third line from the bottom is used for informational messages and the bottom two lines provide a summary of the commands you can execute. Unlike vi, you are automatically put into insert mode, so you can begin typing immediately. To position the cursor, simply use the arrow keys.

To perform functions, PICO makes use of the control commands mentioned above. For example, to delete a line, position the cursor on the line, and type **CTRL-k** (hold down the control key and press the 'k' key). To delete a character, again position the cursor, and type **CTRL-d**. Be sure to look at the help facility by typing **CTRL-g** ('^G') for more information on commands. See the box below for a summary of commonly used commands.

To quit PICO, type **CTRL-x** ('^X'). The message line (three lines from the bottom) will ask you if you want to save your creation or changes before exiting. All you have to do is type **y** for yes or **n** for no. Unless you don't want to save your changes for some reason (perhaps you made too many mistakes and would like to recover the old version), you should always save. The next prompt will ask you what filename to write the changes to. It will default to the *filename* you specified at startup, so just press <RETURN> if you want to write over that file. Otherwise, type a new filename.

Emacs. Emacs stands for 'editor macros', and a lot of people prefer using it over vi. There's a good tutorial available in emacs

PICO COMMANDS SUMMARY

^G	Get Help
^X	Exit
^O	WriteOut (save changes)
^J	Justify (format) the current paragraph
^R	Read file (insert a file at cursor position)
^W	Where is (position the cursor at a specified text string)
^Y	Previous page (position the cursor at the previous screen page)
^V	Next page (position the cursor at the next screen page)
^K	Delete line
^U	Undelete line
^C	Current position of cursor
^T	Spell

that will step you through all the commands you need to know. To get started, type:

emacs *filename*

To learn about emacs, check out the online tutorial by typing **^H T**. This means that you type CTRL-H and then the character 't'.

As mentioned above, you will find new emacs versions to support graphical environments such as X11 under a Unix system. If you use X11, emacs will offer you an integrated workspace with capabilities beyond your belief. Its greatest advantage (the powerful capabilities) is also its greatest disadvantage, for there are so many macros, commands and control sequences that you will grow old just reading them. If you feel you are going mad using emacs, you can type **ALT-x** or **META-x** and then type **doctor** and <RETURN>. Emacs will go directly into the psychologist mode, listening to your problems and providing you with unexpected solutions.

ELECTRONIC MAIL

There are lots of email applications choices available for Unix users. This section offers an introduction to ELM and PINE.

Here's how they work in general. All Unix mail readers access a 'spool' file called the **inbox**. The inbox is where incoming email is stored automatically. The inbox file is probably stored elsewhere on the Unix system, not in your directory. When you execute an email application, it checks your inbox to see if you have any mail. If you do, your email program will display the messages you've received. You can then read, respond and send email.

ELM

ELM is a very popular and intuitive email application. To begin using it, just type **elm**. Message summaries will appear on your screen that will look similar to this:

```
Mailbox is '/usr/spool/mail/cousteau' with 4 messages
[ELM 2.3 PL11]

->  1 Feb 14 Cicil Levaree      (26)    Your Mother in France
   N 2 Feb 15 Whitey Shark       (38)    A great Shark Joke
   N 3 Feb 15 Paul Shaffer       (1039) Bottles filled up
   N 4 Feb 16 Hal Brunier        (10)    Diving turn on Sunday

You can use any of the following commands
                              by pressing the first character:
d)elete or u)ndelete mail, m)ail a message,
                      r)eply or f)orward mail, q)uit
To read a message, press <return>.
                          j = move down, k = move up, ? = help

Command:
```

In this example, there are four messages in Jacques Cousteau's inbox. This screen is ELM's 'index' of messages. The first column indicates the status of the messages, whether they've been read or not. Here, messages two through four have not been read. To read a message, position the arrow or the cursor on the desired message using the arrow keys, or type 'j' for down and 'k' for up. The arrow in this example is pointing at message one. To view this message requires only that you hit the <RETURN> key. You can then page through the message by hitting the space bar (or type **q** to quit the paging process).

If Jacques wanted to reply to Cicil, he would position the arrow or cursor line on message one and type **r**. ELM will ask him if he wants to include a copy of the original message, to which he types '**y**' or '**n**'. (The default is 'n'.) It will then let him edit the subject of the message (at the 'Subject of message:' prompt); he can leave it the way it is (by pressing <RETURN>), or change it. The next prompt, 'Copies to:', lets him specify other recipients of this message by typing in other email addresses (he might decide that Whitey Shark and Hal need to be in on this). After completing this last question, he's whisked into an editor, which will probably be one of the three mentioned above. (And, of course, he should adhere to all netiquette rules when composing his reply.) When he finishes editing, ELM gives him the following prompt:

```
Please choose one of the following options
                          by parenthesized letter:

e)dit message,    edit h)eaders,    s)end it   f)orget it.
```

The default command for send is 's', so if he types **s** or <RETURN>, his message will be sent. Typing **f** aborts the sending process, a very handy command to have. Also, the **h** command is very important. It lets you view your headers, which specify whom the message is going to, among other things. (You should get in the habit of checking the 'To:' and 'Cc:' headers to make sure that this message is going to end up where you want.) Finally, the **e** command will put him right back into the editor.

After Jacques has sent the message, there are several things he can do: save this message, forward it to someone, delete it, or do nothing. To delete it, all he has to do is type **d**, and the letter 'D' should appear to the left of the message. To save it, he types **s**. ELM will ask if he wants to save it in a file that is named for the sender of the message. It will attach a '=' (equals sign) to the filename, which means that it will save it in the mail directory (which is most likely named 'Mail' or 'mail'). In this particular case, it asks if he wants to save the mail folder (as it's called there) as 'clevaree'. If he just types <RETURN>, it will be saved in the mail directory as *clevaree* (this is also written as *Mail/clevaree*). He can, of course, name it anything he wants.

You should save important messages in folders, which are named either by subject or sender. You can then refer to them later in the mail program by typing **c** for 'change folder', and then typing the name of the folder (prefixed by '=' to indicate the standard mail directory). For more information about changing folders, type **?** at the 'Change to which folder' prompt. The help screen will show you the names of the folders in your mail directory and what to type to change to some standard folders (such as inbox, sent and received).

Once you get more proficient with ELM, you may want to customize it a bit to suit you better. You can do that by typing **o** for options at the index command level. Some of the things you can set include your editor, your default mail directory (where you save your mail messages), your name, your editor and how ELM sorts your messages (by date, by sender, by size, by subject and so on).

ELM also lets you create aliases, or your own email directory of names and addresses. Aliases are a really nice feature—they eliminate the need to type long and complicated email addresses. Once you've created an alias in ELM, all you have to do is use *that* name instead of the long address. To enter the alias database, at the index command level, type **a**. To 'make' an alias, type **m**. ELM will prompt you for the alias name (the nickname), the full name of the person and the email address for the person. There are quite a few other things you can do here; type **?** for more information.

To quit ELM, at the mail index, type **q**. If you haven't emptied your inbox, ELM will ask you what you want to do with read or unread messages. It's up to you whether you want to keep them in your inbox (so they're shown next time you read email) or move them to a 'received' folder. Answer the questions ELM asks you, based on what you want to do with your inbox messages. You can also bail out and not save any changes that you've made to your inbox by typing **x**.

PINE

Another very popular email application is **PINE**. PINE was developed by the University of Washington, and stands for 'Pine Is

No-longer Elm'. (It used to stand for 'Pine Is Nearly Elm'.) PINE
is an extremely easy mail agent with lots of help and menus.

To execute PINE, type **pine**. This will bring up the PINE
main menu, which looks similar to this:

```
PINE 3.89      MAIN MENU    Folder: INBOX 1 Message

? HELP                  - Get help using Pine
C COMPOSE MESSAGE       - Compose and send a message
I FOLDER INDEX          - View messages in current folder
F FOLDER LIST           - Select a folder to view
A ADDRESS BOOK          - Update address book
S SETUP                 - Configure or update Pine
Q QUIT                  - Exit the Pine program

          Copyright 1989-1993. PINE is a trademark
              of the University of Washington.
          [Folder "INBOX" opened with 1 message]
? Help                    P PervCmd           R RelNotes
O OTHER CMDS L [ListFldrs] N NextCmd          K KBLock
F1: Help | F2: Main Menu | F7: Reset Emulator
```

The very first thing you should do, of course, is take advantage of PINE's help facility, so type **?** to get started.

To compose and send a message, type **c**. This will put you
into PINE's editor, PICO, which was described above.

```
PINE 3.89     COMPOSE MESSAGE Folder: inbox 1 Messages

To      :
Cc      :
Attchmnt :
Subject  :
----- Message Text -----
```

As you can see, there are four fields to complete for the email
message. Use the arrow keys or tab key to jump from field to
field. You need to specify who you're sending the message to, the
subject and any copies. PINE has the MIME capability, which was
mentioned in Chapter 3, so you can send nontext (binary) files
very easily. Just type the name of the file in the 'Attchmnt:' field.
If it's a file you created on your PC or Mac, remember that you
need to upload it first to the Unix system using a file transfer protocol such as Kermit before you can attach it to your message.

Once you've filled in all the blanks, you can start typing your message in the 'Message Text' buffer. When you're done, type **^X** to send. PINE will ask you if you want to send the message—type '**y**' or '**n**'. If in the middle of editing you decide you want to cancel the whole process, just type **^C**, and then respond with **y** to indicate that you really want to abort the sending process.

PINE has a nice feature that eliminates the need to send yourself a carbon copy. It automatically adds every message you send to the 'sent-mail' folder. The first time you run PINE, it will probably ask you if you'd like to create a 'sent-mail' folder. Type **y** to create it, and all your outgoing email will be saved in this folder. You can then call it up by changing email folders (see the PINE main menu for that option).

The next option on the PINE main menu is the Folder Index. Type **i** to look at your inbox. The screen will look very similar to ELM's above, and many of the commands are the same. Use your arrow keys to position the cursor on the message you wish to read, and hit <RETURN>. You can delete this message by typing **d**, save the message by typing **s**, reply to it by typing **r**, and so on. Make sure that you type **?** to read the help manual. To return to the main menu, type **m**.

Another good feature about PINE is the 'Folder List' menu item. From the PINE main menu, type **l**. PINE will list all of your saved mail; each file is actually a mail folder. You can select which one to open by using your arrow keys to position the cursor on the folder. Then hit <RETURN>, and the folder's index is displayed. It will look a lot like your inbox index. If you saved email from your mother in a folder called 'mum', you could then use this feature to reference all the email your mother sent to you. Or you could ignore it until she calls you asking why you never write her email.

Next on the PINE main menu is an 'Address Book' feature that lets you create an address book. Type **a** to enter this directory. If this is your first time, you probably won't have any addresses listed. To create an entry for Jacques Cousteau, type **a** for add. At the 'New full name (last, first):' prompt, type **Cousteau, Jacques** <RETURN>. You'll be asked for a nickname, so type **jacques** <RETURN>. And lastly, you need to input the email address for Jacques at the 'Enter new e-mail address:' prompt, so type **cousteau@dive.into.ocean.fr**. And there you go! Now when you send email, you don't have to type **cousteau@dive.** **into.ocean.fr** every time in the 'To:' field; you can just type **jacques**! For more information on creating an address book, type **?**.

Last on the PINE main menu (before Quit) is the 'Other' menu. Here you can check on the status of your disk space or set your printer. This is a really nice feature if you're dialled-in. Setting the printer to **attach-to-ansi** will, in many cases, let you print directly to your own printer. Be sure to read the help files while in the 'Other' menu to find out more.

Quitting PINE is easy. From the main menu, all you have to do is type **q**. PINE will ask you if that's really what you want to do. Type **y** if it is.

READING USENET NEWS

The last section in this Unix survival guide will help you get started in reading USENET news. Just by using your news reader, you're able to read articles that have originated from all over the world. Don't worry how they got to your computer, though. That's another book.

The news reader discussed here is called **tin**. There are many other news readers, so if you don't like this one, ask your Internet provider what other applications are available and try them out.

News Reader Basics

Every Unix news reader accesses a file in your home directory called *.newsrc*. Notice that this filename is prefaced by a dot. This means that it's an 'invisible' file, and it probably doesn't show up when you list your files (using *ls*). But it's there, and if it isn't, your news reader will create it the first time you execute it.

The *.newsrc* file lists each and every newsgroup that is accessible on your machine, one newsgroup per line. Part of the file looks like this:

```
rec.arts.anime:
rec.arts.books: 1-73875,78896,80480
rec.arts.drwho:
rec.arts.int-fiction:
```

Free Speech Upheld on the Internet

'Those who want to censor pornography on the Net at the source have missed the point. For the first time in history, we can provide the digital tools to individuals to censor what they receive on their screens according to their own values, while letting those who produce exercise freedom of speech. Which is no longer, as it has been in Broadcast, an obligation to listen. That's why I think computer bulletin boards, locally tailored by parents, teachers, or guardians of young people, can make ideal "front ends" to the Internet. We can have it both ways now.'

Source: Dave Hughes.

```
rec.arts.misc:
rec.arts.movies:
rec.arts.movies.reviews:
rec.arts.poems:
rec.arts.sf-lovers:
rec.arts.tv:
rec.arts.tv.soaps:
rec.arts.wobegon:
```

When you first start reading news, you are automatically 'subscribed' to every single newsgroup in your *.newsrc* file. The operative subscription character in that file is the colon after each name—that indicates a subscription. There are several ways to 'unsubscribe' from newsgroups. One is through your news reader. The other is a 'brute force' way—that is, by editing your *.newsrc*.

Why do you care about unsubscribing anyway? Because you may be a bit overwhelmed by the sheer number of newsgroups— thousands and thousands. You simply cannot read all of them regularly, so don't even try! Paring down to the ones you want to participate in and adding others later on will make reading news a bit more manageable.

To edit *.newsrc*, use your favourite editor, and replace all the colons of the newsgroups from which you want to unsubscribe with an exclamation mark, '!'. You can do this really quickly with vi. Type the following commands:

```
vi .newsrc
:1,$s/:/!/
```

For those who are interested, the second command means 'from lines 1 through the end of the file (**1,$**), substitute (**s/**) every colon (**:/**) with an exclamation mark (**!/**)'.

You can then subscribe to the newsgroups you want by replacing the exclamation marks with colons. This may take you a while, because some sites carry thousands and thousands of newsgroups. You certainly don't have to do this all in one sitting; you can edit your *.newsrc* at a later time when you hear about newsgroups that interest you.

If you decide to go ahead and page through all of these newsgroups, there's an easy way to search for keywords using vi. In command mode, type */keyword*, where *keyword* is the word for which you're searching. For example, using vi to search for the keyword *music*, type **/music**. The cursor will position you at the next occurrence of that word, and you can then change the exclamation mark. To keep searching for that word, just type **n** (for 'next'). When you're finished editing, you can exit and write your changes by typing **:wq**.

Tin

Tin is a full-screen news reader that lets you read and post to USENET newsgroups. It's a very powerful application, and this section cannot cover all the various options and commands, but it will give you enough information to get started. Be sure to check out the manual page, **man tin**, to find out more about this news reader.

Here's how tin works in general. When you fire it up, you'll be at the top level, the Group Selection level. This is a newsgroup table of contents from which you pick a newsgroup to read. When you've selected the desired newsgroup, you advance to the next level, the Article level or Thread Selection list. Here you can select articles within a chosen newsgroup to read (the reading level). You can post an article at any time during your tin ses-

sion. To use this news reader, type **tin**. You'll see some messages
that look like this:

```
tin 1.2 PL2 [UNIX] © Copyright 1991-93 Iain Lea.
Reading news active file . . .
Reading attributes file . . .
Reading newsgroups file . . .
```

If there are newsgroups that have been added since your last
session, tin will ask you if you want to subscribe to each of them.
Type **y** or **n**.

After any newsgroup additions, you'll see the Group Selection screen, which shows you every newsgroup you're subscribed to, one per line. Here's a sample Tin screen:

```
Group Selection (18)
h=help


1   49 alt.fan.dave_barry Electronic fan club
2   4 rec.arts.movies Discussions of movies and mo
3   39 rec.gardens Gardening, methods and resul
4   407 sci.space.shuttle The space shuttle and the
    ST
5   19 de.talk.romance All circling around romance
    and love
6   33 es.alt.anuncios Anuncios varios de interes
    general
7   66 fj.books Books of all genres, shapes, and
    sizes (Canjy letters)
8   8 maus.bigfood All around food and other stuff to
    eat
9   27 uk.education.misc General discussion of UK
    educational matters
10  89 bln.announce.zib Announcements regarding the
    Zuse Centre in Berlin
11  34 rec.music.dylan Discussion of Bob's works &
    music.
12  65 rec.boats.paddle Talk about any boats with
    oars, paddles
13  49 rec.games.trivia Discussion about trivia.
14  2 sci.math.symbolic Symbolic algebra discussion.
15  2 alt.individualism Philosophies where individual
    rights ar
16  8 comp.society.folklore Computer folklore &
    culture, past & pre
```

```
<n>=set current to n, TAB=next unread, /=search
pattern, c)atchup, g)oto, j=line down, k=line up,
h)elp, m)ove, q)uit, r=toggle all/unread, s)ubscribe,
S)ub pattern, u)nsubscribe, U)nsub pattern, y)ank in/
out
```

```
*** End of Groups ***
```

The title says 'Group Selection (18)' at the top of the screen. The number in the parentheses indicates that you're subscribed to 18 newsgroups, but you see only 16 newsgroups on the screen. Tin shows 16 groups at a time; you can go to the next screen (and see the remaining two newsgroups) by typing the <PAGE DOWN> key or the space bar. To show the previous screen, type either <PAGE UP> or **b**. When you actually use tin, you will probably see a lot more than 18 newsgroups.

If you want to quit when you're at the Group Selection screen, type **q**.

This screen has information other than newsgroup names. For example, look at *rec.boats.paddle*. The very first number on the left tells what the newsgroup number is; in this case, it's 12. The second number indicates how many unread articles there are in that newsgroup; here there are 65 unread articles. Next is the name of the newsgroup, *rec.boats.paddle*, and finally there's a short description (if one exists) of the newsgroup.

If you want, you can turn off the newsgroup description column by typing **d**. (This and the next command are toggle switches. To turn the newsgroup description column back on, type **d** again.) You can also ask tin not to show you any newsgroups that have no unread articles (which will have no number preceding them). If you type **r**, this newsgroup will not show on your screen; typing another **r** will show it (with all the other newsgroups).

There's a summary of common commands listed at the bottom of the screen. Here's a brief explanation of them:

<n>	Set current newsgroup at the <n> (a number).
<TAB>	Pressing the tab key will position you at the next unread article in the selected newsgroup.
/<keyword>	Search for a keyword.

c	Mark that newsgroup as read.
g	Go to newsgroup number.
j	Move the selector line down.
k	Move the selector line up.
h	Display summary of commands.
m	Move selected newsgroup to another position on the screen.
q	Quit tin.
r	Toggle switch for 'show all' or 'show only unread'.
s	Subscribe to the selected newsgroup.
S <pattern>	Subscribe to groups whose names match the specified pattern.
u	Unsubscribe from the selected newsgroup.
U <pattern>	Unsubscribe from groups whose names match the specified pattern.
y	Toggle switch to yank in/yank out unsubscribed newsgroups.

Navigating. In order to read a newsgroup, you must first select it. When you start tin, the first newsgroup will be highlighted. To select another newsgroup, move the highlighter bar up and down the screen. You can do this by using the up and down arrow keys, or by typing **j** (for down) and **k** (for up). You can jump directly to a newsgroup by typing the corresponding number. Finally, you can search forward for a newsgroup by typing **/keyword**, where *keyword* is a word you're looking for in a newsgroup name.

Let's read the *alt.fan.pratchett* newsgroup. Since this group is already highlighted, all you need to do is type <RETURN>, and you'll be at the next level of tin, the article or 'thread' level. You'll then see a screen that looks similar to the Group Selection screen above. This one, however, lists all the articles in the *alt.fan.pratchett* newsgroup instead of listing newsgroup names.

To advance to the next unread article from the Group Selection index, you can also press the <TAB> key instead of <RETURN>. You can use the <TAB> key within the newsgroup to advance to unread articles. In this case, when you hit the <TAB> (or <RETURN>) key, you'll get the article index screen for the *alt.fan.pratchett* newsgroup:

```
alt.fan.pratchett (105T 409A 0K 0H R)                         h=help

1  + 20  Salmiakki                                  snail
2  + 3   Useful Information                         Terry Pratchett
3  + 2   killing)                                   Philip Johnson
4  + 16  Toad                                       David Thompson
5  + 12  Discworld game ! ..                        David Thompson
6  + 4   Reality where are you?                     Cath Lawrence
7  + 33  German Lotto                               Cath Lawrence
8  + 35  That ole AFP t-shirt                       Cath Lawrence
9  + 5   Cats and Toast                             Framtidsbygget
10 + 2   Newbie, American, looks at t-shirt thread  fqc4591@acf6.acf.n

        <n>=set current to n, TAB=next unread, /=search pattern,
   ^K)ill/select, a)uthor search, c)atchup, j=line down, k=line up,
      K=mark read, l)ist thread, |=pipe, m)ail, o=print, q)uit,
                r=toggle all/unread, s)ave, t)ag, w=post
```

As you can see, this screen looks a lot like the title screen of newsgroups. Moving around works the same way, using numbers or the arrow key (or the 'j' and 'k' keys).

This level—the thread or article level—will let you follow discussion threads. A thread is two or more postings devoted to one topic in a discussion. For example, you might post an article to the *alt.fan.pratchett* newsgroup about Rincewind and his Luggage. People who are reading your article can then respond to what you said. This creates a discussion thread. At this article level, discussion threads are normally referenced by the original poster's article. From there you can follow the thread and post a follow-up, if you wish.

In the above *alt.fan.pratchett* example, the first line indicates the name of the newsgroup, followed by some numbers in parentheses. These refer to the number of threads (in this case, 105), the number of articles (409), the number of killed (thrown-away) articles (0), and the number of 'hot' (preselected according to a certain standard) articles (0). If you have the 'r' switch toggled to 'on'—meaning, show only articles that haven't been read—that will be indicated here too, in this case, by the 'r'.

The next section lists the articles in this newsgroup. The first column specifies the article number. If there's a + sign after the article number, then there are articles in the thread that haven't been read. If there's another number, it indicates the number of articles—follow-up discussions—in the thread. The next column is the subject of each particular news thread. The last column specifies the author of the original thread.

At this point, if you wish to return to the Group Selection index, either type **q** (for quit the Article/Thread index), or use the left arrow key. The bottom of the screen lists a summary of some of the commands you can use in this level. Here's a brief explanation:

<n>	Set current article selector to article number <n>.
<TAB>	Position the selector at the next unread article.
/<keyword>	Search forward in the article index for <keyword>.
^K	Kill specified threads (for you only).
a <author>	Search forward for articles by a specified author.
c	Mark all articles in newsgroup as read (catchup).
j	Move selector down.
k	Move selector up.
K	Mark the selected thread as read.
l	List all the articles in the thread.
|	Pipe the current article to a Unix command (advanced command).
m	Mail the article or thread to someone.
o	Print the thread or article.
q	Quit; return to Group Selection Level.
r	Toggle: show all or just unread.
s	Save article or thread.
w	Post an article.

Navigating and Reading News. Navigating this level is the same as with the Group Selection level. You can either start at the beginning or move the highlighter bar down to a desired article/thread. Once the article is selected, hit either <RETURN> or <TAB>. The <RETURN> key will advance you to the first article in that thread; the <TAB> key will place you at the next unread article. When you're reading an article, you page through it just as you do using the 'more' program mentioned earlier—that is, by using your space bar. If you want to return to the Article/ Thread index level, type **q**.

SUMMARY OF COMMON UNIX COMMANDS AND APPLICATIONS

To find out more about a command, use the **man** (for 'manual')
command. For example, to find out about the 'change directory'
command, *cd*, type **man cd**.

File Commands

ls	list files
more, page	display a file at your terminal
cp	copy a file
mv	move or rename files
rm	remove files

Editors

vi	editor
emacs	editor

Directory Commands

cd	change current directory
mkdir	make a new directory
rmdir	remove a directory
pwd	print working directory

Command Information

apropos	locate commands by keyword lookup
whatis	display a command description
man	display manual pages online

Useful Information Commands

cal	print calendar
date	print date and time
who	print who and where users are logged in

Email Applications

elm	email
PINE	email

News Applications
rn, trn, tass, tin, nn, vnews

(If you haven't realized by now, the 'quit' command can be
used at any level to return you to the previous level. When you
use it at the Group Selection index, you exit tin.)

Posting. At some point, you'll want to tell the world what you think by posting your own articles. There are several ways to do this in tin. To post an article 'from scratch'—when you're not following up on another discussion—is very easy. At any level, type **w** (for write). You'll be asked for a subject. Type the subject (be descriptive), and hit <RETURN>. Tin will put you in an editor, probably one of the three editors described previously. At this point you can type your article. Make sure you leave a blank space between the headers (*Subject:, Newsgroups:, Organization:, Summary:, Keywords:* and so on) and the text of your article. When you've finished, exit the editor. Tin will then prompt you to do the following:

```
            q)uit, e)dit, p)ost:
```

If you want to abort this article, type **q**. If you want to go back and edit the article again, type **e**. And if it's ready to be posted, just type **p**.

Another common way to post an article is by following up on a discussion. So, when you're reading an article, you can type **f** (which will include the text of the message to which you're replying), or **F** (which won't include the text of the article).

If instead of posting your reply to the entire world you'd rather keep it private between you and the poster of the article, you can send him or her private email. To do this, type **r** (to include the text of the article), or **R** (to omit the text of the article).

Finally, when you're done using tin, you can either keep typing **q** until you exit the program level by level, or you can type **Q**, which will let you make a quick exit.

You may feel as though you've earned an Internet advanced degree by now, and unless you already have access through your office or college, you're probably itching to get connected to the Internet. The next chapter deals with the nitty-gritty of getting on the Internet: finding the right modem and software, deciding what kind of access *you* need, and locating commercial or alternative Internet access. So stay tuned—you're almost at home on the Internet!

Chapter 7

GETTING CONNECTED

*N**ow that you know* what you want to do on the Internet, or at least where you want to go exploring, you'll want to get connected. There isn't just one place you can go to get access; paths and roads to the Internet are many. The best one for you will depend on your circumstances, your needs, and—to some extent—your finances. This chapter tells you what you need to get started, your choices for individual access, where to go for services, and the basics for connecting a business organization. There are a lot of details that apply only to the European market; however, most of the general information applies also to the rest of the world. Demand for Internet access is increasing rapidly worldwide, and there are more connectivity choices for individuals and businesses because of the many competing provider services.

EASY STREET

If you work for an institution or a company with full-time access through a network connection to the Internet, you have the shortest path of all. All you need to do is sit down at your office terminal or workstation and, using the instructions and Internet applications supplied by your in-house computer gurus, log on and get going. Most Internet connections have been made just like that—as connections between two networks, rather than between two computers. For example, a university's LAN might get access to the Internet by making a connection through a leased phone line to a regional network. Once that connection is made, in most cases, every computer on the LAN has 'full-time' access—meaning, the Internet is available all the time, day and night. More and more businesses are getting connections, and some universities provide access. Be sure to inquire locally before starting your search.

ALL YOU NEED TO GET STARTED DIALLING INTO THE INTERNET

Fortunately, these days there are more and more ways to get access to the Internet if you're an individual computer user or small business. All you need is a personal computer (Mac, PC, whatever), a modem, communications software and a phone line. Connecting an entire business or organization's network is more complex than can be covered in detail here, but an overview of the major steps is included later in this chapter (see 'Connecting Your Business or Organization'). Some sources for more information are given, as well.

Modems

If you're in the market for a modem, then read this section before whipping out your credit card. A little planning and research in the modem department on your part will make your journey to the Internet a bit easier.

Modems are, simply put, computer appliances that convert the digital signal from your computer into an analogue sound wave that can be transmitted over telephone lines. A modem at the other end converts the analogue signal back into a digital signal that is understood by the computer you're talking to. Exciting advances are being made in modem technology, with faster speeds and more error-free data transmission. High-speed modems can reduce errors from line noise and even do data compression. As with any computer-related purchase, you should buy the very best modem you can afford—perhaps even a bit better than you can afford. Technology changes fast, and five years from now, today's high-speed modems will be as obsolete as that dinosaur of modems, the 300bps acoustic coupler.

If you have a slower modem, don't despair. Many individuals are still using 2400bps (or slower) modems that they've had for several years to access the Internet and other services. All of the access and information systems support them, and, for the occasional user, the difference in online and/or long-distance charges may not be significant. (The higher your modem speed, of course, the less time it takes you to transfer information.) Using a 2400bps modem, you can access email, Telnet, FTP and terminal client applications such as text-based Gopher and WWW browsers. However, the bigger the message or file, the longer it will take to show on your screen or transfer to your computer. If you've got a 2400bps modem, you're pretty much limited to text-based communication, unless you have a lot of patience.

If you plan to spend a lot of time online and run applications like Mosaic, or if you need quick, error-free access, spring for a high-speed modem with error correction and data compression. Many of the new Internet applications incorporate multimedia, and they require you to drive in the fast lane of the Infobahn. You *can* use Mosaic if you're dialling into the Internet with a modem, but you must be using a modem that runs at least at 9.6Kbps, preferably at 14.4Kbps or faster. Prices for these high-speed modems keep falling and you can probably show savings immediately in connect-time charges alone. See the 'Full-Access Dialup Connection' section to learn how to use Mosaic and other client applications via a dialup link.

The ideal modem for telecommunications not only communicates at high speeds but also has error correction and data compression features. Error correction protocols help filter out line noise, which throws 'garbage' characters—like '{{pdf{{{'—on to your screen, and they ensure an error-free transmission. Most file transfer programs also have a mechanism to ensure accurate file transfers. Data compression, while a useful feature, may not help you much on some bulletin boards and information services that have already compressed their files, in which case your modem can't compress them any further. Shopping for a modem gets you into a complexity of feature combinations: speed, modulation protocols, data compression and more. Claims, particularly for speed, may not be what they appear to be. So it would be wise, especially if you are planning to spend a lot for a high-speed modem, to check some independent sources before you buy. The information box decodes some of the seemingly cryptic modem standards.

Before you go to buy a modem in a European country, find out what requirements it has to fulfil and whether your local telecommunication provider permits its use. For instance, in Germany all modems used in the public phone network are required to have a 'FTZ' number. In the United Kingdom, all modems that are to be connected to the public telephone system must carry a green 'BABT' approval sticker. It isn't, in fact, illegal to sell or possess an unapproved modem, but it is illegal to connect it to the public telephone network. Other countries may not restrict their use. Ask your telephone carrier company or your local modem dealer about the situation.

During the long process of negotiating and ratifying the V.34 standard, a number of modem manufacturers agreed to an interim 'almost-V.34' standard called V.Fast (you may also see this written V.FC, for V.Fast Class). Many V.Fast modems, which communicate at 28.8Kbps, come with an upgrade offer to either swap the modem's ROM chips or download a software upgrade to the full V.34 standard. Now that 'official' V.34 modems are around, it's worth making sure either that you're buying a genuine V.34 modem or that the V.Fast modem does come with an upgrade offer.

There is another 'nonstandard' standard around known as V.32 terbo. Modems built to this standard can communicate at 19,200bps, rather than the 14,100 bps of V.32bis. There are relatively few of these and V.32terbo appears to have largely been overtaken by the debut of V.34.

The development in this sector is a bit fuzzy, so the information coming to you with this book may be outdated by the time you read it. Consult your local dealer for further information.

Communications Software

The second required component is software that will enable communication. Communications software, which is installed on your personal computer, sets up the three-way conversation between your computer, the modem and the remote computer or

COMMON MODEM STANDARDS AND TYPICAL SPEEDS

The following specify some common modem standards. Many of these—the ones that begin with a 'V'—are defined by the Consultative Committee for International Telegraph and Telephone (CCITT), an international organization that develops communications standards.

The third column estimates the time it would take to transfer a 100K file (the average size of many documents or image files on the Internet).

Modulation	Standard Speed	Approx. Time for 100K File Transfer
V.22	1200bps	14 minutes
V.22bis	2400bps	7 minutes
V.32	9.6Kbps	2 minutes
V.32bis	14.4Kbps	83 seconds
V.34	28.8Kbps	27 seconds
PEP	19.2Kbps	varies

Standard Type	
V.42	Error Correction
V.42bis	Data Compression
MNP 4	Error Correction
MNP 5	Data Compression

Notes:

Speeds are represented here in bits per second (bps), not in baud. Baud rates and bps are different terms, and faster modem speeds are always measured in bps.

Be aware that the other end must support the same standards in order to achieve the desired connection rate.

A popular high-speed modem these days is one that conforms to V.32bis with V.42 and V.42bis. You should expect to spend in the neighbourhood of UK£120–300 for a good modem.

PEP is a special protocol used in Trailblazer and Worldblazer modems from Telebit, a modem provider. They are very common in Europe.

There are many other standards.

terminal server. Since you are dialling into the Internet, there are many types of communication packages available, enabling different kinds of connections. These are terminal emulation, off-line access and SLIP/PPP.

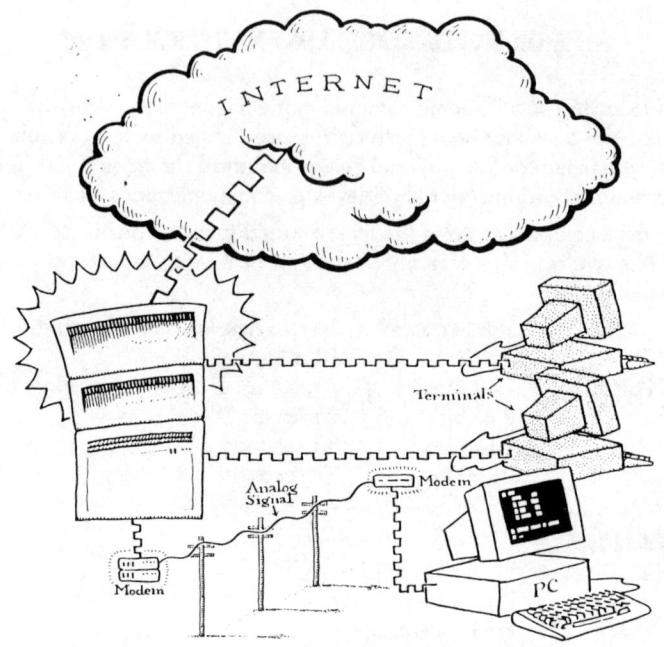

With terminal emulation, your personal computer becomes a terminal
on an Internet computer.

TYPES OF CONNECTIONS

The following sections explain the three basic access options you
have as an individual/independent user. All of these are commonly used and available from a large number of Internet
providers. The best choice for you depends on your existing
equipment situation and how much you're willing to spend.

Terminal Emulation

Terminal emulation is the easiest type of dialup Internet access to
understand. Using your modem and free or commercial communications software, such as Kermit, PROCOMM, WhiteKnight or
MicroPhone, you can dial into an Internet-connected computer
or communications server and basically turn your PC or Mac into
a dumb terminal that will most likely emulate a VT100, a vener-
able terminal produced in the millions by Digital Equipment Corporation (DEC). (You can get communication software from a

number of places. Some modems come bundled with communications software. You can also buy it from any software store. And there are a number of free implementations, like Kermit, that are widely distributed through various channels, such as user groups, bulletin board systems and the Internet.) Once connected, everything you type is from the perspective of the remote computer into which you have dialled. When you read email or news, you are using email and news applications that reside on the remote computer. Similarly, remote logins, file transfers and other tools, are all executed on the remote computer. Your PC or Mac provides only the display.

When you use FTP or Gopher to transfer a file, be aware that you are transferring the file to the Internet-connected computer you are dialled into, *not* to your own computer. If you want the file to reside on your PC or Mac, then you have to execute *another* transfer process by downloading it using a different kind of file transfer protocol, such as Kermit, Xmodem, Ymodem or Zmodem. This is perhaps one of the biggest stumbling blocks for new users—the confusion about where the file actually is and how to make it show up where you want. In this situation, when you're transferring files, just think of this Internet-connected computer as the 'middle guy'. When you transfer a file to the middle guy using FTP or Gopher, remember that you then need to tell the middle guy to transfer it to your own computer. Think of it as a 'two-step transfer' dance.

For example, suppose that you're using Kermit to dial into an Internet-connected computer on CIX (the Compulink Information Xchange, not to be confused with the Internet's Commercial Internet Exchange), a popular London-based commercial conferencing system. You're zipping around the planet checking out the scene, when you find an archive of online books available via anonymous FTP on host *vtucs.cc.vt.edu* in the *Files/infores/books* directory (the URL is *ftp://vtucs.cc.vt.edu/Files/infores/books*). After you browse the digital shelves looking for a book you can curl up with on your laptop and read, you decide on *Walden* by Henry David Thoreau. To get this, you have to change to the *walden* directory (**cd walden**), and then get the file (**get walden**).

At this point, *Walden* is on the CIX computer (the middle guy), *not* on your own computer. You need to initiate another transfer (using Kermit, Xmodem, Ymodem or Zmodem, for example) from CIX to your PC or Mac.

Here's how to do this if the middle-guy computer and your computer both have Kermit. First, fire up Kermit on the middle-guy computer, in this case, the CIX computer. If you're using a Unix system, you can type, **kermit -s walden** (the '-s' means 'send'). Then, on your own computer, you need to select the 'receive file' option. You can do this a number of ways—it depends on what system you're using. Refer to your communication software documentation for the exact details.

(FYI, this online book archive is also available via Gopher on host *gopher.vt.edu*, path *Eris Information Services/Eris Files/Information Resources/Books*.)

'Offline' Software Access

Offline software access brings some of the Internet functions, such as email, USENET news and file transfer, straight to your computer, but lets you work offline. This means that you're not actively dialled-in while you're working (or playing), only when the need arises. When that happens, the software makes the connection, performs the required functions, such as transferring email back and forth, and then disconnects. Providers or services supply you with special software, called **client** or **agent software**. In addition to taking care of the communications, this software also provides email, an editor for composing messages, and perhaps a news reader. This offline software is available in both the commercial and the public domains.

Although you're not *interactively* using the Internet, you can still do a lot of useful things, such as download email and news, reading messages and postings at your leisure on your home computer rather than tying up a phone line and running up connection charges. But be aware that not all of the Internet's applications, particularly remote login, Gopher and Mosaic, are available to you, since you can't issue commands and receive information interactively when you're not connected. Despite this limited functionality, these client connections are recommended for novice users, because they are more user-friendly than many of the public-access systems. With such access, you work with a familiar graphical application on your PC or Mac, not on a foreign computer account. You also don't have to worry about taking the extra step of transferring files from a middle-guy Internet computer to your home computer (as you do with dialup terminal emulation access)—the software does all of this for you.

Full-Access Dialup Connection

A more advanced client connection uses client networking software and a high-speed modem to actually *become* a 'directly connected' computer on the Internet. This type of access differs from the services above because you are skipping the terminal-emulation middle guy, so to speak, and you're interactively using the Internet, not working offline.

What makes this happen is a fast modem (the fastest you can get, at least 9.6Kbps) and software that conforms to a special protocol. There are two protocols available, SLIP and PPP. Either of these, used in conjunction with graphical Internet client applications like Gopher and Mosaic, brings the power and flexibility of the Internet straight to your home computer over an ordinary telephone line. SLIP and PPP are different, but each performs essentially the same function—that is, they make your computer a **peer** computer on the Internet. A SLIP or PPP connection is a great way to connect, but it can be more expensive and a bit more difficult to configure.

When you use this type of connection, you are actually executing Internet applications on your *own* computer, not on an Internet-connected computer that you've dialled into. For example, if you want to transfer a file using FTP from a public-access site, you transfer that file straight to your home computer instead of working with the terminal-emulation middle guy. Similarly, you can use a client Gopher application that lets you point and click your way through Gopherspace. The Gopher menus appear as folders on some systems, which is very intuitive. Or, try exploring the WWW using Mosaic. It's much more interesting when the Web is in colour (if you've got a colour monitor, of course).

You must dial into another computer or terminal server that is running SLIP (if your computer is running SLIP) or PPP (if

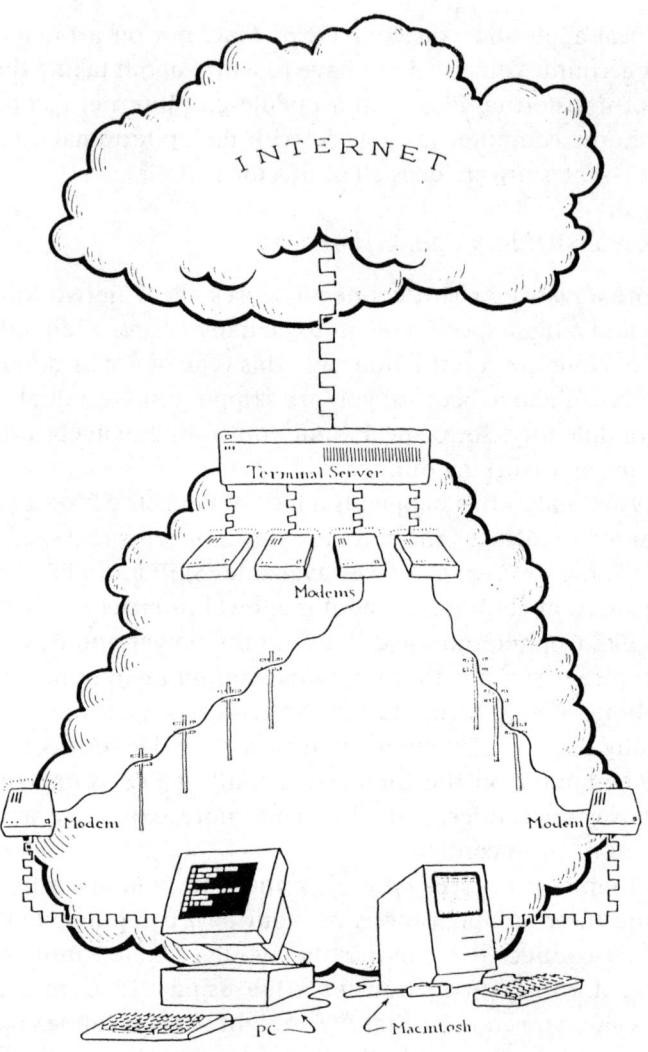

With SLIP or PPP, your computer becomes a host on the Internet.

your computer is running PPP) to make this connection. (These remote ends are known as SLIP or PPP servers. They help you get set up at the beginning of the connection, but they are essentially 'invisible' after you get going.) You'll also need a unique Internet Protocol (IP) address, because your computer must be identified

Internet to the Rescue!

Tired of those busy signals when you're trying to reach technical support for your computer? One high-tech company gets much of its hardware and software technical support over the Internet. Over the past year, they've got bug fixes and patches for their Sun Microsystems workstations and technical support from their router vendor, Cisco Systems. Another hardware vendor uses the Internet to login to their system for problem diagnosis and resolution.

One of the company's software engineers told us about how the Internet recently saved the day (and night) for him when his boss needed a network monitoring problem fixed by Friday morning (and it was 4:59 p.m. on Thursday!) A quick search into the Internet produced a gold mine of network monitoring programs. He chose one of the simpler ones, customized it, and within an hour was done and on his way home. 'Another victory for Truth, Connectedness, and the Internet Way!'

Source: Peter Ho, Unocal Corp. (Note: All opinions are Ho's and in no way reflect Unocal's positions.)

on the network. Your IP address may stay the same, or it may change every time you connect. Your provider will most likely assign you an address, or the remote SLIP/PPP server will assign you a number to use when you make the connection. You may want a registered hostname as well, and as with the IP address and any other required information and parameters, your network provider will probably be able to assist you.

The 'Internet Connectivity' section in the Appendix lists some SLIP and PPP implementations, as well as some popular client applications.

CHOOSING AN INDIVIDUAL ACCESS PROVIDER

Network access for individuals is a new and evolving market, one that is growing very quickly. So finding the services you want, the access, and the right price is not as simple as picking a long-distance phone carrier, or getting phone service through your local phone company. Internet access is offered by private companies, a few universities, academic/research networks and public-private partnerships. Service packages vary a great deal and change constantly, as do rates. Your options are not limited to what is described in this chapter. Use the information here and in the 'Providers' section of the Appendix as a general guide to starting your own research.

Public Dialup Internet Access Systems

Lots of companies offer dial-in access to their large Internet-connected computer systems, giving you terminal emulation or (if available) SLIP/PPP access to the Internet. All of these services offer file transfer, remote login, Gopher and news services, in addition to email and (depending on the system) a variety of other services, including commercial databases. Access is usually via a phone call to the system's nearest number, although some systems also offer access via public data networks. (See below for some information about alternative access methods.)

Many public-access providers are expanding and adding access points in more cities, so you may want to contact them for their latest local dial-in information. Some of them also offer assistance with buying and installing modems and communications software. Pricing structures vary widely, with monthly access fees, connect charges or a combination. The services all provide for a wide range of modem speeds. The service access points are often referred to as Points of Presence (PoPs). Look for the acronym PoP and you almost certainly will stumble over an Internet provider near you.

More often than not, the type of computer into which you're dialled is running the Unix operating system. Don't fret, though, if you don't know Unix. Many providers also offer menu systems that eliminate the requirement of a 'computer science Unix internals degree' and simplify things greatly. If you are forced to wade through the Unix muck, be sure to refer to Chapter 6, which includes information on some common commands, applications and how to get help if you get stuck. To be fair, Unix isn't all that bad, and once you get the hang of the system, it can be quite fun to use. It's just not very intuitive to the novice.

See the 'Providers' section in the Appendix for directions on how to retrieve a list of public access dialup systems compiled by Peter Kaminski.

National and Mid-level Individual Access Providers

As mentioned in Chapter 2, there are lots of regional academic/ research and national commercial Internet providers that offer individual access to their networks. The commercial providers, such as EUnet, PIPEX, Demon, INNET, SURFNET, PING and GARR, offer a wide range of access for individuals, from terminal emulation to full-time SLIP or PPP access. There are also a number of local access providers springing up to provide dial-in services, usually modem-based. Examples in the U.K. are Pavilion in Brighton and Aladdin in Southampton. These organizations are often resellers or agents for the larger national providers. The Appendix has a list of providers and what each offers.

Everything-But-the-Kitchen-Sink Providers

You've probably been shaking your head at all the background work you have to do just to find 'graphical, user-friendly' interfaces and an Internet provider. Well, be on the lookout for commercial products that combine full Internet access, an Internet provider and all the parts needed to make graphical client applications like Gopher, WAIS and Mosaic work. You, of course, supply the computer, modem, phone line and a standard kitchen sink.

Access for Teachers

More and more teachers are using computer networking in the classroom and for their own education and curriculum development. In Germany, the open German schools network offers Internet connections for schools and education organizations within a special program. If you are a teacher, and are interested in finding out more about access to the Internet, contact your district's computer coordinator or regional computing consortium to find out about your access options.

Community Networks

Community networks are springing up in cities all over the world. In addition to acting as online town halls, providing information about city government and local functions, they often offer email and perhaps full access to the Internet.

ALTERNATIVE PHONE ACCESS

The services listed above are great if you live in a big city with local dial-in access points. However, if you live in a rural area, you travel frequently, or your chosen system is an expensive long-distance call away, you should investigate other access methods. Some major options are mentioned below.

CompuServe Packet Network (CPN). CompuServe has hundreds of local-access phone numbers all over the world. You need not subscribe to CompuServe's information service to use CPN; you'll be billed for your use through your provider. If your chosen system allows access via CPN, use your modem to dial CompuServe's information service. If you're outside the United States, call +1 614-529-1340 to obtain access information using a voicemail system. While this service has been available for some time in the United States, Compuserve is only just starting to offer direct Internet access in the U.K. It plans to provide direct Internet connections using modem and network/ISDN connections. Initially this will be separate from the company's own CIS information service, but it is working on software to provide a unified front-end to both. For details about CompuServe's services in the U.K., call Freephone 0800-289-378.

Major City Dial-in Service. Some commercial providers offer dial-in 'ports' around the world, giving teleworkers and travellers local access in major cities. Access is usually made via the local phone system to a **terminal server** or **communications server** connected directly to the Internet. A terminal server is basically a 'bouncing off' point to the Internet, a computer that accepts con-

TeleOlympics

Kids around the world caught the Olympic spirit in 1993 as they participated in their own worldwide 'virtual' Olympics. The Academy One TeleOlympics, organized by NPTN (National Public Telecomputing Network), had more than 12,000 kids from nine countries competing in track and field events in their own school playgrounds. All of the events were held on the same day, after an opening ceremony that included a real-time chat hosted by the Cleveland FreeNet and an exchange of email among all the participating schools. Events included 50-, 400-, 800-, and 1600-metre runs (for different age groups), a long jump, and a tennis ball throw. Results were posted to the network, and the medalists in each event and age category shared an electronic victory platform. The teachers made the most of the accompanying educational opportunities, and the kids had fun!

Source: Linda Delzeit, Cleveland FreeNet.

nections and allows you to use the Internet to remotely login to other computers. Terminal servers have modems attached to them so that users can dial in and, from there, remotely login to any computer on the Internet, or initiate a SLIP/PPP connection to become directly connected.

Who does it: UUNet's TAC Access, EUnet's Traveller (major cities in Europe) and PSI's Global Dialling Service (GDS) offer local dial access in many cities.

Email and News Services

The wonder of the Internet is its many connecting points. If the methods above don't suit you for some reason, an outernet (or indirect) connection may. Some of the so-called indirect (email and news only) access paths are mentioned below; to discover other available options, just ask around. Keep in mind that new services, new software and new technology are being made available almost on a daily basis, creating new opportunities to connect directly or indirectly to the Internet.

Email Access Through Commercial Networks. If email is all you need, you have plenty of choices for an Internet connection. Most commercial online services, such as CompuServe and World, have an email gateway to the Internet. If you have an account on one of these systems, you can send and receive email to and from anyone on the Internet. Note, however, that these services may have a per-message charge for both inbound and outbound Internet email. These charges can add up, so be sure to inquire about prices and then shop around for the best deal.

Email Access Through the UUCP Worldwide Network. As mentioned in Chapter 2, **UUCP** stands for Unix-to-Unix Copy Protocol. Basically, it is used as a method for computers to talk to one another over phone lines. Versions of UUCP are available for VMS and DOS operating systems, as well as for Unix computers.

UUCP provides for file transfer between machines. The files that are transferred often contain commands to be executed on a remote system, including printing on a remote printer or sending email. The UUCP network consists of thousands of computers all over the world that have agreed to communicate with each other via the phone lines. Because of these agreements, it is possible to send email from one computer to another by specifying exactly which computers the email must travel through to get to its destination. This process is called **source routing**. Many UUCP nodes are starting to register in the Internet domain name system (by using MX records), so that they look as if they're directly connected to the Internet (when, in fact, they have an agreement with an Internet-connected computer to act as a 'post office', transferring email back and forth).

Although no central authority controls the UUCP network, there is a public registry that maintains information about computers whose administrators have volunteered (or remembered) to submit information. There are many email gateways between the UUCP network and the Internet, so it is easy to send and receive email. USENET news runs over the UUCP network, so that may also be available. However, UUCP does not allow for remote login or interactive file transfer.

Going the UUCP route is usually much less expensive than other kinds of access, but it may require more research and up-front work. The equipment is simple—your PC or Mac, a modem and a phone line. The software is usually free or very inexpensive. Your expenses may include some long-distance charges. The hard part may be finding someone to agree to connect you, either letting you dial him or her up for information or having him or her dial you up, or both. If you ask, you may find someone in a local computer user group who'll agree to let you send information back and forth from/to that person's computer.

Although some universities may offer similar services, user support and reliability is not always guaranteed, because people are usually connecting you out of kindness of heart. If you don't want to struggle to find someone to help you or spend time debugging problems, you should go with a commercial UUCP email provider, where hand holding and ongoing support are available. (Although, even with hand holding, it can still be hard to set up.)

Bulletin Board Systems

Many local BBSs also provide some type of mail access to the Internet. Through these systems, you may be able to exchange UUCP and USENET news, or you may be able to dialup the system (using terminal emulation) and access mail and news interactively on the BBS system.

Another network that's similar to UUCP is called FidoNet. FidoNet is primarily a hobbyist network whose principal applications are email and conferences (called 'echoes'). It consists of thousands of computers from all over the world, located mostly in the United States, Europe and Australia. Messages are transferred over dialup phone lines, just as in the UUCP network. The FidoNet technology is being used for many different networks; one of these is K12net, a primary and secondary education network that connects schools all over the United States. There are email gateways between most FidoNet networks and the Internet.

Find these systems by asking local computer gurus at user group meetings, or by consulting the NIXPUB list, which currently includes about 127 systems and their services worldwide.

Serious Games

Paralleling world events such as the 1990 Persian Gulf War, university-sponsored computer simulations play out real-world political dramas on the Internet stage. In early 1990 these computer simulations started in the Middle East politics classes at Melbourne University in Australia, connected with foreign relations classes at the University of Texas and Macquarie University, Australia.

Students were divided into teams of one to five people each (simulations generally had 40 to 150 teams), and each team assumed the role of a political leader in the Middle East or of another vitally interested country, such as the United States, the United Kingdom or France. One team played Yasser Arafat, while others played President Bush, the Prime Minister of Israel and the King of Saudi Arabia. The teams extensively researched their characters to help them play the assigned roles in a realistic fashion.

The controllers (usually the class lecturers) then set an initial scenario (typically the assassination of a prominent figure, an invasion or whatever seemed like fun), and the various teams responded, using email (and 'talk' where possible) to communicate with each other. Each team tried to advance its own goals and strategies, almost always at the expense of someone else.

The amount of mail flying back and forth was tremendous. Over the three-week simulation period, most teams

(Continued)

NIXPUB is an access list that's maintained by a volunteer and made available via anonymous FTP and dialup UUCP. (If you don't have direct Internet access, you may have to ask someone with Internet access to retrieve it for you.)

CONNECTING YOUR BUSINESS OR ORGANIZATION

The types of connections discussed above work well for individuals, but if you're interested in offering Internet access to every received 1,500 to 2,000 messages. Many general 'press release' type of missives went out to all players, supplemented by roughly 200 to 250 personal messages for each team. Aside from the mail, lots of the wheeling and dealing took place over 'talk' as well.

In a sense, the Internet became the stage on which these games of global diplomacy were played out. In the past, such simulations used letters that 'runners' carried back and forth. Using email and the Internet improves the concept tremendously. Most of the standard advantages of email apply, including speed, imperviousness to distance and the ability to login from almost anywhere, rather than being confined to one specific location.

During the 1990 Mideast computer simulation, the participants managed to *talk* Saddam Hussein into leaving Kuwait without going to war. Otherwise, events in the simulations tended to mirror real life to an astonishing degree. At one point, one of the 'characters' was killed off in a simulation, only to have his real-life counterpart die a few weeks later. Players threaten, cajole, bribe, fall in love, blackmail and occasionally shoot at each other. A lot of hot air is vented, and generally things don't change very much in the end, which is pretty much the way the Middle East is in reality.

The concept's popularity is growing; other simulations occurred in 1991, and probably are going on right now, as you read this, holding the mirror up to nature and playing out alternate scripts to reality on the Internet.

Source: Joseph D'Cruz, Research Assistant at Melbourne University, Australia.

computer in your business, school or organization, do not run out and buy a large number of modems and phone lines. What you need is a **full-time connection** from your LAN to the Internet. This is the 'traditional' way of connecting to the Internet— that is, interconnecting LANs and WANs. The steps down this path are many and involved, and unfortunately this book is not large enough to fill you in on all the details. Indeed, whole books are written on this subject (see below for information), but the major steps are outlined below.

The first thing you should do is to make sure you're set up locally. This means that the LAN (or LANs) that you're interconnecting needs to be running appropriate software. Remember that the Internet, for the most part, is based on TCP/IP protocols. All computers that are participating must be running the necessary TCP/IP communications programs and applications, or else they won't be able to 'talk' to any other computer on the Internet. TCP/IP implementations, both commercial and public domain, exist for almost every type of computer platform around. The Appendix will point you in the direction of some of these. You may need network consulting assistance to help you find the best solution for your particular situation.

Along with installing the software (if it's not already available on the computers), you're going to need to do some network administration. You will need your own IP network number (for example, 131.108), and a domain name (such as *a-company-in-the-uk.uk*). The IP network number will be one of several classes, depending on how big your network is in terms of number of networks and computers.

Once you obtain this network number, you can assign separate, unique IP addresses based on it to each computer on your network. Similarly, with a domain name, you can uniquely identify your organization and each of your computers by giving them a logical name within that domain. You can obtain these key identifiers from the InterNIC registration services operated by Network Solutions, Inc. (The InterNIC is explained in Chapter 5.) Some countries provide their own registration services; you can contact the InterNIC to find out whom to contact. You will need to complete several registration forms to apply for your IP number and domain name, and send them in to the InterNIC. These registration forms ask for certain information about your network, such as how many computers are connected to it, as well as administrative and technical contact information. If you have problems answering any of the questions on these registration forms, ask your network provider or the InterNIC for assistance. (Your network provider may provide registration services as part of the connection fee.) If you are located in Europe, the RIPE NCC in Amsterdam (see Chapter 5.) will provide the InterNIC services mentioned.

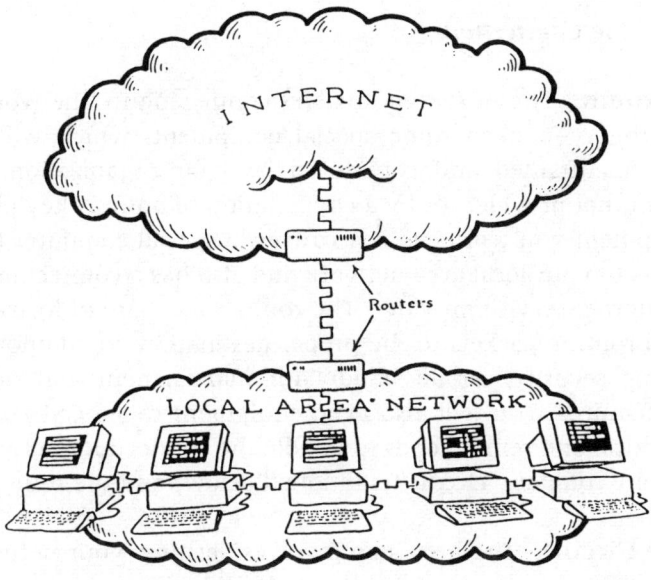

Your business or organization can connect its local area network to the Internet.

You'll also need to provide the names of two computers that will act as domain nameservers for host information on your network. A domain nameserver is a computer that has a database of information about the computers on your network. (The type of information in this database includes each computer's name, Internet address and computer type.) Two servers are required for reliability purposes, one designated primary, the other secondary. (Your organization can have more than one secondary nameserver.)

If one server (perhaps the primary one) is unavailable (probably for hardware reasons or because the network is down), the other will be able to answer queries for computer addresses and names. For this reason, it is recommended that one of these nameservers be located at some place other than your own network. Some network providers offer name service or will act as a domain 'dating service' for you, helping you to find an off-site secondary server.

Making the Connection

Equipment. The next step involves connecting to 'the world'. To do this, you need some special equipment, which will be owned, maintained and configured by your organization, by your Internet provider, or by a combination of both. A key piece of equipment you will need is a **router**, a special computer that connects to your local area network and also has a connection to your Internet service provider. The router takes care of forwarding and routing packets to the proper destination, in addition to providing security, circuit bandwidth management and other useful features. You will also need equipment called CSU/DSUs for the local and remote ends to handle the connections between the phone company circuit (mentioned below) and the routers.

Phone Circuit. The next step involves 'lashing' your network up to an Internet provider. This requires obtaining a wide-area network circuit from a PTO. Your Internet provider may do this for you or assist you with this. There are many different types of circuits and bandwidth choices. Your solution will depend on what's available in your area, what you can afford, and basically what makes sense for your situation.

A phone circuit can be dedicated (full-time) or dialup. A dialup 'dedicated' solution is similar to the individual SLIP/PPP service mentioned above; in fact, it probably uses SLIP or PPP. Using these protocols and the fastest modem around, it is possible to serve a couple of users on a local-area network. This is an on-demand type of connection, and the connection will have to be established each time before it can be used. If you have more than a couple of users and you're planning on running applications like Mosaic or CU-SeeMe, you will want a faster, dedicated circuit, running at least 64Kbps. **Bandwidth** refers to the speed of your connection, or how much data can be pumped through a circuit at a given time. The speed you need depends on the combination of users, applications and amount of money you have to spend. Your organization's connection may be running as slowly as 9.6Kbps or as fast as 34Mbps. See the 'Circuit Choices' box for a list of common circuits and typical speeds.

Internet connections are being made with just about any-thing these days, and some wacky engineers have even demon-strated transmitting TCP/IP over a string connecting two tin cans. A land-line circuit may not be the best solution for you, so be aware that there are other options, such as wireless, microwave or satellites.

The Internet Provider. You can buy the equipment and ob-tain a circuit, but you're not going anywhere unless you've got an Internet provider. In Europe, your choices in providers and service offerings are many. You can decide to subscribe either to a provider who is serving your country or to one serving the whole continent. If you decide to subscribe to an international provider in Europe, you have the choice between PIPEX, a com-pany offering services in the United Kingdom, Benelux and Ger-many, or EUnet, which offers its services in 34 countries on over 200 PoPs. Both providers are members of the CIX. In each Euro-pean country there is at least one national Internet provider of-fering services. To contact a provider near you, see the Appendix.

Circuit Choices

The chart below lists common circuits and typical speeds you can obtain from your PTO. Your circuit will begin at your site and terminate at an Internet provider's Point of Presence (PoP), the closest access point. Circuit costs are a recurring charge, billed monthly, and most commonly are based on speed and distance.

The type of services include both digital and analogue; the lower speeds are usually analogue, and the higher speeds are usually digital. Keep in mind that if you use an analogue service, you'll need a modem (explained at the beginning of this chapter) to convert the digital bits to analogue for the analogue circuit. If you're using a leased digital circuit, you'll need a CSU/DSU in-stead of a modem.

These choices may look complicated, but the good news is that a lot of the Internet service providers will act as a one-stop shop, recommending solutions and packaging the equipment that you need to make the connection. This assistance is not only

POINT-TO-POINT CIRCUITS

Type	Typical Speed	Notes/Explanation
DDS	up to 56Kbps	Dataphone Digital Service (U.S.)
T1	1.5Mbps	U.S.
FT1	128Kbps–768Kbps	Fractional T1 U.S.
T3	45Mbps	U.S.
E1	2.048Mbps	European equivalent of T1
E3	34Mbps	European equivalent of T3

PACKET-SWITCHED CIRCUITS

Type	Typical Speed	Notes/Explanation
X.25	9.6Kbps	CCITT Standard
Frame Relay	56Kbps–2Mbps	
SMDS	64Kbps–N*64Kbps	Switched Multimegabit Data Service
ATM	1Mbps–155Mbps	Asynchronous Transfer Mode

CIRCUIT-SWITCHED CIRCUITS

Type	Typical Speed	Notes/Explanation
POTS	standard modem speeds	Plain Old Telephone Service; analogue service
Switched 56	56Kbps	Digital Circuits
ISDN-BRI	2*64Kbps	Integrated Services Digital Network, Basic Rate Interface. ISDN-BRI comes as ISDN-2, offering 2 lines totalling 128Kbps. (Pedantically, it also uses an extra 16Kbps signalling channel, known as a D channel. ISDN-2 is sometimes described as offering '2Bs and a D channel'.
ISDN-PRI	1.544Mbps	ISDN Primary Rate Interface (PRI)

easier on you but it can also frequently save you money, not to mention time.

Costs of connecting your organization's network can vary widely (and wildly) from provider to provider. Obviously, providers who do much of the work for you will charge more in administrative and monthly or yearly fees. Start-up expenses include special equipment and administrative fees. CSU/DSUs can cost anywhere from 400 to 2,500 ECUs each, depending on the speed of your connection (you'll probably have to buy two of them, one for each end of the circuit). Router prices are falling, but you'll spend at least a couple of thousand ECUs for a good, low-end access router. After your network is connected, recurring costs include monthly administrative fees and circuit charges that run the gamut. Remember, though, that with most providers, the information traffic on your circuits isn't metered—you won't get a monthly long-distance bill on top of everything else for every file transfer an employee or student made from a computer in Norway, or for every email message sent to someone in Alaska. (However, this may not be the case for services in countries that charge by the packet instead of a flat rate.)

Other Connection Issues

Once you're connected, there are several issues that you may have to address constantly. One is technical support. If your network provider doesn't monitor, configure and upgrade your network's connection, then you will have to pay someone to do it (or do it yourself). Someone has to maintain the domain nameservers and establish an email system for your organization. Also, you may want to provide a Gopher or WWW server for your organization's public information; as has been mentioned throughout this book, quite a few businesses offer public information archives that include their catalogues, pricing information, tutorials, books and so on.

User Support. An Internet connection does your business or school no good if no one knows how to use it. Don't underestimate the amount of support and training you'll need; this is one of the most important components of an Internet connection, and unfortunately one of the first things to be ignored. You can get help from the millions of people, the thousands of email lists and the megabytes of documentation available on the Internet, but more than likely you'll need some hand holding for your users. Your network provider may assist in training, and Internet seminars are springing up all over the world. No matter what you do, everyone in your organization needs a copy of this book. :-)

Security. Finally, you or your network provider will be responsible for maintaining security on your network and computers. Security includes making sure you know which users on your network are accessing the Internet (by using proper authorization mechanisms, such as accounts and passwords on computers and terminal servers) and keeping intruders out of your systems. A router can be configured to allow outside access to all, some or none of your internal networks. There are quite a few businesses that use their routers as 'firewalls', allowing only a certain type of traffic to enter their internal networks.

FOR MORE INFORMATION

There are two very good books that provide information on buying and implementing a network connection:

- *Connecting to the Internet: An O'Reilly Buyer's Guide*, by Susan Estrada, published by O'Reilly & Associates
- *The Internet Connection: System Connectivity and Configuration*, by John S. Quarterman and Carl-Mitchell Smoot, published by Addison-Wesley

There it is. Whether you're a retiree or a recluse, whether you have a gigabit-per-second connection or a tin can and a string, *you* can be a part of the Internet. And once you're connected, you can behold the fabulous sites in Cyberspace. Some good advice: keep trying when you're frustrated, keep looking when you can't find it, and keep your sense of humour. You probably couldn't ride a bicycle perfectly the first time you tried either!

The world of the Internet is immense, and so, too, is the body of information about it! The biggest task in writing this book was sorting out what you, the new Internet user, needed to know most to get started. The listing of resources that follows in the Appendix is the most fitting conclusion to this book, because it gives you places to look for even more information. Hopefully, you're excited about further adventures. You've now been given the map, the rules of the road and the keys to the kingdom. Enjoy your Internet journey!

Appendix

This appendix contains pointers to popular resources available on the Internet. The Uniform Resource Locators (URL) system (explained in Chapter 4) was used to describe these resources. Here are some quick examples of how you would use each type of URL:

URL	Commands
telnet://flounder.rutgers.edu:5150	**telnet flounder.rutgers.edu 5150**
ftp://quartz.rutgers.edu/ *pub/baseball/jazz*	**ftp quartz.rutgers.edu** **cd pub/baseball** **get jazz**
gopher://sunsite.unc.edu	**gopher sunsite.unc.edu**
http://galaxy.einet.net/galaxy.html	Use entire URL in your web browser. For example, Choose *Open URL* in Mosaic and type in the URL.

N.B.: Some URLs and commands are split between lines because of their length.

Many of the FTP URLs specify directories of files, not filenames. In this appendix, FTP URLs that end with a "/" are directories. In those cases you'll need to type **dir** to get a listing of files that are available. Remember to read any instructions shown on the screen and check for "readme" files in each directory that will provide more clues.

Remember, the Internet is a moving target. Computer names change. Sites disappear. What works today may not work tomorrow. You're welcome to send comments and corrections to: *tracy@editorial.com*

GETTING CONNECTED

International and U.S. Service Providers

Central Offices

British Telecom
  BT*Net*
  Tel: +44-1442-295828
  Fax: +44-1442-295858
  Email: *internet@bt.net*
  http://www.bt.net/

EUnet Ltd (Europe)
  Kruislaan 409
  1098 SJ, Amsterdam
  The Netherlands
  Tel: +31-20-592-5109
  Fax: +31-20-592-5163
  Email: *info@eu.net*
  ftp://ftp.edu.net/pub/info;
  gopher://gopher.EU.net;
  http://www.EU.net

PIPEX
  Public IP Exchange Ltd
  216 Science Park
  Milton Road
  Cambridge CB4 4WA
  U.K.
  Tel: +44-1223-250120
  Fax: +44 1223-250121
  Email: *pipex@pipex.net*
  or *pipex-info-request@pipex.net*
  ftp://ftp.pipex.net;
  http://www.worldserver.pipex.net

Algeria
EUnet Algeria
  ALUUG
  Mohan Tafat
  Lotissement Benhaddadi
  Lot No 58 Villa No 27
  Cheraga Tipasa
  Algeria
  Tel: +213-236-97-91
  Fax: +213-236-97-62
  Email: *mohant@cashab.uucp*

Austria
EUnet EDV Dienstleistungs GmbH
  Thurngasse 8/16
  A-1090 Vienna
  Austria
  Tel: +43-1-317-4969
  Fax: +43-1-310-6926
  Email: *office@eunet.co.at*
  ftp://ftp.eunet.co.at:~ftp/pub/
    EUnet/EUnet-Austria
  http://www.eunet.co.at/
PING EDV
  Dienstleistungsges.m.b.H.
  Thurngasse 8/3
  A-1090 Vienna
  Austria
  Tel: +43-222-319-4336
  Fax: +43-222-310-6927
  Email: *office@ping.at*

Belgium
EUnet Belgium NV/SA
  Stapelhuisstraat 13
  B-3000 Leuven
  Belgium
  Tel: +32-16-23-60-99
  Fax: +32-16-23-20-79
  Email: *info@Belgium.EU.net*
PIPEX in Belgium
  INNET
  Postelarenweg 2/3
  B-2400 Mol
  Belgium
  Tel: +32-14-31-99-37
  Fax: +32-14-31-90-11
  Email: *luc@inbe.net*

Bulgaria
EUnet Bulgaria
  Digital Systems
  Neofit Bozveli 6
  BG-9000 Varna
  Bulgaria
  Tel: +359-52-259135
  Fax: +359-52-234540
  Email: *info@Bulgaria.EU.net*

Czech Republic
EUnet Czechia
  COnet s.r.o.
  Technicka 5
  166 28 Prague 6
  Czech Republic
  Tel: +42-2-2435-3242
  Fax: +42-2-2431-0646
  Email: *info@EUnet.cz*
  http://www.eunet.cz/

Denmark
EUnet Denmark
  Fruebjergvej 3
  DK-2100 Copenhagen
  Denmark
  Tel: +45-39-17-99-00
  Fax: +45-39-17-98-97
  Email: *info@dknet.dk*

NorduNet/DEnet
UNI-C
DT4, Building 305
DK-2800 Lyngby
Denmark
Tel: +45-42-88-39-99 ext. 2018
Fax: +45-45-93-02-20
Email: *Steen.Linden@uni-c.dk*

Egypt
EUnet in Egypt
Egyptian National STI Network
101 Kasr El-Aini st, 12 floor
Cairo 11516
Egypt
Tel: +20-2-355-7253
Fax: +20-2-354-7807
Email: *ow@estinet.uucp*
PIPEX in Egypt
Neil Ashworth
BankNet Kft
Naphegy ter 8
1016 Budapest
Hungary
Tel: +36-1-202-7083
Fax: +36-1-175-8364

Estonia
EE-NIC
Institute of Chemical Physics
and Biophysics
10 Ravala Blvd.
EE0001 Tallin
Estonia
Tel: +372-2-441304
Fax: +372-2-440640
Email: *jack@anubis.kbfi.ee*
EUnet/Relcom
ul. Raspletina, 4, korp. 1
123060 Moscow
Russia
Tel: +7-95-943-4735
Fax: +7-95-198-9510
Email: *postmaster@USSR.EU.net*

Finland
Datanet
Telecom Finland
Data Services
P.O. Box 228
FIN-33101 Tampere
Finland
Tel: +358-31-243-2242 or
+358-400-625-470
Fax: +358-243-2211
Email: *son@tele.fi*
EUnet Finland
Punavuorenkatu 1
FIN-00120 Helsinki
Finland
Tel: +358-400-2060 or
+358-49-425-722
Fax: +358-622-2626
Email: *helpdesk@eunet.fi*
http://www.eunet.fi/
NorduNet/FUNET
P.O. Box 405
FIN-02101 Espoo
Finland
Tel: +358-457-2704
Fax: +358-457-2302
Email: *info@funet.fi*
http://www.eunet.fi/

France
EUnet in France
Fnet
52, avenue de la Grande Armie
75017 Paris
France
Tel: +33-1-53-81-60-99
Fax: +33-1-45-74-52-79
Email: *contact@fnet.fr*
PIPEX in France
OLIANE—Groupe Apysoft
35 boulevard de la Liberation
94300 Vincennes
France
Tel: +33-1-43-28-32-32
Fax: +33-1-43-28-46-21
Email: *support@oleane.net*
http://www.oleane.net/

Germany

EUnet Deutschland GmbH
Emil-Figge-Str. 80
D-44227 Dortmund
Germany
Tel: +49-231-972-00
Fax: +49-231-972-1111
Email: *info@Germany.EU.net*
http://www.Germany.EU.net/
NTG/XLink
Vincent-Prienitz-Str.3
D-76131 Karlsruhe
Germany
Tel: +49-721-9652-0
Fax:+49-721-9652-210
Email: *info@xlink.net*
PIPEX in Germany
Commercial Link Systems
Sternstr. 2
D-24116 Kiel
Germany
Tel: +49-431-9790161
Fax: +49-431-978126
Email: *Heinen@cls.net*
http://www.cls.net/

Great Britain

SoNet
Aladdin Ltd
5 Alexandria Road
Hedge End
Southampton
U.K.
Tel: +44-1489-782221
Fax: +44-1489-782382
Email: *info@aladdin.co.uk*
ftp://ftp.aladdin.co.uk/
http://www.aladdin.co.uk/
ALMAC
ALMAC BBS Ltd
141 Bo'ness Road
Grangemouth
Stirlingshire FK3 9BS
Scotland
U.K.
Tel: +44-1324-666336
Fax: +44-1324-665155
Email: *postmaster@almac.co.uk*

Atlas
Atlas Internet
Tel: +44-171-312-0400
Fax: +44-171-636-9219
Email: *info@atlas.co.uk*
http://www.atlas.co.uk/
BBC Networking Club
P.O. Box 7
Broadcasting Support Services
London W3 6XY
U.K.
Tel: +44-181-576-7799
Fax: +44-181-576-1130
Email: *info@bbcnc.org.uk*
BT*Net*
Tel: +44-1442-295828
Fax: +44-1442-295858
Email: *internet@bt.net*
http://www.bt.net/
CityScape
CityScape Internet Services Ltd
9 Covent Garden
Cambridge CB1 2HR
U.K.
Tel: +44-1223-566950
Fax: +44-1223-566951
Email: *sales@cityscape.co.uk*
http://www.cityscape.co.uk
CIX
No. 2 The Sanctuary
Oakhill Grove
Surbiton KT6 6DU
U.K.
Tel: +44-181-390-8446
Fax: +44-181-390-6561
Email:
cixadmin@cix.compulink.co.uk
CompuServe
Tel: (in U.K.) 0800-289378
http://www.compuserve.com/

CONNECT
PC User Group
P.O. Box 360
84-88 Pinner Road
Harrow HA1 4LQ
U.K.
Tel: +44-181-863-1191
Fax: +44-181-863-6095
Email: *info@ibmpcug.co.uk*
http://www.ibmpcug.co.uk
DELPHI
Delphi Internet Ltd
The Elephant House
Hawley Crescent
London NW1 8NP
U.K.
Tel: +44-171-757-7080
Fax: +44-171-757-7160
Email: *ukservice@delphi.com*
Demon
Demon Internet Ltd
Gateway House
322 Regents Park Road
Finchley
London N31QQ
U.K.
Tel: +44-181371-1234 (London)
+44-131-552-0344 (Edinburgh)
Fax: +44-181-371-1150
Email: *internet@demon.net*
http://www,demon.co.uk/
ftp://ftp.demon.co.uk/
usenet: Demon.announce
The Direct Connection - TDC
P.O. Box 931
London SE18 3PW
U.K.
Tel: +44-181-317-0100
Fax: +44-181-317-3886
Email: *helpdesk@dircon.co.uk*

Dungeon
Dungeon Network Systems
3 Hazel Close
Mildenhall
Suffolk IP28 7HU
U.K.
Tel: +44-1638-711550
Fax: +44-1638-718623
Email: *info@dungeon.com*
ftp://ftp/dungeon.com/
http://www.dungeon.com/
Easynet
Easynet Ltd
39 Whitfield Street
London W1P 5RE
U.K.
Tel: +44-171-209-0990
Fax: +44-171-209-1891
Email: *info@easynet.co.uk*
ftp://ftp.easynet.co.uk/
http://www.easynet.co.uk/
EUnet
EUnet GB Ltd
Wilson House
John Wilson Business Park
Whitstable
Kent CT5 3QY
U.K.
Tel: +44-1227-266466
Fax: +44-1227-266477
Email: *sales@Britain.EU.net*
http://www.Britain.EU.net/
ExNet
ExNet Systems Ltd
37 Honley Road
Catford
London SE6 2HY
U.K.
Tel: +44-181-244-0077
Fax: +44-181-244-0078
Email: *helpex@exnet.com*

GreenNet
4th Floor
393-395 City Road
London EC1V 1NE
U.K.
Tel: +44-171-713-1941
Fax: +44-171-833-1169
Email: *support@gn.apc.org*
On-line
642a Leabridge Road
London E10 6AP
U.K.
Tel: +44-181-558-6114
Fax: +44-181-558-3914
Email: *mike@mail.on-line.co.uk*
Luna
Lunatech Research Ltd
FREEPOST (RG3101)
Wokingham
Berkshire RG11 1BR
U.K.
Tel: +44-1734-791900
Email: *info@luna.co.uk*
ftp://ftp.luna.co.uk/
http://www.luna.co.uk/
Pavilion
Pavilion Internet plc
Aqua House
24 Old Steine
Brighton
East Sussex BN1 1E
U.K.
Tel: +44-1273-607072
Fax: +44-1273-607073
Email: *info@pavilion.co.uk*
http://www/pavilion.co.uk/
PIPEX
Public IP Exchange Ltd
216 Science Park
Milton Road
Cambridge CB4 4WA
U.K.
Tel: +44-1223-250120
Fax: +44-1223-250121
Email: *pipex@pipex.net*
ftp://ftp.pipex.net/
http://www.worldserver.pipex.net/

RedNet onLine
RedNet Ltd
5 Clivedon Office Village
Lancaster Road
High Wickham
Buckinghamshire HP12 3YZ
U.K.
Tel: +44-1494-513333
Fax: +44-1494-143374
Email: *info@rednet.co.uk*
http://www.rednet.co.uk/
Sound & Vision
Sound & Vision BBS
24 Oatlands Chase
Weybridge
Surrey KT13 9RY
U.K.
Tel: +44-1932-253131
Fax: +44-1932-253131
Email: *info@span.com*
Specialix
Specialix Ltd
3 Wintersells Road
Byfleet
Surrey KT14 7LF
U.K.
Tel: +44-1932-354254
Fax: +44-1932-352781
Email: *postmaster@specialix.co.uk*
ftp://ftp.specialix.co.uk/public/
U-Net
U-Net Ltd
Unit G9
Warrington Business Park
Long Lane
Warrington WA2 8TX
U.K.
Tel: +44-1925-633144
Fax: +44-1925-850420
Email: *hi@u-net.com*
http://www.u-net.com/

WinNet
  PC User Group
  P.O. Box 360
  84-88 Pinner Road
  Harrow HA1 4LQ
  U.K.
  Tel: +44-181-863-1191
  Fax: +44-181-863-6095
  Email: *request@win-uk.net*
  ftp://ftp.ibmpcug.co.uk/
  http://www.ibmpcug.co.uk/
Zynet
  Zynet Ltd
  Minerva House
  Baring Crescent
  Exeter
  Devon EX1 1TL
  U.K.
  Tel: +44-1392-426160
  Fax: +44-1392-421762
  Email: *zynet@zynet.net*
  http://www.zynet.co.uk/

Greece

EUnet in Greece
  Foundation of Research and
    Technology Hellas
  FORTHnet/EUnetGR
  36 Daidalou str.
  P.O. Box 1385
  Heraklion
  Crete
  Greece 71110
  Tel: +30-81-221171 or
    +30-81-229368
  Fax: +30-81-229342 or
    +30-81-229343
  Email: *info@Greece.EU.net*

Hungary

EUnet Hungary—MTA SZTAKI
  P.O. Box 63
  1518 Budapest
  Hungary
  Tel: +361-269-8281
  Fax: +361-269-8288
  Email: *info@Hungary.EU.net*
  http://www.hungary.EU.net/

PIPEX in Hungary
  Molnar Erzsebet
  ODIN Kft.
  Lonyai utca 43. IV. 48
  1097 Budapest
  Hungary
  Tel: +36-1-218-1901
  Fax: +36-1-116-8896
  Email: *Mary@Odin.net*

Iceland

NORDUnet/SURIS and EUnet
  University of Iceland
  Taeknigardi
  Dunhagi 5, 107 Reykjavík
  Iceland
  Tel: +354-1-694747
  Fax: +354-1-28801
  Email: *marius@rhi.hi.is*
  http://www.isnet.is/

Ireland

EUnet in Ireland
  IEunet Ltd
  Innovation Centre
  Trinity College
  Dublin 2
  Ireland
  Tel: +353-1-679-0832
  Fax: +353-1-679-8039
  Email: *info@Ireland.EU.net*
  http://www.ieunet.ie/

PIPEX in Ireland
  International Trade Centre
    Belfast
  Interpoint
  20-24 York Street
  Belfast Northern BT15 1AQ
  Northern Ireland
  Tel: +44-232-231622 or
    +44-232-231715
  Email: *bradley@gpl.com*

Italy
EUnet in Italy
  IUnet Italy
  Viale Monza, 253
  I-20126 Milan
  Italy
  Tel: +39-2-27002528
  Fax: +39-2-27001322
  Email: *info@Italy.EU.net*
  http://www.italy.eu.net/
GARR-NIS
  Giuliana Tamorri
  c/o CNUCE—Instituto del CNR
  via S. Maria, 36
  56126 Pisa
  Italy
  Tel: NIS +39 50 593360
  Fax: +39 50 904052
  Telex: 500371—CNUCE
  Email: *tamorri@nis.gar*
  telnet://wais.nis.garr.it (login
    wais);=20
  ftp://ftp.nis.garr.it/garr/doc
  gopher://gopher.nis.garr.it
PIPEX in Italy
  Joy Marino
  ITnet S.p.A.
  Via Greto di Cornigliano 6
  I-16152 Genoa
  Italy
  Tel: +39-10-353-2997
  Fax: +39-10-56-2628

Lithuania
EUnet/RELCOM
  ul. Raspletina, 4, korp. 1
  123060 Moscow
  Russia
  Tel: +7-95-943-4735
  Fax: +7-95-198-9510
  Email: *postmaster@USSR.EU.net*

Luxemburg
EUnet Luxemburg/CRP-CU
  162a, av. de la Faiencerie
  L-1511 Luxemburg
  Tel: +352-47-02-61-361
  Fax: +352-47-02-64
  Email: *info@Luxemburg.EU.net*

Morocco
EUnet in Morocco
  Ecole Mohammadia
    d'Ingenieurs
  Amine Mounir Alaoui
  BP 765 Rabat-Agdal
  Morocco
  Tel: +212-7-776563
  Fax: +212-7-778853
  Email: *amine@emi.uucp*

Netherlands
EUnet in the Netherlands
  NLnet
  Kruislaan 419
  1098 VA Amsterdam
  Netherlands
  Tel: +31-20-6639366
  Fax: +31-20-6655311
  Email: *info@NL.net*
  http://www.nl.net/
SURFnet (Netherlands)
  Cluetinckborch Office
    (3rd floor)
  Godebaldkwartier 24
  Hoog Catharijne
  Utrecht
  The Netherlands
  Tel: +31-30-310-290
  Email: *info@surfnet.nl*
  ftp://ftp.nic.surfnet.nl
  gopher://gopher.nic.surfnet.nl

Norway
DAXNET
  Scandinavian Airlines Data
  Fornebuveien 40
  N-1330 Oslo Lufthavn
  Norway
  Tel: +47-67-59-65-14
  Fax: +47-67-59-77-77
  Email: *tore@nic.dax.net*

EUnet Norway
Forskningsparken
Gaustadallen 21
N-0371 Oslo
Norway
Tel: +47-22-95-83-27
Fax: +47-22-60-44-27
Email: *info@norway.eu.net*
http://www.eunet.no/
NORDUnet/UNINETT
Postboks 6883 Elgeseter
N-7002 Trondheim
Norway
Tel: +47-72-59-29-91
Fax: +47-73-59-64-50
Email: *sekreteriat@uninett.no*
http://www.uninett.no/
TelePost Communication AS
P.O. Box 335, Skoyen
N-0212 Oslo
Norway
Tel: +47-22-73-37-00
Fax: +47-22-73-37-10
Email:
Gunn.Skogseth@telepost.telemax.no

Poland
EUnet in Poland
PL-net Ltd
Al. Jerozolimskie 65/79,
Room 16.07
PL-00-697 Warsaw
Poland
Tel: +48-2-630-63-02
Fax: +48-2-630-63-05
Email: *info@Poland.EU.net*
NASK Research and Academic
Networks in Poland
Bartycka 18
PL-00-927 Warsaw
Poland
Tel: +48-22-26-80-00
Fax: +48-22-26-80-00
Email: *irek@nask.org.pl*

Portugal
EUnet in Portugal
EUnet Portugal
PUUG/Grupo Portugues de
Utlizadores do Sistema UNIX
c/o UNINOVA
Quinta da Torre
2825 Monte da Caparica
Portugal
Tel: +351-1-395-06-42
Fax: +351-1-397-18-76
Email: *info@Portugal.EU.net*
PIPEX in Portugal
Henrique J. Carreiro
Telepac Servicos de
Telecomunicacoes SA
Rue Dr Antonio Loureiro
Borges 1
1495 Lisbon
Portugal
Tel: +351-10-353-2997
Fax: +351-10-56-2628

Romania
EUnet Romania SRL
Liviu Ionescu
Bd. Unirii 20, Bl. 5C, Ap. 14
Bucharest
Romania
Tel: +40-1-312-6886
Fax: +40-1-312-6668
Email: *info@Romania.EU.net*
http://www.EU.net/EUnet/

Russia and former Soviet Union
EUnet/Relcom
ul. Raspletina, 4, korp. 1
123060 Moscow
Russia
Tel: +7-95-943-4735
Fax: +7-95-198-9510
Email: *postmaster@USSR.EU.net*

Slovakia

EUnet in Slovakia
  EUnet Slovakia
  c/o Computing Centre of MFF
  U.K.
  Mlynska dolina
  842 15 Bratislava
  Slovak Republic
  Tel: +42-7-725-306
  Fax: +42-7-728-462
  Email: *info@Slovakia.EU.net*
  http://www.eunet.sk/

Slovenia

EUnet in Slovenia
  EUnet SI
  NIL Ltd
  Litijska 51
  61000 Ljubljana
  Slovenia
  Tel: +386-61-140-51-83
  Fax: +386-61-140-53-81
  Email: *info@eunet.si*
  http://www.eunet.si/
PIPEX in Slovenia
  Alojz Zadravec
  Quantum
  Stegne 25
  61000 Ljubljana
  Slovenia
  Tel: +386-61-159-17-40
  Fax: +386-61-159-25-66
  Email: *root@stella.quantum.si*

Spain

EUnet in Spain
  Goya Servicios Telematicos
  Clara del Rey 8, 1-7
  E-28002 Madrid
  Spain
  Tel: +34-1-413-48-56
  Fax: +34-1-413-49-01
  Email: *info@eunet.es*
  http://www.eunet.es/

Sweden

EUnet in Sweden: see Norway
NorduNet/SUNET
  UMDAC
  S-901 87 Umeå
  Sweden
  Tel: +46-90-16-56-45
  Fax: +46-90-16-67-62
  Email:
  Hans.Wallberg@umdac.umu.se
Tele2/SWIPnet AB
  Box 6048
  S-164 06 Kista
  Sweden
  Tel: +46-8-632-40-58
  Fax: +46-8-632-42-00
  Email: *info@swip.net*
Telia/TIPnet
  Kaserntorget 11
  S-403 35 Göteborg
  Sweden
  Tel: +46-31-770-8485
  Fax: +46-31-112-800
  Email: *info@tip.net*
Transpac Scandanavia AB
  Strandbergsgatan 61
  S-112 89 Stockholm
  Sweden
  Tel: +46-8-13-60-38
  Fax: +46-8-656-7320
  Email: *info@transpac.se*

Switzerland

EUnet in Switzerland
  CHUUG/EUnet
  Zweierstrasse 35
  8004 Zurich
  Switzerland
  Tel: +41-1-291-45-80
  Fax: +41-1-291-46-42
  Email: *info@Switzerland.EU.net*
  http://www.eunet.ch/

Ping GmbH
    Albis Strasse 48
    8932 Mettmenstetten
    Switzerland
    Tel: +41-1-776-80-16
    Fax: +41-1-776-80-19
    Email: *postmaster@ping.ch*

Tunisia
EUnet in Tunisia
    IRSIT / EUnet Tunisia
    BP 212, 2 Rue Ibn Nadime
    1082 Cite Mahrajane
    Tunis
    Tunisia
    Tel: +216-1-787-757 or
    +216-1-289-853
    Fax: +216-1-787-827
    Email: *mondher@Tunisia.EU.net*

Ukraine
EUnet in Ukraine
    EUnet/Relcom
    ul. Raspletina, 4, korp. 1
    123060 Moscow
    Russia
    Tel: +7-95-943-4735
    Fax: +7-95-198-9510
    Email: *postmaster@USSR.EU.net*

Note: Information on United Kingdom networks is posted regularly to the USENET newsgroup *uk.nets* and is archived at *ftp://ftp.demon.co.uk/pub/doc*. Also, see Susan Estrada's *DLIST* for a comprehensive listing of international networks. (See the 'Lists of Providers' section in this appendix for instructions on getting the *DLIST*.)

Travellers' Connection (Europe)

EUNet Traveller. This service, provided by EUNet, enables business travellers to access their computer at home from most major European cities. For more information, send email to *traveller@EU.net* or try one of the following: *telnet://Traveller.EU.net* (login *new*); *ftp://ftp.EU.net/EUnet/Traveller*; *gopher://gopher.EU.net*; *http://www.EU.net/Traveller*

Public Access Systems

Most of the following information and provider listings were obtained from *Public Dialup Internet Access List (PDIAL)*, compiled by Peter Kaminski and used with permission. Send additions and corrections to *kaminski@netcom.com*. See the 'Lists of Providers' section in this appendix for information on obtaining the latest online list.

Many of these systems run the Unix operating system. All provide dialup terminal emulation. Ask about UUCP, SLIP or PPP access. Typical services include USENET, IRC, BBS and games. Most of these systems offer local area dialup access. (See the 'Dialup' field for the local modem number and a new user login name, if one exists.) A summary of services by area code is provided. (See 'Local Dialup Access Providers Summary'.)

A good number of systems also provide access for users outside their local areas. (See the 'Wide Area Access Providers Summary' section.) Wide-area access is usually offered via a public data network (PDN) and is specified in the 'Long Distance' field. Please note that prices, access and services for each of these may change; use the prices listed for guidance only and not as the definitive pricing structure for each organization.

Lists of Providers

Dedicated Line Internet Providers (DLIST). Compiled by Susan Estrada, made freely available by O'Reilly and Associates. Send email to *dlist@ora.com* to get a copy.

Internet Access Providers. Compiled by SRI International Network Information Systems Center (NISC). *ftp://nic.merit.edu/internet/ providers; gopher://nic.merit.edu:7043/00/internet/providers*. Also available in hard-copy form in the book *Internet: Getting Started*, published by Prentice Hall.

Network Service Providers Around the World. Compiled by Barry Raveendran Greene. Archived at *ftp://nic.merit.edu/internet/providers/ providers.around.the.world; gopher://nic.merit.edu:7043/1/internet- providers*. Or send email to *p00128@psilink.com* for more information.

Open Access UNIX Sites: NIXPUb List. Compiled by Paul Eschallier. Posted regularly to the USENET groups *comp.misc, comp.bbs.misc,* and *alt.bbs*. Archived at *ftp://ftp.cs.widener.edu/pub*. Also available through email from *archive-server@cs.widener.edu*; include the message *send nixpub long* in the body.

Public Dialup Internet Access List (PDIAL). Compiled and maintained by Peter Kaminski. Posted regularly to USENET Newsgroups *alt.internet.access.wanted, alt.bbs.lists,* and *ba.internet*. Archived at *ftp:// gvl.unisys.com/pub/pubnet/pdial; gopher://gopher-chem.ucdavis.edu/1m/ Index/PDIAL-aw*. Or send a message to *info-deli-server@netcom.com* with the subject *Send PDIAL*.

STARTING YOUR INTERNET TOUR
Selected Resources for Navigating the Internet

Lists and Guides for Online Library Catalogs, BBSs, and Databases

Accessing On-line Bibliography Databases, maintained by Billy Barron and Marie-Christine Mahe. Directory of online library catalogs and databases. *ftp://ftp.utdallas.edu/pub/staff/billy/libguide; gopher://squirrel1. utdallas.edu* (Choose *Libraries*.)

AT&T InterNIC Directory and Database Services. Includes white pages, yellow pages, and access to a large number of databases and Internet documents. *gopher://gopher.internic.net; ftp://ds.internic.net/8dirofdirs*

The British Library has a gopher site, available directly at: *gopher:// portico.bl.uk*

Campus-Wide Information Systems (CWIS), compiled by Judy Hallman (*Judy_Hallman@unc.edu*). *ftp://sunsite.unc.edu/pub/docs/about-the-net/ cwis/cwis-l*

Project Gutenberg provides a rich source of classic literature and other texts in electronic format. Access via *http://www.info.cern.ch/roeber/ Misc/Gutenberg.html   gopher://gopher.msen.com:70/11/stuff/gutenberg*
Internet-Accessible Library Catalogs & Databases, by Art St. George and Ron Larsen. Listing of over 100 online library catalogs and databases. *ftp://ariel.unm.edu/library/internet.library*
The Internet Yellow Pages, by Harley Hahn and Rick Stout. Osborne McGraw-Hill, 1994.
SURAnet Guide to Selected Internet Resources, by the SURAnet Network Information Center. This is a monthly updated guide to new and unique Internet resources. *ftp://ftp.sura.net/pub/nic/how.to.get.SURAnet. guide* or call (301) 982-4600 to order.
Special Internet Connections, compiled by Scott Yanoff (*yanoff@ csd4.csd.uwm.edu*) This is a list of Internet services organized by subject. *ftp://cds4.csd.uwm.edu/pub/inet.services.txt*

Network Information Centres

Asia-Pacific: Asia Pacifica Network Information Center (APNIC), c/o Computer Center, University of Tokyo 2-11-16; Yayoi, Bunkyo-ku, Tokyo 113 Japan Phone: 81-3-3580-3781, 81-3-3580-3784 Fax: 81-3-3580-3782 Email: *admin@apnic.net* Information: *gopher:// apnic.net*

Australia: Australian Academic and Research Network (AARNET), GPO Box 1142, Canberra ACT 2601 Australia Phone: 61-6-249-3385 Fax: 61-6-249-1369 Email: *aarnet@aarnet.edu.au* Information: *gopher://plaza.aarnet.edu.au; http://aarnet.edu.au*

Canada: The CA&NET Network Operations Centre (NA-NOC), University of Toronto, 255 Huron St., Room 367, Toronto, Ontario M5S 1A1, Canada Phone: (416) 978-4621 Email: *noc@canet.ca*

Europe: RIPE Network Coordination Centre (RIPE-NCC), Kruislaan 409, NL-1098 SJ Amsterdam, The Netherlands Phone: 31-20-592-5065, Fax: 31-20-592-5090 Email: *ncc@RIPE.NET*

United States: InterNIC Information Services Phone: (619) 455-4600 Email: *info@internic.net* Information: *telnet://gopher.internic.net* (login **gopher**); *gopher://gopher.internic.net*

Information Services: General Atomics, P.O. Box 85608, San Diego, CA 92186-9784 Phone: (619) 455-4600 Fax: (619) 455-4640 Email: *info@is.internic.net* Information: *telnet://is.internic.net* (login **gopher**); *ftp\gopher://is.internic.net/; http://www.internic.net*

Directory and Database Services: AT&T Phone: (908) 668-6587 Fax: (908) 668-3763 Email: *admin@ds.internic.net*
Information: *ftp\gopher://ds.internic.net; http://www.internic.net*

Registration Services: Network Solutions Inc. (NSI), Attn: InterNIC Registration Services, 505 Huntmar Park Dr., Herndon, VA 22070 Phone: (703) 742-4777 Email: *admin@rs.internic.net*
Information: *telnet\ftp\gopher://rs.internic.net; http://www.internic.net*

COMMERCIAL NETWORKING

Organizations and Consortiums

CommerceNet
  459 Hamilton Avenue
  Palo Alto, CA 94301
  U.S.A.
  Tel: (415) 617-8790
  Fax: (415) 617-1516
  Email: *info@commerce.net*
  ftp://ftp.commerce.net
  http://www.commerce.net
The Commercial Internet Exchange (CIX) Association
  Trade Association of Commercial Internet Providers
  3110 Fairview Park Dr, Suite 590
  Falls Church, VA 22042
  U.S.A.
  Tel: (303) 482-2150 FAX: (303) 482-2884 Email: *info@cix.org*
  ftp://ftp.cix.org Gopher://cix.org
Enterprise Networking
  Enterprise Integration Networking (EINet)
  Microelectronics and Computer Technology Corporation (MCC)
  3500 West Balcones Center Drive
  Austin, TX 78759
  U.S.A.
  Tel: (512) 338-3569 Fax: (512) 338-3897
  Email: *info@einet.net*
  Email server: *einet-info@einet.net ftp://ftp.einet.net*
  http://galaxy.einet.net/EINet
The London Internet Neutral eXchange (LINX)
  The UK neutral exchange for Internet Services Providers.
  Tel: +44 171-512-0550
  http://www.cix.org

Commercial Information Services

ClariNet Communications Corporation
  4880 Stevens Creek Blvd., Suite 206
  San Jose, CA 95129
  U.S.A.
  Tel: (408) 296-0366
  Fax: (408) 296-1668
  Email: *info@clarinet.com*
  ftp://ftp.clarinet.com/clarinetinfo/maininfo
Dow Jones News/Retrieval
  Dow Jones Information Services
  Tel (customer service): (609) 452-1511

Knight-Ridder Information, Inc.
 Tel: (415) 858-3810
 Fax: (415) 858-7069
Lexis-Nexis, Mead Data Central, Inc.
 Tel: Ohio: (513) 865-6800 (ask for International Dept.)
 London: +44-71-488-9187
 Zurich: +41-1-361-6608
 Canada: (416) 361-6323

Books and Periodicals

Cronin, Mary (1994). *Doing Business on the Internet: How the Electronic Highway Is Transforming American Companies.* New York: Van Nostrand Reinhold.

Internet Business Journal. Subscriptions $149/12 issues (year). Write to: Strangelove Press, 60 Springfield Road, Suite 1, Ottawa, Ontario, Canada, K1M 1C7. For more information, see *ftp://nstn.ns.ca/pub/ internet-business-journal; gopher://gopher.fonorola.net/11/.*

Internet Business Report. Subscription information available from CMP Publications, Inc., 600 Community Dr., Manhasset, NY 10030, U.S.A.

Schofield, Sue. *The UK Internet Book.* Addison-Wesley. ISBN 0-201-42766-4. 1994

Winder, Davey. *All You Need to Know about The Internet.* Future Publishing. 1994

.net Magazine. Monthly UK periodical about all things Internet. *http:// www.futurenet.co.uk/net.html/* Email: *netmag@futurenet.co.uk*

Hypercard Tours

A Cruise of the Internet. Developed by Steve Burdick in collaboration with Laura Kelleher and Mark Davis for Merit Network, Inc. *ftp:// nic.merit.edu/resources/* (Choose directory *cruise.dos* or *cruise.mac.*) For more information, contact Merit Network, Inc., Information Services, 2901 Hubbard, Pod G, Ann Arbor, MI 48105. Email address: *cruise2feedback@merit.edu*

Tour of the Internet. Developed by the NSF Network Service Center (NNSC), BBN Laboratories, Inc. *ftp://ftp.es.net/pub/networking-info/ internet-tour/* Get the *internet-tour-readme.txt* file for instructions on getting and installing this HyperCard stack.

Books and Online Documents

See elsewhere in the Appendix for a listing of Internet resource guides, both hardcopy and online.

Resource Catalogs and Lists

Finding Sites

New Internet Sites is a database of new WorldWideWeb, Gopher, hytelnet, and WAIS sites. *gopher://liberty.uc.wlu.edu* (Choose *Explore Internet Resources.*)

Nova-Links Internet Access, maintained by Rob Kabacoff, is a
   WorldWideWeb navigator of available WWW, Gopher, and hytelnet
   sites that is updated daily. It also provides software libraries and a
   "fun and games page." *http://alpha.acast.nova.edu/start.html*

Sites to Lose Yourself In

CERN. the home of the WWW, CERN hosts a comprehensive index to
   world-wide www sites, available by subject or geography: *http://
   info.cern.ch/hypertext/DataSources/WWW/Servers.html/*

Macintosh Software. For a comprehensive source of regularly updated
   Macintosh software and PD software, look at *http://web.nexor.co.uk/
   mac-archive/*

Metro. A French site which provides a guide to the metro systems of
   the world, including most major European cities. Access is by
   gopher://gopher.jussieu.fr/11/metro/

NASA. NASA has a large number of Web, Gopher, FTP, WAIS, and
   Telnet sites. In the NASA sites, you can view the latest Hubble Space
   Telescope photographs, read the notebook logs of the JASON project,
   and access NASA's immense databases of astrophysics, oceanogra-
   phy, and geosciences information. For a hypertext gateway to all of
   NASA's resources, try *http://www.jsc.nasa.gov/NASAInternetConnection.
   html* Otherwise, connect to the Goddard Space Flight Center: *ftp://
   ftp.gsfc.nasa.gov/*; *gopher://gopher.gsfc.nasa.gov/*; *http://www.gsfc.nasa.
   gov/NASA_homepage.html*

SunSITE. Telnetting to SunSITE will provide public access to all of the
   most frequently used clients, including lynx, WAIS, and Gopher;
   there is also a large anonymous FTP archive. The SunSITE
   WorldWideWeb site archives the White House papers, has a large
   number of multimedia "exhibits," serves the Cisco K-12 Educational
   Archive and Resource Catalog, and provides Dr. Fun, a daily cartoon; it is so popular that it receives 100,000 visitors per day.
   telnet\FTP\gopher\http://sunsite.unc.edu/

Sony. Sony provides an impressively designed music Web site at: *http://
   www.sony.com* For a more European perspective, it is currently
   setting up a UK Web site; no URL yet available.

For More Information

The Clearinghouse for Networked Information and Retrieval (CNIDR)
   provides information on and promotes the use of Network Information and Retrieval (NIDR) tools. *gopher://gopher.cnidr.org*; *http://
   cnidr.org/welcome.html*

The mailing list, *NEWNIR-L*, discusses new Network Information and
   Retrieval Services. List address: *NEWNIR-L@ITOCSIUM.BITNET*. To
   subscribe: *LISTSERV@ITOCSIUM.BITNET*

The mailing list, *Net Happenings*, distributes announcements of interest,
   including new Internet resources, conferences, and publications. To
   subscribe, send a message to *majordomo@is.internic.net* and in the
   body of the message type: **subscribe net-happenings**

Telnet Resources

List of Sites. A good list of Telnet sites is included in Scott Yanoff's *Special Internet Connections* (see the "Starting Your Internet Tour" section of this Appendix).

Greatest Hits. **Dartmouth Library.** Access Dante's *Divine Comedy* and all the criticism written on it, *The King James Bible*, and Shakespeare's Sonnets. *telnet://library.dartmouth.edu*
Library of Congress. Access a database of all of the Library of Congress' holdings, or find the most up-to-date legislative and copyright information. *telnet://locis.loc.gov*

Anonymous FTP Resources

List of Sites. List of Anonymous FTP Sites, originally by Tom Czarnik, now maintained by Perry Rovers (*Perry.Rovers@kub.nl*). *ftp://ftp.edu.tw/ documents/networking/guides/ftp-list/sitelist*
How to Find Sources and Lists of Mail Servers, originally by Jonathan Kamens, now maintained by Kent Lanfield (*kent@sterling.com*). Includes a list of anonymous FTP sites that allow files to be accessed via email. Posted regularly to the USENET newsgroups: *comp.sources. wanted, alt.sources.wanted, comp.answers, alt.answers*, and *news.answers* To get a current copy, send email to: *send-finding-sources-faq@ sterling.com*

Greatest Hits. **Entertainment Archives.** Includes the largest humor archive on the Internet, as well as directories for TV and music, puzzles, books, cyberculture, Disney, and baseball, among many others: *ftp://quartz.rutgers.edu/pub* Send email to *pirmann@ cs.rutgers.edu* for more information.
NCSA. The home of Telnet, Mosaic, and a large virtual reality archive: *ftp://ftp.ncsa.uiuc.edu/*
UUNET Archives of Everything. All the software you could possibly need can be found here: *ftp://ftp.uu.net/* For more information, send email to *archive@uunet.uu.net*

Gopher Resources

Lists of Sites. Gopher Jewels, maintained by David Riggins (*david.riggins@tpoint.com*). Lists Gopher sites by category. *gopher:// cwis.usc.edu* (Choose *Other Gophers and Information Servers*); *http:// galaxy.einet.net/GJ/index.html* David Riggins also maintains a mailing list for sharing interesting Gopher finds: *GOPHERJEWELS@ EINET.NET* To subscribe, send a message to *listproc@einet.net* and put the following command in the body: **subscribe gopher jewels** *firstname lastname*
All the Gopher Servers in the World (the name says it all). Gopher sites are listed by geographical location: *gopher://gopher.tc.umn.edu* (look in the directory *Other Gopher and Information Servers*).

Gopher-Mail is a guide for accessing Gopher resources via electronic mail. For more information, send email to *gophermail-admin@ calvin.edu*

Greatest Hits. **The Internet Wiretap.** This gargantuan Gopher site maintains a video game archive, archives the White House press releases, and has a large Etext library. *gopher://wiretap.spies.com* Send email to *gopher@wiretap.spies.com* for more information.

UIUC Weather Machine. This Gopher site provides up-to-the-minute weather forecasts for every part of the United States, along with the latest satellite images. *gopher://wx.atmos.uiuc.edu*

The World. The home of the Online Book Initiative, a project for publishing electronic texts, as well as a shopping mall and an archive of newsgroups and mailing lists. Also provides gateways to a large number of other Gopher and Telnet sites. *gopher://gopher.std.com*

Additional Information and Discussion. **Mailing list:** GOPHERN, also called "Let's Go Gopherin'," is dedicated to discussing new and interesting Gopher sites. List address: *GOPHERN@UBVM.CC. BUFFALO.EDU* To subscribe: *LISTSERV@UBVM.CC.BUFFALO.EDU*

Veronica FAQ: Compiled and maintained by Steven Foster and Fred Barrie: *gopher://veronica.scs.unr.edu* (Choose *Search All of Gopherspace Using Veronica.*)

USENET: See *comp.infosystems.gopher* or *alt.gopher*

WAIS

List of Sites. Master Directory of WAIS Servers. Indexes all the WAIS sites. *ftp://quake.think.com/pub/wais/; http://info.cern.ch/hypertext/DataSources/ WAIS/ByHost.html*

Newsgroup-Related Indexes, by Edward Vielmetti. Lists WAIS sites that index some or all of USENET newsgroups. *http://info.cern.ch/hypertext/ Products/WAIS/Sources/NewsGroupRelated.html*

Greatest Hits. **CIA World Factbook.** This immense resource is searchable via gopher and WAIS at *gopher://gopher.uwo.ca* (Choose *Selected Internet Resources,* then *Books, Serials, Music.*)

White House Papers. A WAIS search of all the Clinton papers is available at *telnet://sunsite.unc.edu* (login as **politics**).

Additional Information and Discussion. **USENET:** *comp.infosystems.wais* is a general discussion of WAIS.

WorldWideWeb

All registered UK WWW servers: *http://src.doc.ic.ac.uk/all-uk.html/*

Documents about using the Internet: *http://www.internic.net/ infoguide/gopher/using-internet.html/*

Lists of Sites. CUI Catalog. A powerful searching tool of WorldWideWeb resources: Also regularly announces "what's new" in the Web: *http:// cui_www.unige.ch/w3catalog*

MKGray@MIT.EDU's New 'Wow, It's Big!' Comprehensive HTTP Site List, compiled and maintained by Matthew K. Gray (*mkgray@mit.edu*). Lists every WWW site, and provides information on the growth of the web: *http://www.mit.edu:8001/people/mkgray/compre3.html*

Virtual Library. Lists WorldWideWeb servers by subject: *http://info.cern.ch/hypertext/DataSources/bySubject/Overview.html*

W3 Servers. A geographical listing of WorldWideWeb servers: *http://info.cern.ch/hypertext/DataSources/WWW/Geographical.html*

Greatest Hits. **Doctor Fun.** The Web's own daily cartoon, as well as archives of every Doctor Fun, and a place to grab Doctor Fun thumbnails for your own home pages: *http://sunsite.unc.edu/Dave/drfun.html*

EINet Galaxy. This huge WWW site searches the Internet for any topic imaginable, from multimedia and fun stuff to education, business, medicine, and law, and provides pointers to virtually all the information you could need: *http://galaxy.einet.net/galaxy.html* For more information, send email to: *galaxy@einet.net*

Online BookStore. Find the Mosaic version of the first Stephen King story to be published on the Internet, or order a copy of: *The Internet Companion. http://marketplace.com/obs/top.htm*

Wired. The WWW site of the popular alternative magazine archives back issues, provides discussion on ongoing topics, and has subscription forms: *http://wired.com* To receive update announcements, send email to *infobot@wired.com* with the message **subscribe hotwired.** For more information, send email to: *www@wired.com*

Additional Information and Discussion. **List of FAQs and Guides to WWW.** Starting from here, you should be able to find the answer to any question about anything in the WorldWideWeb: *http://cui_www.unige.ch/OSG/FAQ/www.html*

URL Specifications. The official specifications are available at: *http://info.cern.ch/hypertext/WWW/Addressing/URL/URL_TOC.html*

WWW FAQ, maintained by Thomas Boutell (*boutell@netcom.com*). Posted regularly to *comp.infosystems.www,* and archived at: *http://siva.cshl.org/~boutell/www_faq.html*

USENET: *comp.infosystems.www* is a general discussion of all WWW issues; *comp.os.lynx* discusses lynx, a WWW text browser.

Software, Games, and Video Archives

GameWave: *http://www.iinet.com.au/~nathan/* This site provides a multitude of links to games sites worldwide, catering to both PC and console-based gamers.

Merit/University of Michigan Software Archives, maintained by Fred Swartz (*archive-admin@archive.umich.edu*). *gopher://gopher.archive. merit.net* (Choose *Merit Software Archives.*)

MPEG Archives. MPEG videos that can be accessed through the WorldWideWeb: *http://w3.eeb.ele.tue.nl/mpeg/index.html*

Nintendo Gameboy Home page: *http://www.cs.umd.edu/users/fms/GameBoy/*
PC Game Archives, maintained by Brian O'Neill (*oneill@cs.uml.edu*): *ftp://*
ftp.ulowell.edu/msdos/Games/ (See the *README* file in this directory.)
Other large software archives (for all systems) can be found at: *ftp://*
ftp.uu.net/systems/, ftp://wuarchive.wustl.edu/, and *ftp://oak.oakland.edu/*
pub/ or *pub2/*

Communication Directories, Resources, and Lists

Email Directories of Addresses

How to Find People's E-Mail Addresses FAQ, by Jonathan Kamens, and
maintained by David Lamb (*dlamb@*
qucis.queensu.ca). Posted regularly to the USENET newsgroups:
comp.answers, soc.answers, news.answers, comp.mail.misc, soc.net-people,
and *news.newusers.questions* Archived at: *ftp://rtfm.mit.edu/pub/usenet/*
news.answers/finding-addresses

InterNIC White Pages. Email questions to *admin@ds.internic.net. telnet://*
ds.internic.net (login as **guest**); *ftp://ds.internic.net/internic.info/* (see the
file *whitepages.info*); *gopher://gopher.internic.net/* (Choose *InterNic*
Directory and Database Services.); *http://ds.internic.net/ds/dspgwp.html*

List of Internet Whois Servers, by Matt Power (mhpower@mit.edu): *ftp://*
sipb.mit.edu/pub/whois/whois-servers.list; gopher://sipb.mit.edu (Choose
Internet Whois Servers.)

NetPages, by Susan Estrada, Aldea Communications, Inc., Carlsbad CA.
Email: *netpages@aldea.com* Phone: (619) 929-1100

NYSERNET/PSI White Pages. For more information, send email to: *wpp-*
manager@psi.com. telnet://wp.psi.com (login as **fred**)

Stable Large Email Database (SLED). SLED registers people and provides
a directory service. For more information, send email to *sled@*
drebes.com with the subject *info.*

!%@:: A Directory of Electronic Mail Addresses and Networks, by Donnalyn
Frey and Rich Adams. This is a detailed resource to over 130
networks. Published by O'Reilly and Associates.

In addition, university Gopher servers often maintain directories of
students and faculty. See the "Gopher" section above for lists of
Gopher sites.

Online Address Services

CSO: searches "all the directory servers in the world." *gopher://*
gopher.tc.umn.edu/ (Choose *Phone Books* and then *Phone Books at Other*
Institutions.)

Knowbot: a uniform interface to the white pages services on the
Internet: *telnet://cnri.reston.va.us*

Netfind: a program that queries the network to find addresses: *telnet://*
bruno.cs.colorado.edu (login as **netfind**). Gopher gateway to Netfind:
gopher://ds.internic.net:4320 (Choose *Network Wide E-Mail Searches.*)

X.500: to look up addresses for people and organizations. *gopher:// ds.internic.net* (Choose *Directory and Database Services,* then *White Pages,* then the X500 Gateway.)

WHOIS: another way to look up addresses for people and organizations. *gopher://ds.internic.net:4320*

Lists of Mailing Lists and Misc. Documents

Directory of Scholarly Electronic Conferences, compiled by Diane K. Kovacs *(dkovacs@kentvm.kent.edu).* Provides descriptions of scholarly mailing lists of interest to scholars: *ftp://ksuvxa.KENT.EDU/library/;* (See the file: *ACADLIST.README.*) A print version is available from the Association of Research Libraries; contact Ann Okerson at: *ann@cni.org*

Inter-Network Mail Guide, originally by John J. Chew, now maintained by Scott Yanoff *(yanoff@csd4.csd.uwm.edu).* A guide on how to send electronic mail: *ftp://csd4.csd.uwm.edu/pub/internetwork-mail-guide; http://alpha.acast.nova.edu/cgi-bin/inmgq.pl*

List of BITNET LISTSERV Lists, compiled and maintained at the BITNET Network Information Center (BITNIC), Washington, DC. Available via email by sending a message to *listserv@bitnic.cren.net* with the message, **list global.** For more information, send email to *listserv@ bitnic.cren.net* with the message **info** or contact the BITNIC, 1112 Sixteenth St. NW, Washington, D.C. 20036, (202) 872-4200.

Mailing List Search. WWW search of all available mailing lists and their descriptions: *http://alpha.acast.nova.edu/cgi-bin/lists*

Publicly Accessible Mailing Lists, compiled and maintained by Stephanie da Silva *(arielle@taronga.com): ftp://rtfm.mit.edu/pub/usenet/ news.answers/mail/mailing-lists; http://www.ii.uib.no/cgi-bin/paml*

ripe-118. Available from various online sources (including *ftp.demon.co.uk*), this provides an up-to-date list of Internet Registries in or peripheral to Europe. Usenet NewsMUSs, MOOs, MUSEs and MUSHs

Smiley Server, maintained by David W. Sanderson. Online resource of all the "smilies" in the known universe: *ftp://ftp.uu.net/usenet/ comp.sources.misc/volume23/smiley; gopher://gopher.ora.com* (Choose *Feature Articles,* then *All the Smileys. . . .*) *Smileys* is also available in hardcopy from O'Reilly and Associates (1993).

USENET: *comp.mail.misc*

USENET News

Newsgroup Lists and Descriptions. WWW List of Internet Newsgroups. Also provides instructions for reading news with a WWW client: *http:// info.cern.ch/hypertext/DataSources/News/Groups/Overview.html*

Search USENET newsgroup descriptions (and USENET FAQs): *gopher:// owl.nstn.ns.ca* (Choose *Internet Resources,* then *Search USENET News-group Descriptions.*)

USENET FAQs and Periodic Postings. USENET FAQs. Posted or emailed regularly to newsgroups and mailing lists; also regularly posted on the USENET newsgroup *news.answers.* Archives: *ftp://rtfm.mit.edu/pub/ usenet/; gopher://gopher.physics.utoronto.ca* (Choose *USENET News Frequently Asked Questions.*); *http://www.cis.ohio-state.edu/hypertext/faq/ usenet/FAQ-List.html Periodic Postings,* compiled and maintained by Jonathan I. Kamens. Periodic documents are posted or emailed regularly to newsgroups and mailing lists. Archives: *ftp://rtfm.mit.edu/ pub/usenet/news.answers/periodic-postings*

MUDs, MOOs, MUSEs, and MUSHs

Lists of MUDs. MUD List Archive. Also provides a MUD FAQ and descriptions of a few MUDs. Select "jack in" to login to various MUDs. *gopher://actlab.rtf.utexas.edu* (Choose *Virtual Spaces: MUD.*)

Totally Unofficial List of Internet MUDs, compiled by Scott Goehring: *ftp:// caisr2.caisr.cwru.edu/pub/mud/mudlist.txt*

Zarf's List of Interactive Games on the Web, maintained by Andrew Plotkin (*zarf@cs.cmu.edu*). *http://www.cs.cmu.edu:8001/afs/cs.cmu.edu/user/zarf/ www/games.html*

Greatest Hits. **JaysHouseMOO**. A place where friends hang out. This MOO actually has a WWW server running inside it. *telnet://jayshouse. ccs.neu.edu:1709*

lambdaMOO. This is probably the most popular of the interactive environments. Check the documentation for help and information: *gopher://oac3.hsc.uth.tmc.edu* (Choose *Computer Information,* then *OAC Staff Test Projects,* then *Steve Newton's Goodies,* then *LambdaMoo Documentation.*) To get to lambdaMOO: *telnet://lambda.parc. xerox.com:8888.*

Nails. A MUD with a "Miami Vice" theme: *telnet://flounder.rutgers. edu:5150.* For more information, send email to *rbright@clam. rutgers.edu*

TrekMUSE. Based on the Star Trek universe. *telnet://grimmy.cnidr. org:1701.* For more information, see: *ftp://grimmy.cnidr.org/trek/docs/ trek-manual*

Additional Information and Discussion. **MUD FAQ:** This is the *rec.games.muds.misc* FAQ: *ftp://ftp.math.okstate.edu/pub/muds/misc/mud-faq/*

USENET: For newsgroups discussing various interactive systems, see: *alt.mud, rec.games.mud.announce, rec.games.mud.misc,* and *rec.games. mud.tiny* (devoted to the tinyMUDs)

INTERNET GROUPS AND ORGANIZATIONS

Coalition for Networked Information (CNI), Library Networking, Joan Lippincott, Assistant Executive Director, 21 Dupont Circle, NW, Washington, D.C. 20036 Email: *info@cni.org* Information: *ftp:// ftp.cni.org; gopher://gopher.cni.org*

Computer Professionals for Social Responsibility (CPSR), P.O. Box 717, Palo Alto, CA 94302-0717 Phone: (415) 322-3778 Fax: (415) 322-4748 Email: *cpsr@cpsr.org* Mailing List: *CPSR-Announce_listserv@cpsr.org*; include the message **help** Information: *ftp://ftp.cpsr.org*

Consortium for School Networking (CoSN), K-12 Networking, P.O. Box 65193, Washington, D.C. 20035-5193 Phone: (202) 466-6296 Email: *info@cosn.org* Mailing List: *COSNDISC*; to subscribe, send a message to *listproc@ukon.csen.org*. Information: *gopher://cosn.org*

The Electronic Frontier Foundation, Inc. (EFF), 1001 G St. NW, Suite 950E, Washington, D.C. 20001 Phone: (202) 347-5400 Fax: (202) 393-5509 BBS: (202) 638-6120 Email: *askeff@eff.org* Information: *ftp://ftp.eff.org/pub/EFF/*; *gopher://gopher.eff.org*; *http://www.eff.org*. Mailing Lists: *eff-news-request@eff.org*; *eff-talk-request@eff.org* USENET Newsgroups: *comp.org.eff.talk*; *comp.org.eff.news*; *alt.politics.datahighway*

Federation of Academic and Research Networks (FARNET), 114 Waltham St., Suite 12, Lexington MA 02173, Phone: (617) 890-9445 Fax: (617) 890-9345 Email: *mstone@farnet.org*

Internet Society, 12020 Sunrise Valley Dr., Suite 270 Reston, VA 22091 Phone: (703) 648-9888 Fax: (703) 648-9887 Email: *isoc@isoc.org* Information: *ftp://ftp.isoc.org/*; *gopher://gopher.isoc.org*

CLIENT SOFTWARE OR TOOLS

For an online summary of Internet tools—their uses, their advantages and disadvantages, and where to get them—see the *Internet Tools for NIR* list compiled and maintained by John December (*decemj@rpi.edu*): *ftp://ftp.rpi.edu/pub/communications/internet-tools.readme*; *gopher://nysernet.org* (check the directory *Special Collections: Internet Help*)

Tools and Clients for Accessing Information
(See chart on following pages.)

AmigaMosaic, www browser for the Amiga. Available by anonymous ftp from: *ftp://ftp.demon.co.uk/pub/amiga/mosaic/*

ArcWeb, WWW browser for Acorn Archimedes. Available by anonymous ftp from: *ftp://ftp.demon.co.uk/pub/archimedes/www/*

BinHex

This software program codes Macintosh files for file transfer and emailing: *ftp://mac.archive.umich.edu/mac/util/comm/* It's also available for PCs: *ftp://boombox.micro.umn.edu/pub/binhex/MSDOS* (See the *00readme* file.)

CU-See Me

This Macintosh video-conferencing package enables you to see and "talk" with other Internet Macintosh users. Archived at *ftp://gated.cornell.edu/pub/video/*

Email

There are many Unix email clients, each with its own advantages. **ELM** is easy to use: *ftp://ftp.uu.net/networking/mail/elm/*, or send email

Network Information Discovery and Retrieval Tools

Client Software	Purpose	Quantity of Public Information	Positive Aspects	Negative Aspects	Where to Find Client Software (anonymous FTP)
TELNET	Remote interactive	Over 1,400 sites	Log into thousands of databases worldwide	Need to know where the databases are in advance	*ftp://ftp.ncsa.uiuc.edu/Telnet/* (choose *system*)
FTP	File Transfer Protocol	Gigabytes	Good for moving even large files; lots of software archives	Need to know where the files are in advance	*ftp://wuarchive.wustl.edu/systems/* (pick directory for your computer)
archie	Search and retrieve anonymous FTP	More than 2.2 million files searched	Great for finding software archives if you know an exact filename	Need to know what you are looking for	*ftp://ftp.sura.net/pub/archie/clients/*
WAIS	Multimedia search and retrieval	500+ databases	Fast search; grades quality of information received	Need to know which databases you want to search	*ftp://quake.think.com/wais/*
GOPHER	Publishes and searches information on a distributed network	More than 25,000 sites	Email or FTP results to yourself; menued information is easily navigated	Can get lost in the overwhelming amount of information; links are often poorly maintained	*ftp://boombox.micro.umn.edu/pub/gopher/*
Veronica	keyboard search of Gopher menus	all of Gopherspace	quick way to find a lot of Gopher information on a single topic	widely used and difficult to get a connection	no client available; must be accessed through a gopher client
Jughead	keyboard search of Gopher menus	single Gopher server search	often more accessible than Veronica	limited to one Gopher server	*ftp://boombox.micro.umn.edu/pub/gopher/Unix/GopherTools/jughead/*
WORLD-WIDEWEB	Hypertext interface to Internet resources	More than 2,500 sites	Hypertext links make finding information easy	Easy to get lost or distracted	*ftp://info.cern.ch/pub/www/*

Network Information Discovery and Retrieval Tools (continued)

Client Software	Purpose	Quantity of Public Information	Positive Aspects	Negative Aspects	Where to Find Client Software (anonymous FTP)
Mosaic	Hypermedia browser of the WWW	The entire Internet	Encompasses all tools; multimedia interface	Requires dedicated line and direct Internet connection	*ftp://ftp.ncsa.uiuc.edu/Mosaic/*
Lynx	distributed hypertext browser	The entire Internet	Can be accessed with a dial-up connection	Text-only browser	*ftp://ftp2.cc.ukans.edu/pub/lynx/*
Cello	WWW hypermedia browser for Microsoft Windows	The entire Internet	Good documentation	Requires a direct Internet connection	*ftp://ftp.law.cornell.edu/pub/LII/Cello/*
TKWWW	WWW browser for X Window	The entire Internet	The only WWW client currently available with a text editor	Requires a direct connection to the Internet	*ftp://info.cern.ch/pub/www/src/*

Source: *Netpages*, Aldea Communications, *netpages@aldea.com* or (619) 943-0101.

archive-server@DSI.COM with the message **help** to get more information. **PINE** is a good client for the novice user; it includes many
features, such as folders for storing messages and a stand-alone
editor, PICO: *ftp://ftp.cac.washington.edu/pine/* **MH** is useful because it
allows you to access email directly from the Unix shell prompt: *ftp://
ftp.ics.uci.edu/pub/mh/*

Finger
This client enables you to find out information about specific users:
ftp://wuarchive.wustl.edu/systems/gnu/
Internet Chameleon combines TCP/IP with SLIP/PPP, mail, www
client, news reader, gopher, archie and ftp software for MS Windows.

IRC Chat
This multiuser chat program enables you to talk interactively with
other users: *ftp://cs.bu.edu/irc/clients/* (See the *README* file.)

MBONE
Information on the MBONE is archived at: *ftp://isi.edu/mbone/faq.txt* or
http://www.eit.com/techinfo/mbone/mbone.html The multicast software
needed is available at *ftp://gregorio.stanford.edu/vmtp-ip/*; see the
ipmulticast.README file for more information. Information on
MBONE is also available from the mailing list; send subscription
request to: *mbone-request@isi.edu*

MUDs, MOOs, MUSEs, MUSHs
Clients for text-based, interactive, multiuser environments include
tinytalk, tinyfugue, VT, LPTalk, SayWat, RMF, and **TinyView**,
among others. All are archived in *ftp://ftp.math.okstate.edu/pub/muds/
clients/*
Netscape, WWW navigator for PC, Mac, Unix. Available by anonymous ftp from: *ftp://ftp.mcon.com/netscape/*
Newsbase, mail and news for Acorn Archimedes. Works with Taylor
uucp software and KA9Q. Available by anonymous ftp from: *ftp://
ftp.demon.co.uk/pub/archimedes/developers/*

News Readers
News-reader clients include **tin, nn, rn**, and **trn** for Unix, **thenews**
for Mac, **trumpet** for IBM, and **NewsGrazer** for NeXt. All news
readers are archived at *ftp://news.cis.umn.edu/pub/*
POPmail is a mailserver for PC and Macintosh systems: *ftp://
boombox.micro.umn.edu/pub/* Look in the *POPmail* directory for
Macintosh applications, and in the *pc/minuet* directories for PC.
NUPop is an email client for Windows/Dos systems: *ftp://
casbah.acns.nwu.edu/pub/nupop/* **Eudora** is a popular client for the
Macintosh, and recently a Windows version has been developed: *ftp:/
/ftp.qualcomm.com/* (choose *mac* or *pceudora/*)

INTERNET CONNECTIVITY
Mailing List

info@ripe-ncc.net This mailing list helps you to find an Internet provider near you in Europe. The RIPE NCC forwards your request to all Internet providers in Europe who have contact with the RIPE NCC. The providers themselves will then contact you with all necessary information.

INFO-NETS@THINK.COM This mailing list is for general discussion of networks, particularly internetwork connectivity. Focusses on general worldwide networking questions, connections to particular sites and announcements of new networks and services. Subscription requests and questions should be sent to *info-nets-request@think.com*. Also see the USENET group *info.nets*. Archives are WAIS-indexed: *info-nets.src*.

Getting Started Packages

PIPEX Solo is an all-in-one Internet access software and service package available from PIPEX in the U.K. It includes TCP/IP and PPP software, Email, Telnet and the Netscape www browser.

Chameleon for MS Windows, from Netmanage, will work with any SLIP/PPP service and provides a comprehensive range of Internet access facilities.

PC SLIP and PPP Implementations

SLIP and PPP implementations for the PC are available commercially from the following companies: PC Spry, Inc. (*info@spry.com*), Novell, Inc. (*http://www.novell.com*), FTP Software (*info@ftp.com*) and Netmanage (*info@netmanage.com*).

Books

Estrada, Susan (1993). *Connecting to the Internet: An O'Reilly Buyer's Guide*. O'Reilly and Associates.

Heslop, Brent, and David Angell (1994). *Instant Internet Guide: Hands-on Global Networking*. Addison-Wesley.

Quarterman, John S., and Carl-Mitchell Smoot (1994). *The Internet Connection: System Connectivity and Configuration*. Addison-Wesley. Email *awbook@aw.com* for more information.

TCP/IP AND INTERNETWORKING INFORMATION
Online Documents

Introduction to Internet Protocols. Compiled by the Rutgers Computer Science Facilities Group. *ftp://nic.merit.edu/introducing.the.internet/into.to.ip*.

Knowing About Modems by Patrick Chen. This resource is a good introduction to modems and modem standards. *gopher://gopher-chem.ucdabis.edu/11/Index/Modems-aw/Knowing-About-Modems*.

Network Reading List by Charles Spurgeon. This is an annotated list of
network-related items, such as books and resources describing TCP/IP
protocol sites, Unix networking and Ethernet local area technology.
ftp://ftp.utexas.edu/pub/netinfo/reading-list; gopher://rock.concert.net/11.

PC-MAC TCP/IP and NFS FAQ List by Rawn Shaw (*rawn@rtd.com*). *ftp://
seagull.rtd.com/pub/tcpip; http://www.rtd.com/pcnfsfaq/faq.html.*

Request for Comments (RFCs and FYIs). For an RFC-index search, try
http://web.nexor.co.uk. Archived at *ftp://nic.merit.edu/documents/rfc* and
ftp://nic.ddn.mil; WWW archive at *http://www.cis.ohio-state.edu/
hypertext/information/rfc.html.* RFC list available at *ftp.Germany.EU.net:/
pub/documents/*.* *Internet Handbook,* a list of RFCs, is available at *ftp://
sri.com/netinfo/internet-technology-handbook-contents.* RFCs (and the RFC
index) can be obtained via email also. Send a message to *rfc-
info@isi.edu,* and in the body of the message put the command *help:
waystogetrfcs*. A help message will be returned to you.

Mailing Lists

tcp-ip@nic.ddn.mil. This mailing list is a discussion group for TCP/IP
developers and maintainers. Send subscription requests to *tcp-ip-
request@nic.ddn.mil.*

Organizations

Internet Engineering Task Force (IETF). This organization is an arm of
the Internet Architecture Board concerned with protocol engineering, development and standardization. For a mailing list of IETF
announcements, send email to *ietf-announce-request@cnri.reston.va.us.*
For a general discussion mailing list, send email to *ietf-
request@cnri.reston.va.us.* Futher information available at
ftp://cnri.reston.va.us/ietf.

Books

Arick, Martin R. (1993). *The TCP/IP Companion: A Guide for the Common
User.* QED Publishing Group.

Black, Uyless (1992). *TCP/IP and Related Protocols.* McGraw Hill.

Comer, Douglas E., and David L. Stevens. *Internetworking with TCP/IP:
Principles, Protocols and Architecture,* 2ed. Three volumes. Prentice Hall
Inc.

Hunt, Craig (1992). *TCP/IP Network Adminstration.* O'Reilly and Associates.

Marine, April, Susan Kirkpatrick, Vivan Neou, and Carol Ward (1993).
Internet: Getting Started. Prentice Hall.

Newsletter

ConneXions: The Interoperability Report
Interop Company, a Division of ZP Expos
303 Vintage Park Drive, Suite 201
Foster City, CA 94404-1138
U.S.A.

Tel: (415) 578-6900
Fax: (415) 525-0194
Email: *connexions@interop.com*
http://programs.interop.com

Unix Resources

Gilly, David, and ORA Staff (1992). *UNIX in a Nutshell*. O'Reilly and Associates.

Hahn, Harley (1993). *A Student's Guide to UNIX*. McGraw Hill.

Kochan, Stephen G., and Patrick H. Wood (1989). *UNIX Networking*. Hayden Books.

Libes, Don, and Sandy Ressler. *Life with UNIX: A Guide for Everyone*. Prentice Hall.

Norton, Peter, and Harley Hahn (1991). *Peter Norton's Guide to UNIX*. Bantam Books.

Sobell, Mark G. (1989). *A Practical Guide to UNIX Systems*. Benjamin Cummings Publishing.

SSC Staff (1992). *Beginning UNIX Commands*. Specialized Systems Consultants.

Todino, Grace, and John Strang (1989). *Learning the UNIX Operating System*. O'Reilly Associates.

SECURITY

Online Documents

Ethics and the Internet by the Internet Activities Board (1989). *ftp:// nic.ddn.mil/rfc/rfc1087.txt*. Both this document and the *Site Security Handbook* are available through email from *service@nic.ddn.mil* (put the name of the document in the subject line).

Quadralay Cryptography Archive, maintained by Brain Combs (*combs@quadralay.com*). This is an archive of security and cryptography resources. *http://www.quadralay.com/www/Crypt/Crypt.html*.

Site Security Handbook by Paul Holbrook and Joyce K. Reynolds (1991). *ftp://nic.ddn.mil/rfc/rfc1244.txt*. Also known as FYI8.

Virus Information Documents. Public virus informational documents are maintained by Ken Van Wyk (*krvw@cert.org*) and are available at *ftp://ftp.cert.org/pub/virus-l/docs*.

Mailing Lists

COMP-PRIVACY. Discusses how technology affects privacy. List address: *comp-privacy@pica.army.mil* To request a subscription: *comp-privacy-request@pica.army.mil*

FIREWALLS. Primarily for network administrators, covers the frequently arcane issues surrounding the set-up and administration of Firewalls to secure your own network when providing Internet access. List address: *firewalls@greatcircle.com* Subscription: Send message with subscribe Firewalls to: *majordomo@greatcircle.com*

HACK-L The Hack Report. Reports new occurrences of hacking and computer security violation. List address: *HACK-L@alive.crsys.edmonton.ab.ca* To subscribe: *majordomo@alive.ampr.ab.ca*

RISKS@csl.sri.com The *RISKS Digest* is a moderated discussion group on general computer security issues. To subscribe, send a message to *risks-request@csl.sri.com*.

VALERT-L This list shares urgent virus warnings. It is cross-posted to the VIRUS-L digest. To subscribe, send a message to *listserv@lehigh.edu*.

VIRUS-L@ibm1.cc.lehigh.edu VIRUS-L is an email discussion forum devoted to sharing information about computer viruses. To subscribe, send an email message to *LISTSERV@lehigh.edu* and include this command in the message body: *SUB VIRUS-L* *Your-name*. Also, see the archives: *ftp:/ftp.cert.org/pub/virus-l*.

USENET Groups

The following USENET newsgroups discuss matters of computer security: *alt.security*, *comp.risks* (the same as the *RISKS* mailing list digest), *comp.security.announce* (distribution of CERT advisories), *comp.security.misc*, and *comp.virus* (the same as the VIRUS-L mailing list).

Organizations

Computer Emergency Response Team/CERT Coordination Center
Software Engineering Institute
Carnegie-Mellon University
4500 Fifth Avenue, Pittsburgh, PA 15213
U.S.A.
Tel: (412) 268-7090
Fax: (412) 268-6989
Email: *cert@cert.org ftp://ftp.cert.org*
Mailing lists: *cert-advisory-request@cert.org; cert-tools-request@cert.org*

Electronic Mail Protection

PEM (Privacy Enhanced Mail). Client is available at *ftp://ftp.tis.com/pub/PEM*. For more information, see the PEM FAQ at *ftp://ftp.tis.com/pub/PEM/FAQ* or send email to *tispen-support@tis.com*. There is also a PGP/PEM FAQ at *http://hoohoo.ncsa.uiuc.edu/docs/PEMPGP.html*.

PGP (Pretty Good Privacy) Mail. Client is available at *ftp://ftp.uu.net/pub/security/pgp*. For more information, see the PGP FAQ, posted to the USENET newsgroup *alt.security.pgp* and archived at: *http://www.quadralay.com/www/Crypt/PGP*

Books

Curry, David (1992). *UNIX System Security: A Guide for Users and Systems Administrators*. Addison-Wesley.

Garfinkel, S., and E. Spafford (1991). *Practical UNIX Security*. O'Reilly Associates.

Hafner, Katie, and John Markoff (1991). *Cyberpunk: Outlaws and Hackers on the Computer Frontier.* Simon & Schuster.

Russell, Deborah, and G.T. Gangemi, Sr. (1992). *Computer Security Basics.* O'Reilly Associates.

Sterling, Bruce (1992). *The Hacker Crackdown: Law and Disorder on the Electronic Frontier.* Bantam Books.

Stoll, Clifford (1989). *The Cuckoo's Egg: Tracking a Spy Through the Maze of Computer Espionage.* Doubleday.

Index